HUNGER FOR JUSTICE

"Blessed are those who hunger and thirst for righteousness,
for they shall be satisfied" (Matthew 5:6).

To Betsy, for her love, patience, and support.
To my mother and father, for their spirit of openness and caring.
And to my friends and co-workers at Clergy and Laity Concerned,
whose work, commitment, and vision give credibility to these pages.

HUNGER FOR JUSTICE

The Politics of Food and Faith

Jack A. Nelson

ORBIS BOOKS
Maryknoll, New York 10545

Second Printing, May 1980

The Catholic Foreign Mission Society of America (Maryknoll) recruits and trains people for overseas missionary service. Through Orbis Books Maryknoll aims to foster the international dialogue that is essential to mission. The books published, however, reflect the opinions of their authors and are not meant to represent the official position of the society.

Library of Congress Cataloging in Publication Data

Nelson, Jack A
  Hunger for justice.

  Includes bibliographical references and index.
  1. Food supply. 2. Underdeveloped areas—Food supply. 3. Church and social problems. I. Title
HD9000.6.N38   338.1'9   79-21072
ISBN 0-88344-196-9

Manufactured in the United States of America

CONTENTS

PREFACE

"GOD, GUNS, AND GUTS: THAT'S WHAT'S MADE AMERICA GREAT!" So read a giant billboard seen throughout the midwest in 1975. This oversimplified convergence of God and country, which views the prosperity of America as evidence of God's blessing and sees America's military might as the protector of Christian values and civilization, is being challenged by people throughout our country and throughout the world.

There was a time when love of God meant for me an uncritical acceptance of our country's policies. The pathway leading to a different understanding began when I stepped into new experiences that led to new questions. The poverty and inequality characteristic of Chicago and other American cities, and of countries such as India, Ethiopia, and Sri Lanka, radically called into question my traditional worldview. At first, I was angry that my attitudes about God and country were being challenged. At one point as I walked through the streets of Calcutta, the poverty so enraged me that *I wanted to scream at God*. How could *God* tolerate such suffering? Then I came to a painful realization: *in the suffering of the poor God was screaming at me, in fact at all of us and at our institutions and social systems that cause and perpetuate hunger, poverty, and inequality*.

The emptiness and possibility of that moment defy words. My old support system, defenses, and worldview were passing away. They were replaced not with answers but with questions: why were people poor and hungry? why did American churches and synagogues seem indifferent to the *causes* of human suffering? what were the implications of Judeo-Christian silence for biblical faith? and how could concerned people begin or join organizing efforts for social change and a better future? A journey had begun.

This book is an outgrowth of this journey still in progress. It is impossible to thank all the people whose lives have touched and continue to touch mine along the way. Together we are discovering that legitimate concern about the literal hunger and thirst of others necessarily leads us to a hunger and thirst—and struggle—for justice. The voice of the poor is God's voice. When we open our hearts and minds to that voice we discover that our spiritual and economic well-being are intimately tied to the well-being of our brothers and sisters who live in our neighborhoods and throughout the globe.

To love God we must seek justice. To love our country we must seek to overcome the corporate, government, and military policies that victimize the bodies and spirits of people at home and abroad. What is truly remarkable is that human transformation is possible and that our lives can make a difference.

Chapter 1

THE ROOTS OF HUNGER

Hunger in the Bible

Several years ago I began probing the political and economic roots of the world food crisis. At the same time I reread the Bible, looking for parallels between the causes of hunger in biblical times and our own. I discovered that despite a disparity of several thousand years, the description of the economic roots of hunger in the Bible is helpful in shaping our understanding of the present world food crisis. A passage in Amos is illustrative:

> Hear this, you who trample upon the needy,
> and bring the poor of the land to an end,
> saying, "When will the new moon be over,
> that we may sell grain?
> And the sabbath,
> that we may offer wheat for sale,
> that we may make the ephah small and the shekel great,
> and deal deceitfully with false balances,
> that we may buy the poor for silver
> and the needy for a pair of sandals,
> and sell the refuse of the wheat?"
> The Lord has sworn by the pride of Jacob:
> "Surely I will never forget any of their deeds . . ."
>
> (Amos 8:4–7).[1]

Before examining this passage in detail, we want to look briefly at the social context in which it was spoken. Amos announces the word of God to Israel during the height of its territorial expansion and prosperity. Under Jeroboam II (786–746 B.C.), a capable leader and strong military figure, Israel pursued a successful policy of foreign expansion by exploiting the weakness of its war-torn neighbors.

1

During this time Israel controlled the major trade routes of the ancient world. Expanded trade on which the new prosperity was built transformed the structure of Israelite society. What had once been almost entirely a rural culture became more and more urban, and power shifted to the central marketplace and to those engaged in commerce.

It was also a time of increased social inequality. While foreign trade and the changing social fabric meant wealth and power for merchants and the emerging urban class, they undermined the well-being of growing numbers of people. Amos consistently condemns the wealth of the rich, which has been gained by exploiting the poor (Amos 2:6–7; 3:10; 4:1; 5:11–12), and he is particularly irate that the affluent social classes in Israel live in luxury far removed from the suffering on which that luxury is based (Amos 6:1–7). Indeed, archeological excavations near the site of Amos's prophecy have uncovered distinct sections of the city; one containing large, expensive houses of luxury, the other small, huddled structures.[2]

Farmers were particularly victimized during this period. Small landowners were forced off their land and their property passed into the hands of urban elites. Displaced farmers constituted a new economic class of landless serfs who worked the vineyards and farms for their new overlords. Urban elites transformed independent farmers into tenants, and they built large estates on the backs of the poor. Often a tenant would turn over a major portion of the grain produced as payment for use of the land. Amos, himself a farmer, announced the charge and judgment:

> Therefore because you trample upon the poor
> and take from them exactions of wheat,
> you have built houses of hewn stone,
> but you shall not dwell in them;
> you have planted pleasant vineyards,
> but you shall not drink their wine (Amos 5:11).*

Indeed, a few verses later, Amos says that in the coming judgment the oppressed farmers will bury their oppressors in the ground which had been taken from them:

> "They shall call the farmers to mourning
> and to wailing those who are skilled in lamentation,
> and in all vineyards there shall be wailing,
> for I will pass through the midst of you,"
> says the Lord (Amos 5:16–17).

It is within the context of social injustice, in which the rich grew rich by exploiting the poor and small farmers become landless laborers, that we are to interpret Amos 8:4–7. Amos criticizes the merchants "who trample upon the needy and bring the poor of the land to an end" (v. 4). The merchants were eager to sell debt-ridden people into slavery. In fact, foreclosing on debt was the principle way of wresting land away from small farmers. In the ancient Near East the transfer of footgear was evidence of the transfer of real property. When Amos condemns the merchants for buying "the poor for silver and the needy *for a pair of sandals*" (v. 6) he is condemning them for foreclosing on debt and taking legal title to the land of the poor.[3]

The merchants had enormous power. James Luther Mays writes that the "urban merchants appear to have monopolized the market; they were able to sell to landless peasants at a high price." Also, they "had the resources for stockpiling grain," so that "in a time of poor crops [they] were in a position to control the economy completely."[4] One consequence of monopoly power was that merchants could sell to the highest bidder. Often this meant that grain was exported. Imagine the frustration of poor, hungry Israelites as they saw grain produced on nearby land, in many cases on land they had once owned and cultivated, being transported outside their regions.

Hungry for profits, the merchants reluctantly obeyed the religious laws of the day, which prohibited selling grain on the sabbath or on holidays such as the festival of the new moon (v. 5). The Sabbath as a day of rest was an important religious tradition. It was an occasion to remember "that in six days the Lord made heaven and earth, and on the seventh day . . . rested, and was refreshed" (Ex. 31:17). Practically speaking, it was also an important piece of labor legislation, insuring that workers had one day of rest each week. The merchants were unhappy that their exploitation of the poor was interrupted by a weekly ritual.

Even as they sold on normal business days, they did so deceitfully. They cut down the size of the ephah and made heavier the shekel. In other words they rigged their scales so that poor people paid more money for less grain (v. 5). What's more, the poor paid illegally high prices for the lowest quality wheat (the refuse) (v. 6).

Leviticus 19:35–36 specifically forbids the rigging of scales:

> You shall do no wrong in judgment, in measures of length or weight or quantity. You shall have just balances, just weights, a just ephah, and a just hin.

At the end of verse 36 is this important reminder: "I am the Lord your God, who brought you out of the land of Egypt." What all Israelites were bound by history to remember was that God had delivered them from the oppression and injustice they had suffered at the hands of the Egyptians (Ex. 6:5–8). Therefore, they had no right to oppress others. In fact, to do injustice to the poor was to break the covenant with God.

Yet exploit the poor they did, and ruthlessly. Amos is clear that exploitation was made possible because of the complicity of a variety of powerful groups. In addition to the merchants, there were the bankers without whose cooperation the rigging of scales would have been impossible.[5] Amos also condemns the perversion of justice by the court (5:10, 12), which allowed farmers to be dispossessed of their land.

> The court was the one social institution which stood in the way of the process. The urban group, probably made up primarily of officials in the royal administration and supported by the royal power, were corrupting these courts and shifting the control of social life away from the villages to the royal court.[6]

Finally, Amos condemns the empty religious rituals of a self-indulgent people. Affluent social classes are engaged in the ultimate idolatry: they seek access to God in rituals that reinforce injustice. Their exploitation of the poor makes their religiosity a mockery. Amos goes so far as to say that because they oppress the poor, their sacrifices and tithes actually *multiply their sins* (4:4). And the Lord of the Exodus states forcefully that idolatry is intolerable; what is demanded is justice:

> I hate, I despise your feasts,
> and I take no delight in your solemn assemblies.
> Even though you offer me
> your burnt offerings and cereal offerings,
> I will not accept them,
> and the peace offerings of your fatted beasts
> I will not look upon.
> Take away from me the noise of your songs:
> to the melody of your harps I will not listen.
> But let justice roll down like waters,
> and righteousness like an ever-flowing stream (Amos 5:21–24).

What we learn from Amos is that hunger and poverty are not historical accidents. They are the fruits of social injustice. Poor people in Israel were exploited at both ends of the food chain. Farmers, because of indebtedness and injustice in the court, were reduced to landless serfs, had their production taken from them, or were cut out of production completely. At the same time, poor consumers (including the displaced farmers who migrated from the countryside) could not contend with the monopoly power of the merchants. What's more, as land ownership was concentrated in the hands of a small group, the criterion dictating what was produced was profitability. Therefore, while the laborers who worked the vineyards were hungry, the rich drank wine (a commodity priced well out of reach of the poor) in bowls (Amos 6:6).

Hunger in Amos's Israel was a consequence of economic structures that resulted in great gaps between the wealth and power of the rich compared to the condition of the poor. Once set in motion, these structures of inequality tended to be self-perpetuating. Merchants formed alliances with bankers, members of the court took bribes, and the unjust prosperity of the urban classes spilled over into the coffers of the temple. The result was a mutually beneficial and cozy alliance, complete with economic rewards and religious ideology, which undermined the well-being of the poor.

In Amos's Israel there would seem to be no hope for the hungry, short of a fundamental change in their economic and political position. Such a change would necessarily involve a redistribution of wealth and the wealth-producing resources. Unless the poor could rid themselves of debt and regain control of productive resources, principally land, they would be locked into a state of permanent exploitation.

It is interesting that the biblical writers established clear provisions which, if enforced, could have prevented gross inequalities. Every seventh year was to be a sabbatical year in which all debts were forgiven, all Hebrew slaves freed, and the land allowed to lie fallow to restore its fertility (Deut. 15:1–6, 12–18; Lev. 25:2–7). What's more, every fiftieth year was to be a jubilee in which land automatically returned to its original owner:

> And you shall hallow the fiftieth year, and proclaim liberty throughout the land to all its inhabitants; it shall be a jubilee for you, when each of you shall return to your property and each of you shall return to your family (Lev. 25:10).*

The way to prevent great inequalities in wealth and power is to institutionalize a levelling mechanism that returns productive resources to the people. The theological insight on which the jubilee tradition is founded is that ultimately it is God who owns the land:

> The land shall not be sold in perpetuity, for the land is mine;
> for you are strangers and sojourners with me. And in all the
> country you possess, you shall grant a redemption of the land
> (Lev. 25:23–24).

The principle is clear: God created the earth, and all it contains, for all people. Each person has the right to share the productive resources of society.

The biblical writers were profoundly aware that unjust economic structures prevented a proper relationship with God. So long as inequality and injustice to the poor were built into the fabric of society, faith in the God who had liberated Israel from oppression in Egypt was impossible. In other words, the commitment to build an egalitarian society was inseparable from the struggle against idolatry.

Although it is unlikely that the jubilee was ever successfully enforced, it appears that Jesus announces his ministry by proclaiming a jubilee year:

> The Spirit of the Lord is upon me,
> because he has anointed me to preach good news to the poor.
> He has sent me to proclaim release to the captives
> and recovering of sight to the blind,
> to set at liberty those who are oppressed,
> to proclaim the acceptable year of the Lord (Luke 4:18–19).

The social conditions that served as the backdrop for Jesus' ministry were similar to those described by Amos. The great merchants of the Roman Empire grew rich through the trade of luxury items. The author of Revelation notes with satisfaction the anguish of the merchants of the earth who will mourn the destruction of Rome:

> And the merchants of the earth weep and mourn for her, since
> no one buys their cargo anymore, cargo of gold, silver, jewels
> and pearls, fine linen, purple, silk and scarlet, all kinds of
> scented wood, all articles of ivory, all articles of costly wood,
> bronze, iron and marble, cinnamon, spice, incense, myrrh,
> frankincense, wine, oil, fine flour and wheat, cattle and sheep,
> horses and chariots, and slaves, that is, human souls.
> "The fruit for which thy soul longed has gone from thee,
> and all thy dainties and thy splendor are lost to thee,
> never to be found again."
> The merchants of these wares, who gained wealth from her,
> will stand far off, in fear of her torment, weeping and mourning
> aloud . . . (Rev. 18:11–15).

Jesus' teachings on wealth were aimed at the upper classes, who were the beneficiaries of the traffic in luxuries and indifferent to the suffering of the poor. For example, in Luke 16 Jesus warns that it isn't possible to serve God and riches (v. 13). He then goes on to describe the rich person "who was clothed in purple and fine linen and who feasted sumptuously every day," while being totally indifferent to the suffering of poor Lazarus (vs. 19–31).

Because wealthy merchants were easily and heavily taxed by the empire, land was prized as a sort of tax shelter. According to Walter Wink, "Since land was not so easily converted into the Emperor's coin, liquid assets were quickly converted into large estates."[7] It is not surprising, therefore, that the rich of the Gospels are landowners (Luke 12:16 f.), usually absentee (Matt. 20:1 f., 21:33 f., 22:5, 25:14–30). According to James, the rich landowners will be judged harshly because they grow rich by exploiting the poor:

> Come now, you rich, weep and howl for the miseries that are coming upon you. Your riches have rotted and your garments are moth-eaten. Your gold and silver have rusted, and their rust will be evidence against you and will eat your flesh like fire. You have laid up treasure for the last days. *Behold the wages of the laborers who mowed your fields, which you kept back by fraud, cry out; and the cries of the harvesters have reached the ears of the Lord of hosts* (James 5:1–4; emphasis added).

Foreclosure on debt continued to be the principle vehicle by which the rich stripped the poor of their ancestral rights to land. The common plight of peasants is described in Matthew 18:24–25:

> When he began the reckoning, one was brought to him who owed him ten thousand talents; and as he could not pay, his lord ordered him to be sold, with his wife and children and all that he had, and payment be made.

Given the plight of the poor farmer turned tenant it is not surprising that, according to Wink, "the first act of the Zealots [Jewish nationalists who fiercely fought against Roman domination] at the outbreak of the Great Jewish War in 66 A.D. was to burn the temple treasury, where the records of indebtedness were stored."[8] The Lord's Prayer, which for years I recited with little emotion, may well be a jubilee prayer that gave hope to the oppressed. "Forgive us our debts as we also have forgiven our debtors" (Matt. 6:12), should probably be understood quite literally, and Jesus depicts a king doing just that (Matt. 18:23 f.).

Immediately following the Lord's Prayer there is further evidence linking Jesus' teaching to the jubilee and sabbatical year. Jesus warns that devotion to wealth precludes devotion to God (Matt. 6:19–24), and tells the people not to be anxious about their lives. They are to trust in God:

> Therefore I tell you, do not be anxious about your life, what you shall eat or what you shall drink. . . . Look at the birds of the air: they neither sow nor reap nor gather into barns, and yet your gracious God feeds them. Are you not of more value than they? (Matt. 6:25–26).*

When we remember that, according to the provisions of the sabbatical year (Lev. 25:3), every seventh year *the land is to lie fallow*, and that during the year of jubilee, "you shall neither sow, nor reap what grows of itself, nor gather the grapes, from the undressed vines (Lev. 25:11), we can understand why the people might be anxious: they, like the birds of the air, are to neither sow nor reap; their well-being depends on God who will provide a bountiful harvest in previous years (Lev. 25:21).

When Jesus announces his mission in terms of jubilee, he is attacking hunger, poverty, and idolatry at the root. He is aware that injustice to the poor and great inequalities in wealth and power militate against knowledge of the true God. Without a radical change in the social structure, including a cancellation of debt and redistribution of wealth, there is little hope for the hungry.

For the exploited laborers in Israel, who are like exiles in their own land, the words of Isaiah must have been a beautiful promise:

> They shall build houses and inhabit them;
> they shall plant vineyards and eat their fruit.
> They shall not build and another inhabit;
> they shall not plant and another eat;
> for like the days of a tree shall the days of my people be,
> and my chosen shall long enjoy the work of their hands
>   (Isa. 65:21–22)

Summary

As we move on to examine the political and economic causes of the present-day world food crisis, we will keep in mind this biblical overview. While it is inappropriate simply to transfer the social setting of the Bible to our present situation, it is possible to keep the following points in mind. During biblical times:

1. Foreign trade generally concentrated on the movement of lux-

ury goods (Rev. 18:11–15). While this was beneficial to merchants and affluent social groups, it undermined the position of the poor.

2. Foreign trade was made possible by an aggressive foreign policy (e.g., Israel's foreign policy under Jeroboam, and the foreign policy of the Roman Empire).

3. Food was sometimes exported while poor people were hungry.

4. The growth of foreign trade led to a changed social fabric marked by increased urbanization and a centralization of wealth and power in the hands of urban elites who controlled the economy and gained control over the lands of the rural poor (Amos 8:4–8).

5. The ability to foreclose on debts was a powerful tool of oppression (Amos 8:6).

6. As landowning was concentrated in the hands of a small group of people, small farmers were reduced to a class of landless serfs. Displaced farmers were a cheap labor supply. Some worked the fields and vineyards of their new overlords (Amos 5:11; Job 24:10–11) while others migrated to the city, where they were exploited by the merchants (Amos 8:4–5).

7. With the demise of the small farmer, subsistence agriculture was undermined because production was geared to the "needs" of the rich (Amos 5:11; 6:6). Land was valued as a location for the summerhouses of the rich (Amos 3:15), and as a sort of ancient-day "tax shelter."

8. Monopoly control over the food supply provided merchants with the opportunity to exploit the poor (Amos 8:6).

9. The merchants were hungry for profits and resented the fact that the Sabbath and holidays were days of rest (Amos 8:5).

10. The exploitation of the poor, which resulted in hunger and poverty, involved the complicity of a variety of powerful groups, including merchants, bankers, government officials, members of the court, and religious authorities (Amos 8:4–7; 7:10–12; 5:12; 2:6–8).

11. The people of Israel ignored the biblical teaching that ultimately it is God who owns the land (Lev. 25:23–24). As a result, poor people were denied access to both the fruits and the means of production (Amos 5:11; Job 24:10–11).

12. Wealth and power were unevenly distributed. As a consequence, the affluence of the rich rubbed shoulders with the misery of the poor (Amos 4:1; 3:10; 2:6–8; 5:11; 6:6).

13. Hunger was a consequence of social injustice and not some fateful accident. As such, it was an affront to God, and served as evidence that people were worshiping idols and not the liberating God of the Bible (Amos 5:21–24; 3:13–14; 4:4–5; Hos. 10:1).

Chapter 2

THE ECONOMICS OF HUNGER

Generally, the countries most seriously affected by the world food crisis have three things in common. First, their economies are firmly integrated into the international free-enterprise system. Second, their economic production is geared to international markets and is based on the principle of comparative advantage. And third, their domestic economies are free-enterprise economies. These statements are not as controversial as they might seem to many readers. Most economists would agree with them. The controversy centers on whether these common features are themselves responsible for causing hunger.

Most poor countries are firmly integrated into the international free-enterprise system. They depend heavily on foreign aid and foreign investment to provide capital for development. They purchase technology from multinational corporations and provide incentives for these corporations to locate production facilities on their soil. In addition, the economic cycles in the world economy deeply affect them. Inflation in the United States, for example, means that they must pay higher prices for the American goods they purchase. Or a recession in the developed countries (which is accompanied by a downturn in production and consumption) results in a sharp reduction in the foreign exchange earnings of poor nations because demand for the goods they export declines.

Production for the international market based on the principle of comparative advantage is the logical extension of integration into the international system. Comparative advantage is an economic principle that asserts that different localities, states, regions, or countries should concentrate production on the commodities they can produce most efficiently and exchange those commodities for others produced elsewhere. Each country, according to the logic of comparative advantage, should produce goods for the *international* market, and use revenues from sale of those goods to purchase the products of other nations. The mechanism for making such exchanges is international trade. So, for example, a poor country can export coffee (a commodity which it has an advantage in producing and selling compared to, say, the United States, which produces no coffee), earn foreign exchange, and use that foreign exchange to buy computers or wheat from the United States, where they are efficiently produced.

Finally, the economies of poor countries are free-enterprise economies. This means that the wealth produced through foreign trade or domestic production accrues to private individuals and groups. The practical consequence of this is that decisions about what goods and services to produce, how they will be produced (that is, who will produce them, and what resources will be used), and who will use these goods and services are *private* rather than *public* decisions.

To understand how many poor countries came to share the above characteristics, including hunger, we need to explore briefly the nature of their economies.

Colonialism

Without understanding how colonialism affected the land-use patterns (what crops were produced) and who benefited from colonial agriculture, it would be impossible to explain the food crisis adversely affecting today's underdeveloped nations. During the colonial period, wealth and resources needed to raise living standards in colonies were diverted to Europe. Economic production, instead of being organized to produce and distribute goods and services for the well-being of colonial populations, was geared instead to the marketing desires of the colonizing power. This profoundly affected colonial land- and labor-use patterns.

When I visited Sri Lanka (formerly the British colony of Ceylon) in 1972, the colonial agricultural pattern, in which colonies served as "agricultural establishments" exporting cash crops to Europe, was apparent. Tea and rubber plantations occupied much of the best agricultural land while canals formerly utilized for rice production were in disrepair. There was clear evidence of malnutrition, and yet the lush countryside tended to obscure this reality. Several years after my visit, I read that tea-plantation workers were selling their children because they couldn't afford to feed them. Only then did I appreciate fully the implications of the British neglect of the production of a necessary staple in favor of the production of export crops. From the point of view of the British Empire, Ceylon had simply been one colony among many, and it had a specific role to play in the overall scheme of things. On such logic a world food crisis is founded.

In colony after colony, diversified systems of food production were simplified, and prime agricultural land was planted with cash crops, such as coffee, tea, cocoa, bananas, sugar cane, cotton, sisal, or rubber. Agriculture, divorced from nutritional considerations, became a means by which to extract wealth. Often a colony concentrated production on one particular crop. As Lappé and Collins report:

> Rice farming once had been common in Gambia. But with colonial rule so much of the best land was taken over by peanuts (grown for the European market) that rice had to be imported to counter the mounting prospect of famine. Northern Ghana, once famous for its yams and other foodstuffs, was forced to concentrate solely on cocoa. Most of the Gold Coast, too, became dependent on cocoa. Liberia was turned into a virtual plantation subsidiary of Firestone Tire and Rubber. Food production in Dahomey and southeast Nigeria was all but abandoned in favor of palm oil; Tanganyika (now Tanzania) was forced to focus on sisal and Uganda on cotton.[1]

Colonialism, of course, was not a voluntary affair. Colonies were conquered, not peacefully persuaded. Following conquest, the transition to "agricultural establishment" began. Often land utilized by local farmers to produce subsistence crops was simply confiscated and consolidated into plantations. Displaced farmers, like those in ancient Israel, became the cheap, and in many cases, slave labor supply. Taxation also proved an effective means of encouraging the shift to production of cash crops for the empire. Because taxes had to be paid in royal coin, farmers were *forced* to produce and sell cash crops, or to earn wages through work on the plantations, or both. And as Walter Rodney points out in his book *How Europe Underdeveloped Africa*, the term *forced* is not an overstatement: It was not uncommon for cash crops to be grown under the threat of guns and whips.[2]

Colonial agriculture, then, neglected food production in favor of export crops, such as coffee, tea, sugar cane, and cocoa. The beneficiaries were the European colonizers and, as we shall see, a small group of people within the colonies who profited by participating in the colonial system.

Neocolonialism

The economies of today's underdeveloped countries reflect their colonial economies to such a high degree, and their economic situation remains so precarious, that the postcolonial period is often referred to as neocolonialism. The essense of neocolonialism is that economic dependence continued even after colonies achieved political independence. Poor countries still depend on export of agricultural products and raw materials to the United States and their former colonial overlords for the bulk of their foreign exchange earnings, and their economic situation is deteriorating. In 1900 people in poor countries had a per capita income about one half that of people in rich nations. By 1970 it was about one twentieth that of the rich nations measured in 1900 dollars, and one fortieth in 1970 dollars.[3] Since 1970 the gap has widened still further.

It *isn't* surprising that after political independence former colonies faced serious economic problems, including dependency. For hundreds of years their economies had been designed to transfer wealth to the colonizing powers. Efforts to break their economic dependency by diversifying their economies were bound to be difficult and take time. It would require a serious commitment on the part of development planners and government officials to establish local industries utilizing indigenous resources, to restore balance to agricultural systems divorced from the nutritional needs of the people and skewed in favor of export production, and to build infrastructures facilitating internal development. What *is* surprising, at first glance, is that such a commitment was and is almost totally lacking. In fact, as we hope to demonstrate, the development models pursued by most poor countries, including their reliance on export of agricultural products, raw materials, and more recently light manufactured goods, to earn foreign exchange, have led to increased dependence and further underdevelopment.

To understand why newly independent countries would follow a development path similar to the one that underdeveloped them as colonies, it is helpful to recall several findings from our overview of biblical passages about hunger. First, foreign trade, while beneficial to certain social classes, often undermines the position of the poor. Second, the exploitation of the poor involves the complicity of a variety of powerful groups. And finally, unless wealth and power are evenly distributed, the affluence of the rich will rub shoulders with the misery of the poor.

During the colonial period, wealthy nationals, including large landowners, merchants, colonial administrators, and other urban elites, prospered by cooperating with the colonizing nations. After achieving political independence, these elites were in an excellent position to solidify their wealth and power. But to do so, they could not rock the economic boat too drastically. Plantation owners, for example, depended on American and European corporations to purchase, transport, process, and market their coffee, sugar cane, tea, and tobacco. To alienate these corporations was bound to take money out of their own pockets. No wonder cooperation, although under slightly different circumstances, continued after political independence.

While diversification of production and a redistribution of wealth-producing resources were vital for the development of newly independent countries, they conflicted with the interests of powerful groups. From the vantage point of internal elites, exporting agricultural products and raw materials was highly profitable. It provided personal profits enabling luxury consumption and foreign exchange earnings for "development." What's more, by avoiding radical changes in economic structures, the elites reinforced the system on which their privilege, status, wealth, and power depended. From the vantage point of their foreign allies, transporting, processing, and marketing agricultural products was profitable, and the raw materials of poor countries were essential for the industries of developed countries. Also poor countries were important consumers of industrial products and surplus food supplies.

Aid: Tool of Neocolonialism

Our self-image is that we Americans are a generous people and a peaceful nation. As a consequence, Americans who travel to poor countries are often surprised when local people treat them disrespectfully. When twenty-eight other students and I spent a month in Ethiopia in 1972, our professor from the University of Addis Ababa was blatantly unfriendly and antagonistic. His conduct seemed inconsistent with my recollection that the United States had for many years provided economic and military assistance to the government of Haile Selassie. (From 1946 to 1976 the U.S. provided $283.9 million in military assistance to Ethiopia and trained nearly four thousand soldiers in American military schools.) What I realized later was that the root of the hostility was, in fact, American aid. The United States supported a government that during our visit arrested students simply for talking to us. Our aid propped up a ruler who profited from a feudal economy under which most of the people were tenant farmers too poor to feed their children. I remember feeling puzzled that a country unable to deliver basic goods and services to the majority of its people was able to distribute Coca-Cola to tourists in the remotest parts of the land.

On this same occasion India refused to grant us a group visa. This was hardly the respect one might expect from a country where American grants of food had saved millions of lives during periodic famines in the 1960's. The Indian government had recently expelled

the local contingent of the United States Peace Corps, which it said
had been infiltrated by the Central Intelligence Agency. Also relations between the two countries had cooled because the United
States was sending economic and military support to General Khan,
a brutal dictator from West Pakistan, who was committing well-
documented genocide in East Pakistan. Refugees poured into India,
creating a problem little appreciated by the Indian government,
which later went to war to settle the dispute.[4]

Finally, while I was in Sri Lanka, members of our group went to
the theater in Colombo, where the movie *Tora, Tora, Tora,* was
playing. The movie describes a series of blunders by American
government and military officials that made it possible for the
Japanese to launch a successful "surprise" attack on Pearl Harbor.
What was interesting for an American viewer was not the movie but
the reaction of the crowd. Each sinking of an American ship was
greeted with a standing ovation, complete with thunderous clap-
ping, screams, and laughter. The Americans and British were apparently both regarded as imperialists.

Events and experiences like these prompted me to ask several
questions. If the United States is a generous, aid-giving nation, why
has our aid been so ineffective in combating poverty? Why have we
won so few friends? Why do we give aid to repressive governments?
There are other Americans who wonder why American aid programs
haven't earned us the respect of the world's poor. Some are down-
right angry and lash out at the ungrateful victims. For example, in
December 1974, immediately following the World Food Conference
in Rome, the United States Industrial Council (a nationwide association of conservative business people) offered a press release entitled, "America: Abused and Fed Up." Here is an extract from the
report, which was printed in the *New York Times:*

> . . . the American people aren't about to . . . support new, mas-
> sive giveaways of food to third world nations. . . . For an entire
> generation, Americans have been shipping food to India and
> elsewhere. They have lavished billions of dollars on food
> giveaways without receiving any thanks in return. By and large,
> the American people are very tired of all types of foreign aid.
> Today, the United States faces severe economic difficulty at
> home. The Nation can't afford to be as generous as it was in the
> past. . . . Each country will have to solve its food problems. To
> be sure, the problems facing some countries are horrendous.
> But in many cases, the suffering nations have brought on their
> troubles. . . . Many of the countries now short of food are in-
> competent nations. To use a fashionable word, they aren't "via-

ble" countries. They lack the leadership, resources, educational elites and the capitalist economic structures necessary for effective production of food and long-term national existence. The United States cannot save all the inadequate nations of the world from their inadequacies or follies. . . . Indeed, we are in a period when our Government must stress economic nationalism. We need to maximize all our advantages, including sale of our food. Dependent nations must look to their own resources and attempt to curb their extravagant population growth. . . . The food crisis will worsen in many nations that can't carry out their basic responsibility for feeding their people. Unfortunately, the American people will be subjected to emotion-laden appeals and to threats of third world retaliation if the United States doesn't come across with more food giveaways.[5]

According to this view, poor nations have only themselves to blame for their plight. The United States has generously given aid, but all for naught. The aid-receiving nations are ungrateful, incompetent, and overpopulated. America has been abused long enough, faces severe economic problems of its own, and can no longer fall prey to emotion-laden appeals. *Underlying this view is the basic assumption that aid is designed to help the poor.* Given acceptance of this assumption, it is appropriate to state the problem, as the Industrial Council has, in these terms: *despite* American food and other forms of aid, poor countries face serious food and economic problems.

Unfortunately, the basic assumption of the Industrial Council and of millions of well-meaning Americans about the purpose of aid is faulty. *Aid, in its variety of forms, is an instrument of American foreign policy. Its primary purpose is not and never has been to help the poor and hungry.* This fact is well stated in a 1957 report of the Senate Committee on Foreign Relations on the concept, purpose, and evaluation of American technical assistance:

> The subcommittee has conducted its study on the premise that the sole test of technical assistance is the national interest of the United States. Technical assistance is not something to be done, as a Government enterprise, for its own sake or for the sake of others. The United States is not a charitable institution, nor is it an appropriate outlet for the charitable spirit of the American people. That spirit finds its proper instrumentality in the numerous private philanthropic and religious institutions which have done so much good work abroad.

Technical assistance, according to the report, is a vehicle by which the United States pursues its national interest. Unfortunately, as we shall see, the United States often victimizes the poor in pursuit of that interest. The role that the committee assigns to religious institutions should give pause to Christians who have long been engaged in relief work. Apparently we are to care for people who are victimized in the course of the United States' pursuing of its foreign-policy interests. The committee report continued:

> Technical assistance is only one of a number of instruments available to the United States *to carry out its foreign policy and to promote its national interests abroad.* Besides technical assistance, these *tools of foreign policy* include *economic aid, military assistance,* security treaties, tax and commercial treaties, overseas information programs, participation in the United Nations and other international organizations, the exchange of persons program, tariff and trade policies, *surplus agricultural commodity disposal policies,* and the traditional processes of diplomatic representation. None of these tools has any particular inherent merit; any of them may be useful in a given situation.... The proper measure of a program's cost ... is the relationship of cost to benefits.... The cost of any foreign activity of the United States becomes significant only when it is related to the benefits which the United States receives from that activity.[6]

If aid is ineffective in helping poor countries we would seem to have found the reason: it is designed to serve United States interests. Also it is important to understand that according to the committee, aid is *one among several* tools of foreign policy. It is, therefore, one component in an overall strategy designed to serve the foreign policy interests of the United States. As such, we might expect that American aid programs will have changed over the past thirty years reflecting the changing needs and objectives of American foreign policy. This, as we shall see, is the case.

Aid: Securing Access to Foreign Markets and Raw Materials

In the aftermath of World War II, the United States faced serious economic problems, including excessive productive capacity and increasing dependence on foreign raw materials. "For all our own material might," President Eisenhower stated in his inaugural address in 1953, "even we need markets in the world for the surpluses of our farms and factories. Equally, we need for the same farms and factories vital materials and products of distant lands." World War II had helped bring the United States out of the depression, but as early as 1944 fears about insufficient markets for American goods were voiced in the government. Secretary of State Dean Acheson, testifying before a special Congressional committee on Postwar Economic Policy and Planning, stated:

> We cannot go through another ten years like the ten years at the end of the twenties and the beginning of the thirties, without having the most far-reaching consequences upon our economic and social system. . . . When we look at that problem we may say it is a problem of markets. You don't have a problem of production. The United States has unlimited creative energy. The important thing is markets. We have got to see that what the country produces is used and is sold under financial arrangements which make its production possible.

In an exchange with the chairperson of the committee, Acheson added this interesting anecdote:

> *Acheson:* We could argue for quite a while that under a different system in this country you could use the entire production of the country in the United States.
> *Worley:* What do you mean by that?
> *Acheson:* I take it the Soviet Union could use its entire production internally. If you wish to control the entire trade and income of the United States, which means the life of the people, you could probably fix it so that everything produced here would be consumed here, but that would completely change our Constitution, our relations to property, human liberty, our very conceptions of law. And nobody contemplates that. Therefore, you find you must look to other markets and those markets are abroad. The first thing that I want to bring out is that we need these markets for the output of the United States. If I am wrong about that, then all the argument falls by the wayside, but my contention is that we cannot have full employment and prosperity in the United States without the foreign markets. That is point one, and if anyone wants to challenge me on that we will go over it again.
> *Worley:* I think we are agreed on that.
> *Acheson:* How do we go about getting it? What you have to do at the outset is make credit available.[7]

Acheson firmly believed that freedom, full employment, and prosperity were impossible without an international free-enterprise system. His views were well accepted by numerous government and business leaders and prompted the Marshall Plan—an aid program to rebuild war-torn Europe. The major fear was that war-torn nations would adopt a development path similar to the Soviet Union, thus cutting themselves off as markets for American products. The Council of Economic Advisors warned:

> Without new foreign aid . . . Europe would be forced into an entirely different character of production and reorientation of trade. European resources would have to be organized in such a manner that all but the most essential imports from the Western Hemisphere were dispensed with. This would have a detrimental influence on a number of our important industries which have been accustomed to considerable exports to Europe.[8]

Until 1952, 95 percent of American aid went to Europe. However, during the 1950s the focus of American aid shifted to underdeveloped countries. We mentioned previously that a common feature of poor countries that are seriously affected by the world food crisis is that their economies are firmly integrated into the international free-enterprise system. The shift in American aid programs from Europe, where political stability and economic recovery were well under way, to poorer countries was designed to insure poor country integration into that system.

During World War II poor countries began making strides toward agricultural and industrial self-sufficiency. War-enforced isolation necessarily led to a diversification of their economies. For example, numerous coffee trees in Brazil were torn up and replaced with food crops. The United States resisted these movements toward self-reliance. If poor countries would have broken their dependence on the export of cash crops and raw materials to industrialized countries, or restricted their markets to American exporters, it would have posed serious problems for American corporations.

Of special concern to United States policy makers was access to strategic minerals, most of which came from poor countries. In 1954 the President's Commission on Foreign Economic Policy noted that America's increasing dependence on foreign sources of metals and minerals:

> . . . constitutes one of the striking economic changes of our times. The outbreak of World War II marked the major turning point of this change. Both from the viewpoint of our long-term economic growth and the viewpoint of our national defense, *the shift of the United States from the position of a net exporter*

of metals and minerals to that of net importer is of over-shadowing significance in shaping our foreign economic policies.[9]

Public Law 480

One of the "tools of foreign policy" mentioned in the Senate report on technical assistance is Public Law 480 (P.L. 480), referred to in the report as "surplus agricultural disposal policies." P.L. 480, the Agricultural Trade Development and Assistance Act of 1954, was this nation's first comprehensive food aid program. Written into its statement of purpose were two principle goals: to dispose of agricultural surpluses and to develop future markets for American agricultural products. Not until the bill was amended in 1961 did it mention in its statement of purpose the goals of combating hunger or encouraging economic development in poor countries. Even then, as we shall see, its primary function was as a foreign-policy tool.

During World War II the United States became the world's largest agricultural exporter, and agricultural exports were vital to the health of the overall economy. In 1940 agricultural exports accounted for only 10 percent of total exports, but by 1945 that figure was 37 percent. Surpluses became problematic as war-torn nations rebuilt their agricultural systems and reduced their purchases of American farm products. The Korean War, which ended in 1953, also resulted in declining exports. Agricultural surpluses, which depressed farm prices and forced numerous small farmers out of business, threatened to undermine the American economy. This prompted Edward O'Neal, president of the American Farm Bureau, to state that farm surpluses "will wreck our economy unless we can find sufficient markets to sustain the volume of production." He urged American policymakers to spread the Monroe Doctrine around the world. "Let us spread it all over. . . " O'Neal said, "let us run it into China, if necessary, and run it into Russia."

The problem facing United States policymakers was how to turn damaging surpluses into an instrument of American domestic and foreign economic policy. The short-term need was to dispose of surpluses thus bailing out the domestic economy. But over the long term it was essential that poor countries become permanent markets for American farm products. Achieving these goals was made more difficult by the fact that poor countries were less than ideal customers. Their scarce foreign exchange earnings provided only a limited amount of dollars with which to purchase American goods. Under normal marketing conditions, therefore, American agricultural exporters would have been forced to compete with American industrial exporters, who were also desperate for markets, for the limited foreign-exchange earnings of poor countries.

The genius of P.L. 480 was that it was a multifaceted program serving a variety of American interests. It contained three major sections. Title I permitted poor nations to purchase grain at concessional prices (prices below world market prices); Title II provided grants to nations during famines and other disasters; and Title III authorized the barter of American food for strategic materials. Title I, which has accounted for nearly 80 percent of all commodities shipped under the law, is far and away the most important. It allowed poor countries to purchase American farm products *without using dollars*. Until 1971 concessional sales were financed through loans repayable in the recipient country's local currency. The United States, therefore, made optimal use of poor nations as consumers of American products. Dollars were utilized for industrial imports while food imports were paid for in local currencies.

P.L. 480 was essentially an aid program for American farmers and business leaders. Secretary of Agriculture Orville Freeman noted in 1964 that agricultural exports under P.L. 480

> effectively serve our farm and business communities by building future markets for our efficiently produced abundance. Hundreds of thousands of jobs on our farms and in our towns and cities depend wholly or substantially on the production, processing, transporting, and related activities brought about by Public Law 480.[10]

It is important to remember that Title I involved concessional sales and not grants. In the first twenty years of the program P.L. 480 turned an economic liability (agricultural surpluses) into $20 billion of indebtedness for poor countries at virtually no cost to the United States.

Revenues from concessional sales were used to support a variety of American political and economic interests. For example, in 1957 Congress established the Cooley Loan Program whereby local currencies generated through sale of P.L. 480 commodities were loaned to American corporations at a very low rate of interest. Cooley loans have gone to such corporate giants as CPC International, Cargill Corporation, Chrysler Corporation, Deere & Company, Exxon Corporation, International Telephone & Telegraph (ITT), and the Ralston Purina Company. Loans have also been made to financial institutions such as the Chase Manhattan Corporation, First National City Bank, and Bank of America. All told, 420 subsidiaries of American firms have expanded operations in thirty-one countries through this program.

P.L. 480 funds were often used for military related purposes. The 1964 Conference Bill authorized the use of Title I currencies in support of counterinsurgency programs. The same year, Secretary of Agriculture Orville Freeman aggressively promoted the use of P.L. 480 funds for "internal security," including "activities in support of counterinsurgency programs, such as the Vietnamese strategic-hamlet program." Freeman's recommendations were taken seriously. According to Representative John J. Rooney, 90 percent of the local currency funds generated under Title I sales in Vietnam in 1964 were used to support the military effort.[11]

Two years later Freeman again cited Vietnam in testimony supporting P.L. 480. "The victory," he said, "won't hold unless agriculture goes forward with the troops. This is truly a two-front war. . . . Agriculture is the key element in securing villages and hamlets won in the shooting war."[12] To clarify Freeman's intention we have only to remember that in 1961 the U.S. began destroying growing crops in Vietnam as part of its "resource denial" program. This was accomplished by aerial application of chemical defoliants known as Agents Blue and Orange. In the first eight years of the program Agent Blue was dropped on more than 9 percent of South Vietnam's cropland and 13 percent of its forests, while twelve million gallons of Agent Orange were sprayed over five million acres of Vietnam jungle. Applications were carried out near harvest time, rendering the land useless for at least a year, sometimes much longer. After destroying the people's food supply, it was easier to herd them into camps where their activities could be monitored. American food aid was vital to the success of this effort. In the aftermath of the war Agents Blue and Orange continue their destruction. The defoliants have hampered Vietnam's efforts to rebuild its agricultural system, stillbirths and birth defects are unusually high among native people exposed to the herbicides, and United States veterans exposed to Agent Orange have complained of a variety of ailments.

Since the beginning of P.L. 480, nearly all American food aid has gone to military allies. "Food for Peace," as the program is often called, has more often than not become food for war. About 80 percent of all the money collected in South Korea and South Vietnam through concessional sales was used for the "common defense." The government in South Vietnam took the food from the Food for Peace shipments, sold it to the people, and used the revenues, among other things, to build the "tiger cages" in which political prisoners were tortured. When Senator Proxmire heard testimony from the General Accounting Office in 1971 that, over the previous five years, the Food for Peace program had permitted foreign countries to purchase nearly $700 million in military equipment, he was outraged. According to Proxmire, the use of Food for Peace funds to purchase weapons smacked of an "Orwellian operation," an example in "doublethink" in which "Food for Peace has been converted into Food for War."[13]

Even during the peak of the world food crisis in 1974, 70 percent of Title I shipments went to South Vietnam and Cambodia, while countries which, according to the United Nations, were most seriously affected went without food aid or received very little. Thomas Enders, the Assistant Secretary of State, justified such priorities at hearings of the Senate Agriculture Committee:

> Mr. Chairman, let me add a word about the controversy between "political" and "humanitarian." Few would argue that our programs are designed to achieve both ends. All the countries we assist with P.L. 480 are developing; all are relatively poor; all have deficient dietary standards; many are threatened with disaster, either natural or through war; all have major food needs. The question is not whether to choose between Korea and Pakistan, between Vietnam and Cambodia, between Chile and India. *The question is how to find a basis on which our national interests can be served in each country* (emphasis added).[14]

The need for counterinsurgency programs to control unrest in the countryside was a necessary consequence of P.L. 480. Food aid shipments undercut poor-country food producers while reinforcing producers of cash crops for export. In effect, P.L. 480 gave support to large landowners who were integrated into the international market system. They were able to capitalize on their comparative advantage in producing coffee, sugar cane, bananas, and other tropical commodities. At the same time, P.L. 480 shipments undermined small food producers whose markets were destroyed by cheap imports. In Colombia the government marketing agency sold P.L. 480 wheat at prices low enough to eliminate the greater part of domestic production. Between 1955 and 1971 Colombia imported 1,140,000 tons of wheat. At the same time, prices received by farmers declined sharply. While in 1954 Colombia produced more than 160,000 tons for itself and imported only 50,000 tons, by 1971 it produced less than 50,000 tons, and imported 400,000 tons—almost 90 percent of Colombia's domestic consumption. Meanwhile, Cooley Loans went to American corporations such as Ralston Purina, Parke Davis, Pfizer, Abbott Labs, and Quaker Oats to build feed and fertilizer facilities, and to Goodyear, Gillette, General Electric, and Singer to expand their plant operations in Colombia.[15]

A major goal of P.L. 480 was to usher poor countries through a transition from food aid (concessional sales at below market prices) to dollar sales at full market prices, a process which the U.S. Department of Agriculture refers to as graduating from P.L. 480 status. Surplus disposal was seen as a stepping stone to food dependency and thus an assured dollar market. Often potential food-aid recipients had to agree to future purchases at full market prices as a condition for receiving aid.

South Korea is an interesting example of a country that has graduated from P.L. 480 status. It has been the second largest recipient of American food aid. The South Korean government is a dictatorship closely aligned with the United States government and American corporations. In its effort to please American corporations, the South Korean government has encouraged migration of rural peasants to urban areas to provide a reserve of cheap labor. Food aid facilitated this process by undercutting domestic food producers, thus causing a forced migration from the countryside. It also allowed the government to keep food prices low, which meant that wages could be kept low.

While P.L. 480 benefited American farmers, food processors, and other American-based corporations which shifted productions to Korea to take advantage of cheap labor, it stifled the incomes of Korean peasants and workers. In rural areas poverty is increasing, while the gap between the affluent and the poor widens. And according to an internal memorandum from the United States Agency for International Development (AID), the situation of the urban poor is no better: "One in four is unemployed, and those who are employed make an average of 28 cents an hour, often working for U.S. corporations aided by P.L. 480 loans."[16]

P.L. 480, which undercut poor-nation food producers, has also led to food dependency. In 1970 South Korea produced 81 percent of its food needs; by 1975 this had dropped to 68 percent. South Korea today is a $700 million annual cash customer for American grains and will soon import 50 percent of its food to meet domestic demand. "In the last seven years," Orville Freeman told a Senate Foreign Relations Committee in 1974, "our agricultural exports to Taiwan have climbed by 531 percent and those to [South] Korea by 643 percent because we created a market."

P.L. 480, as we have demonstrated, was by design an important foreign-policy tool. Through this program the U.S. was able to:
• profitably dispose of harmful surpluses and bail out the U.S. economy,
• create future markets by undermining local food producers and encouraging production of agricultural products for export based on the principle of comparative advantage,

- make optimal use of poor countries as consumers of U.S. agricultural and industrial goods,
- encourage poor nations to abandon policies directed toward self-reliance and to integrate their economies into the international free-enterprise system,
- facilitate U.S. corporate expansion abroad through Cooley loans,
- fund counterinsurgency and other military efforts that protect U.S. political and economic interests,
- and finally, foster poor-country indebtedness and dependency.

P.L. 480 was not a master plan mechanically devised and implemented over the years. It was a flexible tool of foreign policy, which evolved into various strategies appropriate to particular needs and opportunities. However, while there was no master plan, there is throughout the history of P.L. 480 a deep awareness among American policymakers that food is power! The more dependent a nation is on the United States for a commodity as essential as food, the more leverage this government has in pursuing its political and economic interests regardless of whether those interests conflict with the needs of the majority of people of a poor nation. Just as displaced farmers and other poor people in Israel were ruthlessly exploited by merchants who monopolized the grain trade, so it is or will be with poor people in countries dependent on the United States for food.

Since its inception, a conscious goal of P.L. 480 has been to create food dependency. In 1957 a State Department official told the Senate:

> We have a real problem in connection with the dependency created by some of these programs. If dependence upon the U.S. goes too fast . . . we may be helping weaken a country and its economy in the long run.

Senator Hubert Humphrey responded:

> I have heard this morning that people may become dependent on us for food. I know that was not supposed to be good news. To me, that is good news, because before people can do anything, they have got to eat. And if you are looking for a way to get people to lean on you and be dependent on you, in terms of their cooperation with you, it seems to me that food dependence would be terrific.[17]

During a severe famine in 1966, India experienced the consequences of food dependency. The United States used food power to pressure India to abandon its intention of having its fertilizer industry domestically controlled. In its issue entitled "Feeding the World's Hungry Millions: How It Will Mean Billions for U.S. Business," *Forbes* magazine reported:

> The U.S. government is putting a great deal of pressure on the underdeveloped nations to make it attractive for U.S. companies to build fertilizer plants abroad. For a long time, India insisted that it handle all the distribution of fertilizers produced in that country by U.S. companies and that it also set the price. Standard of Indiana understandably refused to accept these conditions. AID put food shipments to India on a month-to-month basis until the Indian government let Standard of Indiana market the fertilizer itself at its own price.[18]

Later in 1967, AID requested $50 million so that India could buy fertilizer with the stated purpose of helping United States oil companies. "Much of what is happening now," the *New York Times* commented at the time, "is the result of steady pressure from the United States and the International Bank for Reconstruction and Development, which for the last year have been urging a substantial freeing of the Indian economy and a greater scope for private enterprises."

When the world plummeted into a food crisis in the early 1970s, the United States capitalized on a golden opportunity. The world food crisis hit at a time when the United States was facing an economic crisis more severe than any since the depression of the 1930s. We will discuss the causes of the American economic crisis in more detail in chapter 5. Briefly, the American balance of payments had worsened by 1970 to the point that our trade relations with western Europe and Japan were threatened. Confidence in the dollar was shaken as the Nixon Administration refused to redeem gold for foreign-held dollars. And in 1971 the U.S. experienced its first trade deficit of the century (that is, we imported more goods than we exported).

Many American leaders regard the world food crisis as an opportunity whereby the United States can restore its economy to health and revitalize its political position throughout the world. In 1974 Secretary of Agriculture Earl Butz openly stated that food is a weapon. He made this comment several months after the Central Intelligence Agency (CIA) completed a study on American food power. This study indicated that, in the future, world food shortages could give the United States "virtual life and death power over the fate of the multitudes of the needy." "Twenty years ago," the CIA

study states proudly, "North America exported mainly to Western
Europe; most other regions were basically self-sufficient. Now, the
whole world has become dependent on North America for grain—
feed grains mainly to Europe and Japan, food grains elsewhere."[19]

Monopoly food power is profitable. As the food crisis intensified,
food aid all but disappeared while sales skyrocketed. In 1969 revenues from agricultural exports were $5.9 billion of which 17 percent
was related to concessional sales under P.L. 480; in 1974 sales were
$21.9 billion, of which only 3 percent was concessional.[20] Those are
impressive figures, which would bring a nod of approval from the
monopoly merchants in Amos's Israel.

In 1974, twenty years after sponsorship of original P.L. 480 legislation, Senator Hubert Humphrey was involved in an exchange with
Donald Paarlberg, director of agricultural economics for the United
States Department of Agriculture, which highlights the ultimate
purpose and consequence of American food aid policy. Senator
Humphrey was concerned that the agricultural export boom during
the world food crisis would mean a shortage of disaster relief funds
for immediate assistance to Pakistan, Sahelian Africa, and Nicaragua:

> *Senator Humphrey:* . . . it is my understanding that the De-
> partment of [Agriculture] is not asking for additional funds for
> Public Law 480; is that correct?
> *Dr. Paarlberg:* Senator, it is my understanding that the De-
> partment of Agriculture considers Public Law 480 to be what it
> was legislated to be, namely a trade development and surplus
> disposal operation.
> *Senator Humphrey:* Yes.
> *Dr. Paarlberg:* And under the present situation we do not
> have surpluses and with concern about excessive flow of ex-
> ports from this country, we can't really consider a trade devel-
> opment proposal. It [P.L. 480] has become very largely a part of
> our foreign economic policy and a part of our diplomatic policy,
> and those things seem to us to be of a different character from
> those with which we are primarily concerned in the Depart-
> ment of Agriculture.[21]

Perhaps food dependence wasn't so terrific after all. Hubert Humphrey was a considerate and thoughtful person. He used to visit my
father and other workers at a small printing company outside Minneapolis, Minnesota, chew the fat, tell jokes, and listen to their
problems. He was regarded as one of the most progressive liberals in

the Democratic party. But he was victimized by a bitter contradiction that strikes liberals and conservatives alike: they expect it to be possible for the United States to pursue its corporate interests with a vengeance throughout the globe, create dependency, exploit vulnerability, distort poor-nation economies, cooperate with elites, and not inflict intolerable suffering on the poor. Exploiting others is supposed to be good business and ethical too. Our victims are to be grateful beneficiaries, and when they do not act that way, we are somehow surprised.

In 1975, Earl Butz told the Senate Committee on Agriculture and Forestry that "agriculture has now become our number one source of foreign exchange, and it is a powerful factor in maintaining the economic health of this country." Unfortunately, the American economy *is not* healthy, and what Butz and other leaders regarded as "economic health" is a death trap for the poor:

> O my people, your leaders mislead you,
> and confuse the course of your paths.
> The Lord takes a place to contend,
> and stands to judge the people.
> The Lord enters into judgement
> with the elders and princes of the people:
> "It is you who have devoured the vineyard,
> the spoil of the poor is in your houses.
> What do you mean by crushing my people,
> by grinding the face of the poor?"
> says the Lord God of hosts (Isa. 3:12–15).*

In the minds of many Americans, it would be impossible for the United States to act like the merchants of ancient Israel. Yet it is impossible only to the extent that our worldview denies such a possibility. It is impossible because of our distorted sense of consciousness and patriotic faith. As American Christians we have for the most part been mesmerized by the ideology of our nation. This ideology, which has seeped deeply into the fabric of our churches, portrays America as the global Messiah. Yet what recently seemed impossible to many of us has now become historical fact:

> Hear this, you who trample upon the needy,
> and bring the poor of the land to an end,
> saying, "When will the new moon be over,
> that we may sell grain?
> And the sabbath,

that we may offer wheat for sale . . .
that we may buy the poor for silver
and the needy for a pair of sandals,
and sell the refuse of the wheat?"
The Lord has sworn by the pride of Jacob:
"Surely I will never forget any of their deeds" (Amos 8: 4–7).

Chapter 3

HUNGER TODAY

Poor countries today are well integrated into the international free-enterprise system, and poor people within them are paying a heavy price because food production for local consumption was subordinated throughout the 1960s and '70s to other developmental goals. As we have seen, American aid programs, including P.L. 480, were transition tools to the neocolonialism designed to encourage such integration and to discourage food production. "There was a general belief both in and out of government," according to a vice-president of the Rockefeller Foundation, "that other nations should not be encouraged to increase production of . . . [basic food] crops for fear of competition with U.S. efforts to sell its surplus stocks or even give them away."[1]

Discouraging food production in poor nations paid political and economic dividends to a variety of groups in the United States. Food is a vehicle for power and profit. Also cheap food imports enable large producers in poor nations to concentrate agricultural production on export crops, that is, to exploit their comparative advantage in international markets. Unfortunately, as we hope to demonstrate, subordinating food production for local consumption to other developmental goals, integration into the international free-enterprise system, and determining production priorities on the basis of the principle of comparative advantage have resulted in human hunger.

Victims and Beneficiaries

In the lobby of the luxurious Hotel La Romana in the Dominican Republic there is an oil painting of a shantytown. Of course, it is a quaint shantytown. While no people are visible on its dirt road, one imagines that they too are quaint and full of song.

The Hotel La Romana stands like a mirage against a sea of

30

cane fields. There is a high fence around the hotel grounds but armed guards casually wave the white American past the gate.

Many of the guests arrive in their private jets on a small landing strip that bisects the Pete Dye-designed golf course. Others dock their yachts at the private marina on the Caribbean.

The sweet smell of molasses from the nearby sugar mill pervades the entire setting. It is so strong at times that it reminds one of a household air freshener or deodorant designed to mask some terrible reality.

The hotel, sugar mill, and 275,000 acres of surrounding land are owned by Gulf & Western Americas Corporation, part of Gulf & Western Industries, Inc., with assets in 1972 of almost $2.3 billion.

José Juan lives in a battey, or small congregation of dwellings, near the town of El Siebo. He has never dined at the grand hotel, swum at their private beach nor for that matter has he even seen it. Sr. Juan lives alone in a shack unfit for human habitation. There is a sweet odor here not unlike that at the hotel. But one realizes that it is the mixture of sweat and urine. For José Juan is a cane cutter and an employee of Gulf & Western Americas Corporation. And José Juan is dying. . . .

He came to work for "the company" as a cane cutter in 1914. One can see that his body was once strong and firm. But the years . . . have taken their toll. He is weak and in pain. He is frightened he will die in his lonely shack. Without strength he does not work and cannot earn his meager wages. He has nothing to eat but the scraps his neighbors, who are as poor as he, bring to him in pity. . . . José Juan usually goes hungry.

Having heard about a company hospital, he begs his visitors to help him gain admittance. But the local priest informs him that the company says it is only for employees and José Juan has not worked in over a year.

He insists he is due a pension. The priest explains that the company grants a $6 per month pension for an employee who has worked 48 years or more. But again the management says that records were poorly kept so many years ago, and José Juan must be patient while they investigate.

But it is difficult to ask a dying man for patience.

Charles G. Bluhdorn lives in a duplex penthouse on the fashionable East Side of Manhattan. He is also an employee of Gulf & Western Industries. As Chairman of the Board he earned $252,600 for the fiscal year ending July 31, 1972. This sum does not reflect such benefits as stock options and savings plans [which would bring his yearly income to approximately $600,000]. When Mr. Bluhdorn retires, it is estimated he will receive $74,829 per annum in pension benefits. He will not go hungry. . . .

But if Mr. Bluhdorn is on top of the G & W Empire, and Sr. Juan on bottom, there are many thousands of average people in between. And neither they nor the 45,000 common shareholders in G & W feel any particular responsibility toward José Juan and his fellow cane cutters.

It is probably a foolish question to ask whether any one of them, . . . would care to work in the fields for even a day. Perhaps it is not so foolish, though, to consider the consequences of such mundane experience for managerial personnel. Which Vice President could work in ninety degree heat cutting cane from sunrise to sunset? Which Director would permit his young children to labor beside him in order to cut enough cane to eat that night? Which economist would approve of his wages being paid by the ton of cane instead of by the hour or the day? How many stockholders could feed their children on earnings of three or four dollars per day, seasonable employment? [2]

José Juan is dying. The cane cut with the labor of his hands has produced wealth for others, not himself. One can hardly imagine a more vivid description of a modern-day situation that parallels the one described by Amos. The luxury hotel, private jets, yachts, marina, and golf course are all symbols of affluence built on the backs of the poor. They are enjoyed inside armed camps well insulated from the victims. The vineyards of Israel have become cane fields which, like a green plague, devour the land and lifeblood of the poor.

José Juan is dying in a country that shares the three common characteristics of nations seriously affected by hunger. The economy of the Dominican Republic is a free-enterprise economy; it is well integrated into the international free-enterprise system; and its economic production is based on the principle of comparative advantage. In the Dominican Republic 25 percent of the cultivated land is planted with sugar cane, and this percentage is increasing. Over the past twenty years acreage devoted to sugar production has almost doubled while acreage devoted to rice, beans, fruits, and yucca—the mainstay of the people's diet—has declined significantly. [3]

The logic of comparative advantage dictates that the Dominican Republic should export sugar. Foreign-exchange earnings from sugar are supposed to finance economic development by enabling the country to import needed foodstuffs, raw materials, and capital goods that are not produced domestically. But an important yet rarely asked question is: comparative advantage for whom?

In the Dominican Republic the answer is clear. Large landowners, government leaders, and executives of Gulf & Western Industries, Inc., a United States-based multinational corporation, applaud the sugar boom. Gulf & Western, the country's largest private sugar producer, owns 275,000 acres of land on which it produces beef and sugar for export. It also operates the world's largest sugar-producing mill at La Romana, where it processes sugar cane from its own land as well as that of large landowners. In addition to its sugar operations, the company has plowed profits into the Dominican tourist industry and operates—under a thirty-year contract with the Dominican government—a massive industrial free zone where it rents space to American corporations. Industries settling in the zone are granted a twenty-year tax exemption, which allows them the duty-free import of raw materials from domestic and foreign sources, duty-free export of all manufactured goods, and complete exemption from American corporate taxes, profit and dividend taxes to shareholders as well as production, sales, patent, and municipal taxes. And most important is corporate access to an unlimited cheap labor force of unskilled employees, who, according to Gulf & Western advertisements, earn 40 cents per hour.

The darker side of the sugar boom is the imminent death of José Juan. He and hundreds of thousands of others like him do not share in the wealth produced by the sugar boom. The problem for small farmers, subsistence farmers, and landless laborers—who together comprise about 75 percent of the rural population—is that foreign-exchange earnings from sugar exports do not put more food on their plates. In fact, the opposite is true. They are not consulted when decisions are made about how to use foreign exchange. Wealth in a free-enterprise society accrues to private individuals and groups. Investment decisions about what goods and services to produce, how they will be distributed, and who will use them are private decisions. Consequently, investments go to projects that are most profitable, such as tourism, rather than to those that are socially desirable or necessary. As a consequence, not far from the luxury hotel at La Romana, José Juan is living in a shack unfit for human habitation; he is hungry and dying.

Malnutrition is a serious problem throughout the Dominican Republic. Because the land devoted to food crops is declining and the population is increasing, people are migrating to urban areas. But food prices are high and jobs are scarce. In the rural areas premature death is common among rural families. Sugar cane, which dominates the countryside, is not a nutritious crop. Even if it were, poor people could not afford to eat it. A worker for Gulf & Western is paid about $1.30 to cut a ton of sugar cane. At the local store (usually controlled by Gulf & Western), he or she will pay about 55 cents for a pound of refined sugar. In the rural areas approximately 60 percent of Dominican children die before age five.[4] Death is sometimes welcome.

The situation of José Juan and the great majority of people in the Dominican Republic is similar to that of numerous other poor people in underdeveloped countries. Large landowners in conjunction with American multinational corporations profit from export of agricultural products. Comparative advantage is cited as the rationale, and the profits accrue to private individuals and groups who utilize foreign exchange to support developmental goals that further private interests and victimize the poor. In 1977 alone poor countries exported $9.59 billion worth of agricultural products to the United States.[5]

The agricultural exports of poor countries are of high nutritional quality. The United States, for example, is the world's largest importer of beef and fish products. Beef makes its way to the U.S. from poor nations like Argentina, Brazil, Costa Rica, Dominican Republic, El Salvador, Guatemala, Haiti, Honduras, Mexico, Nicaragua, Panama, Paraguay, and Uruguay. "Although more meat can be produced," writes nutritionist Alan Berg, "it is another question whether it will be available for domestic consumption or whether the nutritionally needy can afford it. More meat is being raised in Central America than ever before; it seems, however, to be ending up not in Latin American stomachs but in franchised restaurant hamburgers in the United States." In Nicaragua, a 75 percent increase in meat production was accompanied by only a 3 percent increase in average consumption; in Guatemala a 40 percent increase in production was accompanied by a 6 percent decrease in average consumption; and in Costa Rica, a 92 percent increase in production was accompanied by a 26 percent decline in per capita consumption.[6]

Mexico produces a variety of fruits and vegetables for export to the United States, including asparagus, cabbages, cantaloupes, cauliflowers, cucumbers, eggplants, garlic, green beans, peas, peppers, squash, strawberries, tomatoes, and watermelons. During the winter and spring Mexico supplies over one half of the American domestic consumption of several of these vegetables. In search of cheap labor and higher profit margins, American corporations have been quick to shift production sites to Mexico, or to contract with large Mexican producers. Until recently white asparagus consumed in the United States was produced in California. No longer is this so. In 1975 Del Monte shifted contracts to Mexico, where it is one of two firms controlling 90 percent of Mexican asparagus production. In 1973 Del Monte paid American asparagus growers 23 cents a pound for their crop; in Mexico contractors receive only 10 cents a pound. The Mexican contractors pay laborers 23 cents an hour, thus enabling Del Monte to translate cheap labor into high profits.

For the most part it is American firms that are facilitating the shifts from Mexican production for local consumption to production for export to the United States. They are in effect financing malnutrition in Mexico. The shifts are dramatic. From 1960 to 1974 onion imports from Mexico to the United States increased over five times to 95 million pounds, and cucumber imports soared from under 9 million to over 173 million pounds. From 1960 to 1972 eggplant imports grew tenfold, and squash imports multiplied forty-three times. United States-based suppliers have turned areas of Mexico into strawberry fields. By 1970 over 150 million pounds, three quarters of which were frozen, were being exported to the United States annually, approximately a third of United States consumption. Early-childhood deaths due to malnutrition have gone up 10 percent over the last ten years in Mexico, while the acreage devoted to basic food crops—corn, wheat, beans, and rice—actually declined 25 percent over the same period. In the period 1975–77 Mexico imported 15 percent of its corn, 25 percent of its wheat, and 45 percent of its soybeans.[7]

More than a third of the cultivated land in the Philippines is producing export crops. Del Monte and Castle & Cooke (Dole), in response to their workers' successful efforts to increase wages in Hawaii, have shifted pineapple production to a variety of under-developed countries, including the Philippines, where wages can be as low as 15 cents an hour. Del Monte has cut its Hawaiian production by 40 percent while it has expanded production and canning in the Philippines and is opening plantations in Kenya. Castle & Cooke, which had all of its operations in Hawaii as late as 1959, had only 25 percent of them there in 1975. Castle & Cooke now owns 19,000 acres in the Philippines and has expanded operations in Thailand.[8]

Del Monte, Castle & Cooke, and United Brands are also utilizing the rich soils and cheap labor of the Philippines to produce bananas for the Japanese market where a single banana sells for 25 cents. While these corporations own some land in the Philippines, they prefer to contract production with large landowners who are more than willing to cooperate both in farming and in evicting tenants and small farmers. Contract farming allows United States-based multina-tionals to hire farmers to whom they supply credit, fertilizers, pes-ticides, and other agricultural inputs for the purpose of producing bananas for export. These same landowners also do the dirty work of evicting tenants, wresting land from small farmers, and enforcing slave wages. (Wages average between $1.00 to $1.50 per day, although an average family needs at least $1.70 per day to eat on only a minimum diet.) In this way United States-based corporations are able to assume a low profile and disclaim responsibility for the oppression of people in the countryside.

Much of the land now producing bananas for export was formerly used by small farmers and tenants to produce coconuts, corn, rice, and hemp, much of it for local use. The tenants have simply been evicted while the small landholders have lost their land through a variety of insidious maneuvers by the large landowners and companies. In their efforts to obtain additional landholdings, some landlords have used tactics that include "acts of dispossession like bulldozing farms, demolition and/or burning of homes, manhandling, mauling, intimidations, etc." Often peasants whose families have farmed a piece of land for decades have been evicted because they did not have proper titles to the land. There is evidence to suggest that the Philippine Packing Corporation, which is often known as Philpak or PPC, Del Monte's most diversified international subsidiary, has directly been involved in land takeovers. In one instance a small farmer was told to leave his land. When he refused, some thirty Philippine Packing Corporation employees protected by armed guards drove more than a hundred cattle onto his land which had just been carefully prepared for planting.[9]

American agribusiness companies along with other American corporations have had their interests protected by Ferdinand Marcos's regime of martial law. In declaring martial law in 1972, Marcos stated:

> We're interested in all forms of capital and I would like to emphasize two things: we will offer as much incentive as is possible, and foreign capital will be protected. There will be no confiscation while I am President. Such things as the amortization of investment, retirement of capital and transmittal of profits are guaranteed.

Under the Marcos regime American business firms enjoy unrestricted repatriation of earnings and investments; tax exemptions and credits; protection from government competition; prohibition of all strikes, walkouts, and picketings; liberalized rules for employment of women and children, including the abolition of Sunday as a compulsory rest day for workers; government-controlled labor unions; frozen wages; and a government-controlled press.

In its 1977 annual report Del Monte claimed that "wherever we work, Del Monte and Del Monte people are active contributors to the cultural, civic, humanitarian and educational life of our communities." Del Monte's reinvested capital has gone "towards the creation of more jobs, more taxes and dividends—recycled through the corporate ecosystem, nourishing not only Del Monte's growth but the prosperity of society as a whole."[10] In the August 1977 issue of the *Del Monte Shield*, an in-house publication for stockholders, chairman of the board Alfred W. Eames, Jr., writes:

> The overseas investments of American agribusiness like ours have benefited just about everyone concerned—the Third World Countries themselves, their farmers and factory workers, our shareholders, and certainly not least a world full of consumers who enjoy the benefits of this enterprise—a more abundant food supply.[11]

The picture painted by the company is similar to the oil painting of the quaint shantytown hanging in the lobby of the luxurious Hotel La Romana in the Dominican Republic. However, just as outside the sweet-smelling, fenced-in world of the hotel, there is the tragedy of José Juan and 75 percent of the Dominican people, so too outside Del Monte's boardroom and slick publication there is the tragedy of the majority of the Filipino people. The gap between the rich and poor that was common in Amos's Israel and is symbolized today by the contrast between José Juan and Charles G. Bluhdorn, is repeated in the Philippines. For example, Philpak has established a classical plantation society in its Bukidnon plantation. The center of plantation life is Camp Phillips. Built around a plaza and ball park are a Catholic church, a cooperative store, Holy Cross High School, a management compound, a post office, and a hospital. Filipino middle-management people and plant supervisors and their families are housed nearby in uniform bungalows. Those who have positions of importance have larger yards and are located closer to the hospital. Agricultural workers, seasonal employees, and drivers live several miles away in Camp Uno. Its houses are run-down, the roads are dusty, and recreational facilities are nonexistent. The American executives live far away on the other end of the plantation in a bamboo-shaded, idyllic area called Kawayanon. Here California-type bungalows are built around an artificial twenty-acre lake adjoining an eighteen-hole golf course. This luxurious enclave is serviced by its own private airstrip.[12]

Despite the claims of Del Monte and other American corporations that their operations benefit just about everybody, the real situation is similar to that described by Amos in which the rich grow rich by exploiting the poor. According to a recent estimate 80 percent of the rural labor force—once landholders—are now landless laborers! Many work as tenant farmers on land they once owned![13]

Export agriculture is reinforcing an economy in which production, while profitable for American corporations, large landowners, and urban elites, has little or nothing to do with the basic needs of the people. As a consequence the quality of life for most Filipinos is declining. The inflation rate is approaching 80 percent, real wages (what wages are worth in actual purchasing power) declined by 40 percent between 1972 and 1974, and unemployment and underemployment is over 40 percent.[14]

Although agriculture is a major industry in the Philippines employing about 55 percent of the entire labor force, one half of all rural families in 1971 could not afford to provide themselves with a minimally nutritional diet. Del Monte may be creating a more abundant food supply, but it is not putting nutritious food on the plates of hungry Filipinos. Ninety percent of its production is exported, much of it to affluent consumers in Japan. It is now estimated that one half of all Filipino children under four years of age are afflicted by a serious deficiency of proteins—in fact, one of the highest rates of undernutrition in the world.[15] According to data of the Food and Agricultural Organization of the United Nations (FAO), the average Filipino consumes just 100 calories more a day than the average inhabitant of Bangladesh (1,940 versus 1,840 calories).[16]

The description of American corporate involvement in export agriculture in the Dominican Republic, Mexico, and the Philippines, and the devastating impact such exports have on the poor, is meant to serve as an example of a widespread phenomenon.[17] By focusing on these countries we have touched on three common types of American corporate involvement in export agriculture. In the Dominican Republic Gulf & Western is a large *landowner,* produces and processes a *nonnutritious* crop, largely *for export to the United States.* In Mexico, American firms have encouraged a shift from the production of staples for local consumption to the production of *fruits and vegetables for export to the United States* (in some cases displacing American producers), but the principle vehicle is *contract farming.* Finally in the Philippines, subsidiaries of American corporations encourage the production of *pineapples and bananas* for export to *both the United States and other foreign markets.* Once again the principle vehicle is *contract farming.*

Although the operations and strategies of United States-based companies differ in each of these countries, the motivations and results are the same. In all cases the aim is to capitalize on cheap labor and earn higher returns on the investments. And in all cases wealth earned through exports is unevenly distributed, and the situation of the poor deteriorates. Injustice in the rural areas of each of these countries gives rise to movements for social change that challenge the interests of American corporations and their foreign collaborators. And groups in the United States are also beginning to organize opposition to American corporate and governmental policies that victimize the poor.

After our brief exploration of both the biblical and modern-day roots of hunger, we can better understand the wisdom of the writer of Proverbs 13:23: "The . . . ground of the poor yields much food but it is swept away through injustice."

Agricultural Exports and the Meaning of Development

Millions of poor people throughout the world are hungry because agricultural production is not designed to meet their nutritional needs. At the same time, the developmental goals that are pursued have little or no relationship to the people's well-being. Instead, these countries have economies based on free-enterprise, they are well integrated into the international free-enterprise system, and their production priorities are based on the principle of comparative advantage. In such countries *agriculture* is *a means to other developmental ends*. Agricultural exports finance development. However, the critical question is: development of what nature, and for whose benefit?

In the United States we have developed an exaggerated respect for the objects we associate with economic development. These include private cars, refrigerators, dishwashers, color television sets, processed foods, jet-fresh pineapples, fast-food restaurants, Coca-Cola, and grain-fed meat. Corporate advertising creates needs where none existed before, and shapes our understanding of the meaning of development. Average American youngsters view approximately 350,000 commercials by the time they are eighteen.

We pursue development through privately controlled production and individual consumption, almost forgetting that development should be a social goal. Perhaps this explains why we scarcely notice that our private pursuit of the objects of development has resulted in an increased inequality among various social classes in the United States. We rarely read the book of Amos anymore, although that prophet would feel quite at home in many of our cities and rural areas. Basic necessities—adequate health care, food, housing, and clothing—are priced beyond the reach of many Americans.

Gradually we have learned to associate freedom with the right to acquire the objects of development. So long as we have purchasing power, we think that we are free, and we hardly notice the poverty of others. Even less do we perceive that the wealth of some people is linked to the poverty of others. Corporate and government leaders who are faced with the need for foreign markets and the raw materials of poor countries have consciously or unconsciously defined freedom as freedom of access to the raw materials needed to produce these objects of development as well as the right to sell them worldwide. *Freedom,* as Dean Acheson indicated in chapter 2, *is understood to mean freedom of enterprise.* "Following World War II," Orville Freeman, president of Business International, said in a recent interview, "the U.S. followed a very enlightened policy of free trade and free investment, . . . a very open world, and a very stable world. So this was one of the periods of freedom: freedom to invest, freedom to trade, freedom to have economic intercourse. Stability and freedom."[18]

The multinational corporation by definition seeks to universalize this understanding of freedom by exporting an exaggerated respect for the objects associated with western development. The key to the global market, according to Lee S. Bickmore, former chairperson of the National Biscuit Company, is "the tendency for people all over the world to adopt the same tastes and same consumption habits." According to E. M. de Windt, chairperson of the Eaton Corporation, "The World Company, owned, managed, and operated without regard to the physical, political, and philosophical boundaries of nationalism, can well become a reality in this century." This will happen, he says, "if we make things happen, if we look at the entire world as a market, and as a factory site, if we count customers before counting populations."

Associating freedom with free-enterprise and the freedom to consume masks a good many "un-freedoms." Gulf & Western is free to produce and process sugar cane in the Dominican Republic, invest profits in tourism, pay laborers $1.30 to cut a ton of cane, and repatriate profits to shareholders who freely consume the luxuries of development. But José Juan and 75 percent of the Dominican people are not free. Large landowners in the Philippines are free to evict tenants, force small farmers off their land, and contract banana production with United States-based corporations. With earnings from such production these landowners can freely purchase the best luxury goods the West can offer. But evicted tenants and small farmers are not free. The United States is free to promote free enterprise in India by withholding food aid during a severe famine; but, the majority of the Indian people live and die in bondage to hunger and poverty.

Business consultant Peter Drucker, who first labeled the world economy "a global shopping center," points out that within the "vast mass of poverty that is India" there is "a sizeable modern economy, comprising 10 percent or more of the Indian population, or 50,000,000 people." Fifty million free customers in a sea of poverty. According to an executive of Best Foods, future markets in Latin America are promising, although limited to certain social groups:

> Within ten years . . . Latin America will have 444 million in-habitants. . . . Of this number, a fifth will be able to buy, through their economic power, almost all the products which the industrialists here presently manufacture, while a third will be able to buy some of these products only very infrequently. The rest of the population, about half of the total, are not customers except for the most simple and basic products and probably will continue on a subsistence basis. . . . Those with a continental vision realize that the potential market of 1985 in Latin America will double compared to today.[19]

The search for corporate profits is bringing inappropriate and dangerous products such as Coca-Cola, American cigarettes, birth control pills and untested pharmaceuticals, and a host of highly processed and expensive food products to some of the poorest countries in the world. Such products are given high profile advertising making lavish promises to the poor, who are looking for a way out of their desperate situations. Perhaps most insidious are the sales promotion practices of infant formula manufacturers such as Nestlé, American Home Products, Bristol Myers, and Abbot/Ross.

Slick promotion of artificial formulas convinces many mothers that abandoning traditional breastfeeding in favor of bottle feeding, a symbol of Western progress, is best for their babies. "The onslaught," says Dr. Michael Latham of Cornell University, "is terrific, the message is powerful, the profits to be made are high, and high also is the resultant human suffering." Another industry critic, Dr. Derrick Jellife, Director of the Division of Population, Family and International Health at UCLA, estimates that ten million infants each year suffer severe malnutrition, diarrhea, dehydration, and often death or permanent brain damage, as a result of the shift from breast to bottle feeding in areas of the world where lack of sufficient income, basic knowledge of sterilization, literacy, and clean water make safe use of formulas impossible.

The continental vision has created global alliances that victimize the poor. Increasingly, development in poor countries refers not to the process by which the basic needs of the entire population are met, but to the process whereby foreign economic interests and privileged groups in underdeveloped countries enrich themselves at the expense of their great bulk of the populations. Foreign exchange earned through agricultural exports is the vehicle by which elites in poor countries finance their way into the global shopping center both as producers and consumers. Their road to development is paved with the blood of the poor. This is a situation well-known to Job:

> People remove landmarks;
> they seize flocks and pasture them.
> They drive away the ass of the fatherless;
> they take the widow's ox for a pledge.
> They thrust the poor off the road;
> the poor of the earth all hide themselves.
> Behold, like wild asses in the desert
> they go forth to their toil
> seeking prey in the wilderness
> as food for their children.
> They gather their fodder in the field
> and they glean the vineyard of the wicked one.
> They lie all night naked, without clothing,
> and have no covering in the cold.
> They are wet with the rain of the mountains,
> and cling to the rock for want of shelter.
> (There are those who snatch the fatherless child from the
>   breast,
> and take in pledge the infant of the poor.)
> They go about naked, without clothing;
> hungry, they carry the sheaves;
> among the olive rows of the wicked they make oil;
> they tread the wine presses, but suffer thirst (Job 24:2–11).*

Malnutrition and Brazil's "Economic Miracle"

Brazil is no longer considered poor. With a Gross National Product (GNP) in 1974 of $920 per capita it is considered by economists to belong to the "upper middle-income countries." Although ruled by a military dictatorship since 1964, Brazil is a model of freedom according to the definition of Orville Freeman quoted above. The generals have fostered economic freedom by instituting policies to encourage foreign investments and trade. Unfortunately they have also suppressed all political dissent in order to insure the stable investment climate so highly prized by foreign investors.

The United States government and United States-based corporations, such as General Motors Corporation, Ford Motor Company, Chrysler Corporation, United States Steel Corporation, Bethlehem Steel Corporation, General Electric Company, Pfizer, CPC International, Anderson Clayton & Company, International Business Machines (IBM), and others, have been strong supporters of Brazil's military government. American foreign aid to Brazil was drastically cut between 1962 and 1964 during the liberal presidency of João Goulart. Goulart was committed to policies unfavorable to powerful domestic and foreign groups, including agrarian reform, higher minimum wages, expansion of the internal market, restrictions on foreign investment, and diplomatic and trade relations with socialist countries. In 1965, after a military coup guaranteed a favorable investment climate, the aid faucet was turned back on. Aid to Brazil fell from $81.6 million to $15.1 between 1962 and 1964; it increased dramatically to $122.1 million in 1965.[20] Only South Korea, South Vietnam, India, and Pakistan have received more bilateral aid from the United States than Brazil. During the mid-1960s the Agency for International Development's programs in Brazil averaged between $200 and $300 million per year.[21] At the same time foreign capital flowed in. In 1960 American direct investment in Brazil was $953 million. By 1972 it had increased 260 percent to nearly $2.5 billion. In 1977 it was estimated that Brazil's borrowings from U.S. banks and their foreign branches totaled $10 billion.[22]

Brazil's efforts to achieve rapid economic growth have been successful. Between 1964 and 1976 Brazil's GNP increased by more than 150 percent, with growth spurts of 10 percent a year between 1968 and 1974. Brazil's 1976 GNP of $116.8 billion was ninth highest in the world. In the eyes of many observers Brazil's model of economic development should be emulated by other poorer countries. According to this view, the result of the Brazilian government's decision to allow foreign corporations and capital unrestricted access to its resources has been nothing short of an "economic miracle."

Unfortunately, the benefits of the "economic miracle" are confined to foreign corporations and Brazil's upper classes. Foreign corporations account for 50 percent of all manufacturing sales in Brazil. And while the Brazilian government boasts of a high growth rate, 41.6 percent of Brazilian industry, including 94 percent of the chemical industry, 100 percent of the automobile industry, 82 percent of the rubber industry, and 71 percent of the railways, is in foreign hands.[23] Brazil's rapid economic growth has been accompanied also by a radical redistribution of wealth in favor of the richer economic elements. According to government statistics, real wages for unskilled workers have declined almost 40 percent since 1964 while skilled workers and executives received annual wage increases (after adjustment for inflation) of 2.6 percent and 8.1 percent respectively.[24] A 1970 United Nations study estimated that the richest 5 percent of Brazil's population had one half of the national income.

Alliances between Brazilian elites and foreign corporations have made it possible for Brazil to import the technology and capital needed to produce luxury goods for export and for consumption by internal elites. But the "economic miracle" has not met the basic food, clothing, housing, and health-care needs of the majority of the Brazilian people. "The naked truth," Protestant theologian José Míguez Bonino writes, "is that Brazil has become, not even a colony of a foreign power, but a factory of multinational corporations; the Brazilian population, a reserve of cheap labor, and the Brazilian government and police, foremen and wardens of these corporations."[25]

Perhaps the most devastating aspect of Brazil's "economic miracle" is that it is being financed through agricultural exports. Brazil's agricultural growth rates of more than 5 percent a year under the military government have outpaced the rest of Latin America. But impressive growth rates have not improved the nutritional well-being of the people. The New York Academy of Sciences sponsored in 1976 a conference on food and nutrition that was attended by more than three hundred experts from sixteen countries. According to a *New York Times* article summarizing the conference:

> Brazil was singled out as a country whose impressive agricultural growth had not improved the nutritional levels of its people. The critics said that agricultural expansion here had concentrated on cash crops for export—including soybeans, sugar and coffee—while domestically consumed food crops had lagged behind population growth. . . .
> *The rationale . . . for concentrating on cash crops for export rather than on cheaper, more abundant food for domestic consumption is that the country needs foreign-exchange to finance further development.* This argument is even stronger, now that rising prices for oil and capital-goods imports have thrown Brazil's trade balance into deficit.[26]

Agricultural exports make up the bulk of Brazil's exports. In 1972, for example, 70 percent of the country's export earnings were from agricultural products. Between 1967 and 1977 Brazil increased its agricultural exports from $1.4 billion to $9 billion. By 1977 Brazil had become the world's second-largest agricultural exporter. That same year half of all Brazil's exports were devoured by debt service payments.[27] In 1979 Brazil will utilize 60 percent of its export earnings to service its staggering $41 billion debt, the highest in the developing world. In other words foreign-exchange earnings from exports of coffee, sugar, soybeans, and other agricultural products are being utilized to pay back foreign loans that fuel Brazil's "economic miracle." Food production for domestic consumption, on the other hand, is being ignored because of what Romulo do Almeida, an economist and former president of Brazil's Northeast Bank, refers to as "the immediate objectives of attending the needs of our foreign markets." "That is," he continues, "agriculture for the domestic market remains inefficient and expensive and has few prospects of overcoming this rut."[28]

Brazil is second only to the United States as an agricultural exporter. It is the world's largest producer of coffee, harvests more sugar than Cuba, and has cattle herds twice as large as those of Argentina. Over the past twelve years the production of soybeans has increased fortyfold. The beneficiaries of this agricultural bonanza in Brazil are foreign corporations and banks, urban industrial elites whose exaggerated respect for the objects of development resemble that of our own country; American food processors like Anderson Clayton and General Foods; and the landed elites who accumulate profits from export production. One percent of the farms in Brazil comprise over 43 percent of the country's total farmland, while 50 percent of the farms have less than 3 percent of the land. According to the *New York Times*, despite promises, "agrarian reform has never been carried out." About "50 million of the nation's 110 million people still live in rural areas as subsistence farmers—or, more likely, as poorly paid employees." And, nutritionists agree that "40 percent of the Brazilians are suffering from malnutrition, the major cause of infant mortality."

In 1976 black beans, a staple of the Brazilian diet, were in such short supply that there were riots in Rio de Janeiro. The rioters were quickly suppressed by the police. The 17 percent decline in black-bean production in 1976 was caused in part by "bad weather and in part because the bean growers receive only 1 percent of the total subsidies given Brazilian farmers. The Government subsidies benefit mostly the more affluent farmers, who concentrate on cash crops for export rather than food consumed domestically."[29] Later the Brazilian government imported black beans from Chile, another country ready to sacrifice the nutritional needs of its people to earn foreign exchange.

Brazil's development experience provides additional evidence that freedom is not to be identified with free enterprise. After all, no one is against economic development. The question is: development of what nature, and for whom? A Pastoral Committee of Bishops of Northeast Brazil wrote recently:

> If the Church, in some way, goes back over the decade of development in Latin America, it will have to denounce the fact that after ten years of "development" the result is: hunger, more hunger, and greater undernutrition; food more expensive and inaccessible for the poor; a lessening of basic consumption for the mass of people.[30]

The misuse of resources in Brazil is characteristic of what happens in many underdeveloped countries seeking to "develop" in the international free-enterprise system. Countries with free-enterprise economies often use the GNP as a yardstick of successful development, assuming that the wealth will somehow trickle down to the masses. Unfortunately a by-product of neocolonialism is that poor countries ignore the needs of the majority of their people for food and a balanced kind of development.

> By the end of the Decade of Development (1960–1970) . . . , despite dramatic economic growth in a few poor countries, it had become abundantly clear that the gap between the rich and poor throughout the world was widening. A succession of studies by the U.N. and other international agencies established statistics of global poverty. For 40 percent to 60 percent of the world's population the Decade of Development brought rising unemployment, decreases in purchasing power, and thus lower consumption. . . . A World Bank survey of income-distribution patterns in poor countries around the world . . . found that the development track of the 1960's shows a "striking" increase in incomes, in both absolute and relative terms, for the richest 5 percent while the share of the poorest 40 percent shrinks. While according to such gross indicators as GNP the countries are developing, millions in the bottom 40 percent of the population actually have less food, worse clothing, and poorer housing than their parents had. As Brazil's President Emilio Medici once put it, "Brazil is doing well but the people are not."[31]

The Consequences of Inappropriate Development

A developmental path that enriches the elites of a poor country and foreign groups while impoverishing the majority of people in the

Third World is inappropriate. It is also profitable. What has evolved over the years, often with the assistance of United States aid programs, is a symbiotic relationship between the elites and foreign corporations. It is in the interest of both groups to continue economic relationships similar to those of the colonial era. Both accept similar definitions of freedom and development: freedom is equated with freedom of enterprise and consumption while development is viewed as a private rather than social goal whereby certain objects of development are made available for individual consumption. These objects often do not correspond to the basic goods needed to meet the needs of most of the population for food, clothing, housing, employment, or health care.

Many poor countries are pursuing export-led development strategies. Investment is plowed into export production while production for domestic self-sufficiency is placed on the back burner. Comparative advantage is still the order of the day, and in free-enterprise economies earnings from foreign exchange are utilized by private individuals and groups to finance their participation, as producers and consumers, in the global shopping center. Wealth, as we have demonstrated, ends up in the hands of the elites. By describing some of the consequences of inappropriate development we can get a sense of the spiral of violence inflicted on the poor.

Poverty, Hunger, and Malnutrition

Although there are varying definitions and estimates of poverty, it is clear that the magnitude and extent of poverty in poor countries are severe, with approximately 920 million to 1.2 billion people living in a state of serious or absolute poverty. It is difficult to obtain precise statistics on how many people are poorly nourished, but it is reasonable to assume that there is a high correlation between poverty and hunger. Our review of certain biblical passages suggests that hunger is an expression of poverty, and that poverty is a consequence of social injustice. The preparatory document for the 1974 United Nations World Food Conference confirms this view:

> The causes of inadequate nutrition are many and closely interrelated, . . . but the principal cause is poverty. This in turn results from socio-economic development patterns which in most of the poorer countries have been characterized by a high degree of concentration of power, wealth and incomes in the hands of relatively small elites of national or foreign individuals or groups.[32]

Inequality

In Amos's Israel injustice was accompanied by inequality. The wealth and power of the merchants, bankers, and large landowners was enormous, relative to that of the tenants or landless laborers. The situation is similar today. José Juan would not be dying in a shack unfit for human habitation if his wealth and power were comparable to that of large landowners and executives of Gulf & Western. A recent study of eighty-three countries indicates that slightly more than 3 percent of all landholders, those with 114 acres or more, control nearly 80 percent of all farmland.[33] It is this 3 percent, including or in cooperation with foreign corporations, that determines what is produced, where and to whom products are sold, who receives the profits, and how the profits are utilized. The international free-enterprise system, that luxurious global shopping center, offers elite producers in poor countries an *international market, thereby insulating them from the poverty of their own people.* The fact that the local people are too poor to purchase domestically produced goods is of little consequence because there is a world full of consumers.

Inequality is an unavoidable consequence of exploitation; it is the foundation on which the wealth of the elites is based. Poor people are valued as a cheap labor force producing the agricultural and manufacturing goods which poor countries export to earn foreign exchange. For this reason the workers' wages are kept inhumanly low. Higher wages would pose several problems for the domestic elites and their foreign allies. First, higher wages would put more purchasing power in the hands of the poor. This would increase the amount of goods they consume, and in all likelihood force a reordering of economic priorities to reflect domestic needs rather than international markets, thus reducing both the goods available for export and the foreign-exchange earnings. Second, higher wages would cut into the profits of elites and subsidiaries of United States-based and other foreign corporations. Finally, and this is related closely to the previous point, higher wages would reduce the competitive position of exports from poor countries in the markets of developed countries. *In many cases it is the blood, sweat, and subhuman wages of the poor that constitute the "comparative advantage" of the producers in poor countries.*

The alliances between domestic and foreign elites that perpetuate inequality are remarkably flexible. The common features of such alliances are that they build on mutually perceived interests and victimize the poor. The adoption by poor countries of the "Green Revolution" as a means to increase food production is illustrative. Throughout the 1950's and early part of the 1960's the United States discouraged food production in poor countries. Disposal of agricultural surpluses and creation of future markets were the crux of American policy. Poor countries, for their part, were able to import "cheap food" and concentrate their agricultural production on export crops needed to earn foreign exchange.

By the mid-1960's the situation for both the United States and poor countries had changed somewhat. From the standpoint of the United States, it was clear that the poor countries would be substantial consumers of American agricultural products. A major concern at this time, however, was that domestic markets for the American producers of agricultural *inputs*, such as farm machinery, pesticides, seeds, and fertilizers, were saturated. For example, a high figure for the number of tractors and other farm machinery on American farms was reached in 1964.[34] Once again American producers looked to the markets of poor countries to overcome domestic economic problems. Just as the giant agribusiness firms needed to expand their markets, it was recognized that the poor countries could not neglect their food production indefinitely. And so the time was ripe for a new alliance centered around the Green Revolution.

The Green Revolution is a technological approach to increasing the yields of basic food crops. It is an integrated package of techniques and technology that includes varieties of new seeds, irrigation, mechanization, and an intensive use of chemical fertilizers, pesticides, and herbicides. For American agribusiness firms that export these inputs of the Green Revolution, all this makes good economic sense. For the elites in the poor countries it provides an opportunity to increase food production *without implementing structural changes*. Therefore, it pays both economic and political dividends. Agricultural inputs that are part of the technological package of the Green Revolution are expensive; only relatively well-off farmers can afford them. Therefore, the benefits of increased food production go to the large landowners. This results in greater inequality and a further victimization of small farmers, tenants, and landless laborers. In effect, the Green Revolution is a counter-revolutionary strategy. While increasing food production, it has resulted in more hunger for the poor. Nutritionist Alan Berg writes:

> In the formation of supply strategies, the relation between food supply increases and the circumstances of the malnourished is seldom explicitly taken into account. . . . Explicit measures are

almost never taken to raise the effective demand of the poor.
Nor are agricultural research efforts usually designed with an
acknowledged concern for the nutritional content of output—
especially of food largely eaten by the poor.[35]

Urbanization and Unemployment

Two major consequences of developmental strategies that perpetuate inequality are urbanization and unemployment. A 1974
United Nations study notes:

> In the rural areas, land and water, capital, technical knowledge,
> credit and institutional assistance are distributed in a most
> uneven way. The majority of the rural population is either
> landless or has to make a living from the exploitation of meagre
> land and water resources. In spite of the fact that annually
> millions of rural inhabitants migrate to the urban areas, unem-
> ployment and underemployment are usually very high and
> rural wages generally extremely low. In some instances the
> irregular employment profile gives rise to acute unem-
> ployment during the slack seasons. In other instances produc-
> tion patterns, geared to the satisfaction of the needs of external
> markets, or those of the smaller middle and high-income na-
> tional groups, do not favour diversification and proper utiliza-
> tion of available indigenous resources. Land tenure and struc-
> tures constitute therefore one of the basic reasons for rural
> poverty and malnutrition.[36]

Injustice and inequality in the countryside lead to unemployment
and poverty. This in turn leads to a steady migration of the rural poor
to urban areas. But few jobs await the poor. Investment decisions are
made by private individuals and groups who are concerned with
maximizing profits rather than employment. Manufacturing and industrial production are often geared to foreign markets, and foreign
technologies are imported to insure the standards of developed
countries. Barnet and Müller in their study of multinational corporations conclude that one of the more devastating impacts global corporations have on poor countries is that they transfer technologies
that destroy jobs. Poor countries abound in human resources; yet
global corporations export a technology that is capital-intensive and
laborsaving. This is what these corporations developed in the
United States in response to high labor costs. Alliances between
elites in poor countries and foreign corporations effectively turn the
human resources that are their biggest assets into social liabilities.[37]

The Exploitation of Women

Women make up the majority of the agricultural labor force in many Third World countries, and they have long been the primary food producers within the important subsistence agricultural sector. The rapid expansion of large-scale commercial farming of export crops has had a significant and negative impact on the status, wages, and workload of women, as well as on their ability to produce food sufficient for their families' needs. Commercial export cropping takes up more and more land leaving less for subsistence farmers. Women often end up working longer hours on less (and often less fertile) land. They also make up a significant portion of the seasonal workforce that is the key to high profits for plantation owners. They are the cheapest of the adult workforce and receive wages about four-fifths less than men.[38] Also, women are seldom absorbed into the expanding non-agricultural sector, which, as we have noted, creates relatively few jobs.

Rapid Population Growth

Later, in chapters 6 and 7, we shall consider relationships among development priorities, rapid population growth, hunger, and poverty. Here we simply wish to note that poverty breeds rapid population growth, and not vice versa. In the absence of an authentic development that meets basic human needs, parents desire large families because their children provide the only form of social security available to them.

Food Dependency

American food aid programs effectively discouraged food production in poor countries and fostered dependency. If food is power, it follows that food dependency is an indication of vulnerability or powerlessness. In an earlier period, American aid programs were transitional tools to neocolonialism. Food power may be the guarantor. We will discuss the implications of food dependency in greater detail in chapter 4. With the annual food deficit of underdeveloped countries expected to jump from 36 million metric tons in 1978 to between 120 and 145 million metric tons in 1990, the Central Intelligence Agency's projection of the U.S. holding "life and death power over the fate of the multitudes of the needy" is frightening. Food will probably become the primary tool of American foreign policy.

Dependency, Indebtedness, and Lack of Autonomy

Integration into the international free-enterprise system has left poor countries highly dependent on developed countries for certain basic goods, for luxury items, and for imported technology, spare parts, capital, and manufactured goods. It has also left the poor countries with a staggering debt that threatens to stifle any economic progress. Between 1967 and 1976 the total outstanding debt of the non-oil-producing, underdeveloped countries increased more than fourfold, from $43.7 billion to approximately $180 billion. Poor countries owe this massive debt to international agencies (the World Bank, the International Monetary Fund, and other international agencies), to governments, and to private institutions (banks and other private creditors). In 1967 about $12 billion, or some 28 percent of the total debt, was owed to private sources. By 1976 an estimated $65 billion, or some 40 percent, was owed to private sources, including $45 billion to U.S. banks.[39] The increasing proportion of loans received from private sources is significant because private debt usually carries stiffer lending terms than public debt. Recent figures cited by Gamani Corea, secretary general of a recent United Nations Conference on Trade and Investment, indicates a steadily worsening debt situation. Corea estimates that at the end of 1977, the total external debt of poor countries (both government and commercial borrowings) was $250 billion, and that the annual cost of servicing this debt absorbed 21 percent of the export earnings of the poor countries.[40]

Poor country indebtedness is in part a consequence of the international free-enterprise system, which is not really free. For the most part, it is the developed nations that dictate the world market. They determine the prices of raw materials and primary products, fix the tariffs and quotas that place restrictions on the exports of manufactured and other processed goods from poor countries, and establish the prices poor countries must pay for the processed goods they import. Between 1950 and the present, the prices poor countries received for the raw materials and primary products they exported have progressively dropped relative to the manufactured and high-technology goods they import. For example, according to the government of Tanzania, one tractor cost five tons of sisal in 1963. In 1970 the same tractor cost ten tons of sisal. In 1960 twenty-five tons of rubber purchased six tractors, but by 1975 the same amount of rubber would pay for only two.[41]

Rising costs for food and fuel imports have also aggravated the debt crisis of poor countries. The cost of their imports of cereals, for example, more than tripled from $3 billion in 1971 to $10 billion in 1974. In 1974 the import cost of oil for these same countries had risen to about $10 billion. At the same time, their export earnings declined. The Overseas Development Council described their situation in 1975 in these terms:

> Prices of some industrial raw materials (especially those traded on the world's free markets, such as base metals, cotton, rubber, and fibers) have collapsed. The prices of commodities other than petroleum have declined by 50 percent since last year. The export earnings of non-oil producing developing nations probably will fall by about $8 billion in 1975.[42]

Indebtedness hangs over the heads of poor countries like a guillotine. The ability to foreclose on debts was a powerful tool in the hands of merchants in Amos's Israel. Because of indebtedness and the ruthlessness of the merchants, autonomous small farmers were reduced to landless serfs (Amos 8:4–7). The situation was similar during the time of Jesus' ministry (Matt. 18:24–25). Today the creditors of poor countries hold a similar kind of power. International and private lending institutions are dictating economic policy to the indebted countries.

Indebtedness locks poor countries into the very system that has impoverished them. Creditors such as the International Monetary Fund and private banks have a vested interest in maintaining the integration of poor countries into the international free-enterprise system. Loans, therefore, are tied to certain policies that insure continued integration. First, poor countries must expand their exports. This means more emphasis must be given to export agriculture, and economic production in general is geared to international rather than domestic markets. Second, loans are conditional upon wage reductions and price hikes for basic goods and services. This reduces the purchasing power of the workers, thus diminishing their demand for goods and services. Also, by reducing wages, a country becomes more attractive as a production site for foreign corporations that produce for export and capitalize on cheap labor. Finally, government spending for social services must be drastically cut.

The result of these austerity measures imposed from without is a further victimization of the poor. Increased reliance upon export agriculture to finance debts results in even greater food dependency, vulnerability, and indebtedness. "Most of the developing countries," a United Nations study notes, "continue to depend heavily on agricultural exports for their earnings of foreign exchange. . . . Many of them have to use a large part of their foreign exchange earnings to import food and the fertilizers and other inputs needed to produce it."[43]

For the poor the consequence of indebtedness and continued integration into the international free-enterprise system is accurately described by Job:

> They gather their fodder in the field
> and they glean the vineyard of the wicked one. . . .
> They go about naked, without clothing;
> hungry, they carry the sheaves;
> among the olive rows of the wicked they make oil;
> they tread the wine presses, but suffer thirst (Job 24:6, 10–11).*

Denial of Basic Human Rights

Poverty is a denial of human rights. Unemployment, inadequate housing, health care, and education, hunger and malnutrition all are evidence of violations of human rights. This is particularly true in the case of countries with free-enterprise economies where poverty exists side by side with the affluence of elites. It is, in fact, a by-product of the economic structures that produce such affluence. The denial of basic economic rights necessarily leads to the violation of traditional political rights. It is not a coincidence that many countries that violate traditional political rights, such as free speech, free elections, free press, and the right to a fair trial, are countries where wealth and misery rub shoulders. Torture is the likely consequence of inequality. When land is owned by an affluent minority, when the food needs of local people are ignored in favor of cash crops for export, when foreign-exchange earnings accrue to private individuals and groups that become international consumers, when millions of workers are paid less than human wages in order to maximize the incentives and profits of foreign corporations that produce goods for domestic elites and foreign markets, when millions are unemployed, hungry, and without adequate clothing and shelter, there is little likelihood of democracy. Economic degradation and political repression are blood brothers, and their alliance is consummated in the blood of the poor.

As Americans we have been mesmerized by a corporate definition of freedom and development to the point that we hardly notice that *poor countries most open to U.S. economic penetration, that is, those which encourage free enterprise, are military dictatorships.*

In light of this fact, the Council of the Americas, a mutual-support association of the two hundred principal United States-based corporations with operations in Latin America, suggests as a slogan for its members: "Consumer democracy is more important than political democracy."[44] As we will demonstrate in chapter 4, the Council's slogan is a capsule statement explaining why the U.S. supports dictatorships throughout the globe.

Chapter 4

UNITED STATES MILITARY POWER AND THE THIRD WORLD

Almost anyone who has lived in or visited underdeveloped countries, or poor areas in our own country, can understand why high military spending is often referred to as a mistaken priority. Bloated military budgets exist side by side with the bloated bellies of undernourished children. World military spending increased from $200 billion in 1970 to an estimated $400 billion in 1977. These are alarming figures, given the fact that out of a world population of 4.2 billion, 1 billion are undernourished, 800 million adults are illiterate, 1.4 billion have neither safe water nor effective medical care, and 800 million cannot afford basic housing.[1]

The United States Department of Defense budget for fiscal year 1979 was $126 billion, about 40 percent of net federal spending. For hungry people in this nation and throughout the world, military expenditures of this magnitude represent mistaken priorities. Weapons production utilizes human, technical, and physical resources that are then unavailable for the production of socially useful products to meet human needs. But to call high levels of military spending a mistaken priority is somewhat misleading. American military policies often promote and protect the global economic interests of American corporations. Once produced, weapons are often used to reinforce unjust political and economic structures in poor countries. These structures, as we saw in the previous chapter, reinforce alliances between domestic elites and American-based multinational corporations, but at the same time perpetuate hunger and poverty. "Mistaken priority" rhetoric is often contradicted by actual practices. For example, in 1953 President Eisenhower told the nation that "every gun that is made, every warship launched, every rocket fired signifies, in the final sense, a theft from those who

56

hunger and are not fed, those who are cold and are not clothed." Yet in 1954 most of the thirteen Latin American presidents who were military officers were receiving military assistance from the United States. That same year Eisenhower authorized the overthrow of a democratically elected government in Guatemala that was committed to land reform, and he presented the Legion of Merit to two Latin American dictators—Pérez Jiménez of Venezuela (for his "spirit of friendship and cooperation" and his "sound foreign investment policies"), and Manuel Odría of Peru.

Another qualification must be added to the common understanding of military spending as a "mistaken priority." While it is true that the poor are victimized by high levels of military spending, it is also true that making weapons is a highly profitable business for some of the largest corporations in America that dominate this kind of production. These corporations have a vested interest in maintaining excessive military production, even though it is harmful to the overall American economy. As we hope to demonstrate, the United States is increasingly trying to overcome its economic difficulties brought on by excessive military spending through food power; this results in a further victimization of the world's hungry.

Americans concerned about hungry people in our own country and abroad must be prepared to examine critically the impact of United States military spending and policies on the poor. The 1980s are likely to be a time when our nation's leaders will attempt to rally people around the flag, enlisting uncritical support for interventionist policies in the name of "defense." We must ask ourselves in defense of whose interests and at what cost to the world's hungry.

American Military Policy in a Hungry World

Foreign Expansion: From Jeroboam II to Johnson

"We are the number one nation," President Lyndon Johnson told the National Foreign Policy Conference at a crucial moment in the Vietnam War, "and we are going to stay the number one nation."[2] The United States, which is determined to stay number one, has long prided itself on being the world's leading military and economic power. In a speech to a convention of Junior Chamber of Commerce Executives in 1967 Johnson boasted:

We own almost a third of the world's railroad tracks. We own almost two-thirds of the world's automobiles—and we don't have to wait three years to get a new one, either. . . . We own half the trucks in the world. We own almost a half of all the radios in the world. We own a third of all the electricity that is produced in the world. We own a fourth of all the steel. . . . Although we have only about 6% of the population of the world, we have half its wealth. Bear in mind that the other 94% of the population would like to trade with us. Maybe a better way of saying it would be that they would like to exchange places with us. I would like to see them enjoy the blessings that we enjoy. But don't you help them exchange places with us—because I don't want to be where they are. Instead, I believe that we are generous enough—I believe that we are compassionate enough—and I believe that we are grateful enough that we would like to see all of them enjoy the blessings that are ours.[3]

The historical context in which the United States emerged as the world's number one nation is similar to that of Israel during the reign of Jeroboam II. Jeroboam, an effective military leader, capitalized on the impotency of Israel's war-torn neighbors and pursued a successful policy of foreign expansion. During this time, Israel gained control of the major trade routes of the ancient world. Foreign expansion brought unprecedented affluence to Israel (Amos 6:4–6). But according to Amos, the rich stored up "violence and robbery in their strongholds" (Amos 3:10) because their wealth was based on exploitation of the poor.

World War II was a turning point in world history. The United States, which since the turn of the century had been *a* world power, was now *the* world power. In 1941 Henry R. Luce, publisher of *Life* magazine, wrote his widely circulated editorial, "The American Century." Luce noted that the previous hundred years could be called the British Century, but that the next one hundred years would be the American Century. It has now become time, Luce wrote, "to accept whole-heartedly our duty and our opportunity as the most powerful and vital nation in the world and in consequence exert upon the world the full impact of our influence, for such purposes as we see fit and by such means as we see fit. . . . It now becomes our time to be the powerhouse from which the ideals spread throughout the world."

The United States emerged from World War II with its industrial plant intact. Britain, Germany, France, Japan, Italy, China, and the Soviet Union, on the other hand, in addition to losing millions of their finest men, found their industrial plants in ruin and millions of their people homeless. The historical setting was right for American foreign expansion, and the United States, like Jeroboam's Israel centuries before, capitalized on the opportunity. In 1946 Leo D. Welch, treasurer and later chairperson of Standard Oil of New Jersey, stated the challenge:

> American private enterprise is confronted with this choice; it may strike out and save its position all over the world, or sit by and witness its own funeral. That responsibility is positive and vigorous leadership in the affairs of the world—political, social, and economic—and it must be fulfilled in the broadest sense of the term. As the largest contributors to the global mechanism, we must set the pace and assume the responsibility of the majority stockholder in this corporation known as the world. . . . Nor is this for a given term of office. This is a permanent obligation.

Not surprisingly, Welch, who viewed the world as a corporation and the United States as its majority stockholder, assigned to American foreign policy the task of making the world safe for American corporate investment. "Our foreign policy," he stated in the same speech, "will be more concerned with the safety and stability of our foreign investments than ever before."[4]

Henry R. Luce was an idealist who promised a century of American power in service to globalized American values. Leo D. Welch was a pragmatist who understood that without foreign markets and resources the American free-enterprise system would collapse. During the post-World War II period, the values of the idealist and pragmatist converged to form a powerful ideology. Freedom was associated with the objectives of American expansionism. What was good for American corporations was good for America and the world. Austin Kiplinger, in an article in the *Chicago Journal of Commerce* in 1949, writes:

> . . . the United States . . . is in a position in the world which demands that its foreign trade policy be carefully thought out. In trade and industry we now occupy the position Britain did in the 19th century. The United States must be an imperialist if it is to do its world job properly. "Imperialism" has become a nasty word, of course, but the facts and the logic of our position are inescapable. In ABC's, the facts are these: The United States can produce more than its present capacity to consume. Increased consumption at home will sop up some of this excess, but still more excess will remain. We sell this excess abroad. And since the rest of the world is not up to our standard of production, we must decide what to take in payment. We can let

the deficit stand as a debt which probably will never be paid. Or—and this is where imperialism comes in —we can take ownership of properties throughout the world, and help to run them. And if we do this, *we shall have to cooperate with our own government and foreign governments to arrange the political weather under which American ownership abroad will be carried out.*

This is not exactly like the older style British imperialism which frequently disregarded the rights of the countries in which Britain traded. But rather than shrinking in fear from the word "imperialism," we would do better to meet it head-on, and make a virtue of it. Let us distinguish between Russian "despotic imperialism" and *American "democratic imperialism."* Since we are going to be stuck with the role of imperialist, let's dramatize the new imperialism as an extension of the American way of life and the American productive system.[5]

The American government did arrange the political weather by cooperating and in some cases toppling foreign governments. This enabled American private enterprise to strike out and save its position. In September 1945 American military forces controlled 434 bases around the world. By 1969 approximately 1,222,000 men were manning 399 major and 1,930 minor overseas installations. Since 1945 the United States has conducted a major military campaign or a paramilitary Central Intelligence Agency-sponsored operation in a former colony or dependent country on an average of once every eighteen months—Greece (1948), Iran (1953), Guatemala (1954), Indonesia (1958), Lebanon (1958), Laos (1960), Cuba (1961), Congo (1964), British Guiana (1964), the Dominican Republic (1965), and Vietnam.[6] In addition to overt or covert intervention, the United States has provided the governments of poor countries with billions of dollars in military assistance to insure a proper investment climate.

By briefly examining several of these military or paramilitary interventions in defense of American corporate interests, we can gain insight into how American military policy often perpetuates hunger.

Guatemala

In 1952 the United Fruit Company (today United Brands) owned or controlled about 3 million acres of land worldwide, of which only about 241,000 acres were actually planted with crops such as sugarcane and bananas. The rest was left idle or grazed by a few cattle to keep landless peasants from cultivating it. Thomas McCann, a former vice-president of United Fruit, describes the situation in Guatemala:

> Guatemala was chosen as the site for the company's earliest development activities because a good portion of the country was prime banana land and also because at the time we entered Central America, Guatemala's government was the region's weakest, most corrupt and most pliable. In short, the country offered an "ideal investment climate," and United Fruit's profits flourished for fifty years. Then something went wrong: a man named Jacob Arbenz became president.[7]

United Fruit's problems actually began before the election of Jacob Arbenz. In 1944, General Jorge Ubico, a brutal dictator who played a central role in maintaining the ideal investment climate for the United Fruit Company, was overthrown. Ubico, who proudly compared himself to Hitler, banned labor unions and declared the word "worker" subversive. Following Ubico's loss of power, Juan José Arévalo was elected president in a popular election. Arévalo abolished forced labor on the banana plantations, raised minimum wages to 26 cents per day, permitted unions, and began prying the Guatemalan economy from its near total dependency on United Fruit and other foreign corporations. In response to Arévalo's reforms W. R. Grace and Pan American Airlines stopped promoting tourism; several oil companies discontinued prospecting; United Fruit restricted banana exports; the World Bank withheld loans, and the United States government, which accused Arévalo of being a communist, cut off military assistance.[8]

In March 1953 Jacob Arbenz Guzmán, the democratically elected president whose principal concern was land reform, expropriated 234,000 uncultivated acres of land owned by United Fruit. What Thomas McCann referred to as prime banana land was really first-class agricultural land suitable for the production of a variety of food crops. Arbenz offered as compensation an amount of money equal to United Fruit's assessment of its value for tax purposes. On June 18, 1954, American pilots bombed Guatemala City. Arbenz was overthrown with weapons shipped on ships owned by United Fruit in a Central Intelligence Agency-initiated coup. His replacement, Colonel Carlos Castillo Armas, was a graduate of the United States Command and General Staff College at Fort Leavenworth, Kansas. Castillo Armas immediately returned United Fruit's expropriated land and abolished taxes on interest and dividends to foreign investors.

United Fruit Company had friends in high places. At the time of the American intervention, John Foster Dulles, a long-time legal advisor to the company, was U.S. Secretary of State; his brother Allen Dulles was director of the Central Intelligence Agency; Henry Cabot Lodge, a large stockholder and member of United Fruit Company's board of directors, was the U.S. ambassador to the United Nations; John Moors Cabot, a large shareholder, was Assistant Secretary of State for Inter-American Affairs; and, Walter Bedell Smith, a predecessor of Allen Dulles as director of the Central Intelligence Agency, became president of the United Fruit Company after the Arbenz government was overthrown.

The cozy relationship between government leaders and United Fruit should not obscure the fact that the interests of a large number of American corporations were protected by the paramilitary operation and subsequent military assistance. In 1969 American firms in Guatemala accounted for 86 percent of the country's total foreign investment of $115 million. In that year seventy-seven American companies ranking among the top 1,000 companies in the United States had investments in Guatemala, including giants like Beatrice Foods, Coca-Cola, CPC International, Del Monte, General Mills, Gulf Oil, I.T.T., Nabisco, Pillsbury, and Ralston Purina.[9] In defense of these corporate interests, the United States between 1946 and 1976 provided $74.6 million in military assistance to the Guatemalan government. Between 1950 and 1976 more than 3,200 members of the Guatemalan armed forces were trained in American military schools.[10]

The victims of Guatemala's free-enterprise economy are the majority of its people. According to Susan Demarco and Susan Sechler of the Agribusiness Accountability Project:

> Guatemala must import diet staples such as corn and beans while using land for coffee, bananas and cattle for export. Eighty-seven percent of the Guatemalans are subsistence farmers with just enough land to keep them alive between work on the plantations. One percent of the population owns 80 percent of the land, and two-thirds of the population has an annual income of $42.[11]

Hunger, poverty, and inequality are characteristic of Guatemalan society. Statistics do not fully document the human tragedy of poverty, but they do convey a general picture of underdevelopment. In Guatemala today there is one physician for every 4,344 citizens, life expectancy is 52 years, and the infant mortality rate is a high 79 per thousand. There is one teacher for every 97 school-age children, only 46 percent of the adult population can read and write, and only 29 percent of school-age children attend school.[12] A good investment climate, protected by American military assistance and intervention, has not brought Guatemala closer to meeting the basic needs of its people. In fact the opposite is true.

Cuba

In 1959 Cuban dictator Fulgencio Batista was overthrown by a revolutionary movement led by Fidel Castro. Under Batista the United States dominated the entire Cuban economy. Prior to the Cuban revolution, the United States controlled 40 percent of Cuba's sugar industry, 50 percent of its public railways, 80 percent of its utilities, 90 percent of its mines and cattle ranches, and nearly 100 percent of its oil refineries. When the then American Vice-President, Richard M. Nixon, visited Cuba in 1955, he praised the Batista dictatorship for its "competence and stability."

The darker side of Batista's competence was a variety of social ills that eventually led to his overthrow. A third of the Cuban workforce was unemployed, three quarters of the sugar workers worked only three or four months a year, more than a third of the population was totally illiterate, and another third was partially so. Only 9 percent of rural homes had electricity, 2 percent had inside piping for water, and 3 percent indoor toilets. Ninety percent of the people in farm sections suffered from worm diseases like dysentery or from anemia.[13]

In 1960 presidential candidate John F. Kennedy stated in a campaign speech in Cincinnati his understanding of the social forces that had brought Castro to power:

> We refused to help Cuba meet its desperate need for economic progress. . . . We used the influence of our Government to advance the interests and increase the profits of the private American companies which dominated the island's economy. . . . Administration spokesmen publicly hailed Batista, hailing him as a staunch ally and a good friend at a time when Batista was murdering thousands, destroying the last vestiges of freedom and stealing hundreds of millions of dollars from the Cuban people. . . . Thus it was our own policies, not those of Castro, that first began to turn our former neighbor against us.[14]

A year later President Kennedy approved an ill-fated Central Intelligence Agency-initiated invasion of Cuba by United States-trained Cuban exiles. The invasion attempt, which is known as the Bay of

Pigs operation, failed in its endeavor to overthrow Castro, and caused the United States considerable embarrassment.

In Cuba today there is no unemployment. People are adequately clothed, housed, and fed, and they receive adequate medical care. In sharp contrast to Guatemala, there is in Cuba one physician for every 941 people, life expectancy is 71 years, and the infant mortality rate is 29 per thousand. There is one teacher for every 28 school-age children, 83 percent of the adult population is literate, and 70 percent of school-age children attend school.

Critics will no doubt say that these gains have been made in a socialist country at the expense of personal freedom. But I wonder how free José Juan and millions of other landless laborers really are. How many "unfreedoms" are the result of Gulf & Western's operations in the Dominican Republic or United Fruit's successful efforts to thwart land reform? Workers in Cuba are unionized. They participate in the decision-making process on farms and in factories, and they share more or less equally the benefits of production. This, it seems to me, is significantly more freedom than is available to the workers or unemployed masses in poor countries with free-enterprise economies. In most of these countries, unions are banned, strikes are forbidden, arrests and torture are common, and political and economic rights are denied by military governments. Guatemala's infant mortality rate is a full fifty points higher than Cuba's, and the Dominican Republic's rate is sixty-nine points higher. These figures force me to pause when I associate freedom with free enterprise. I wonder what the infant mortality rate would be in Cuba today had the Cuban Revolution not taken place, or had the Bay of Pigs invasion been successful.

"Learning" from the Cuban Experience:
The Dominican "Showcase"

American corporate and government leaders regarded the Cuban revolution as a serious threat to their interests. The fear was that movements for social change in other underdeveloped and dependent countries might be encouraged by events in Cuba. The existence of a good investment climate alongside massive poverty was a breeding ground for revolutionary activity that had to be contained. Senator Barry Goldwater, even after the failure of the Bay of Pigs invasion, recommended that the United States invade Cuba to "rid this hemisphere of the threat of extending Communism." He was willing to invade even if this meant nuclear war with the Soviet Union.[15]

The Kennedy Administration learned several valuable lessons

from the Cuban revolution. First, it is poverty, inequality, and human degradation that give rise to rebellion. Second, the security of the governments of poor countries which provide favorable investment climates for American corporations is threatened by *internal* rather than *external* forces. American economic interests in poor countries will not be threatened by invasion from without but by rebellion from within against intolerable living conditions.

Kennedy translated both Cuban lessons into American foreign policy. In March 1961 he announced the Alliance for Progress, a new aid program to improve living conditions for people in Latin America. The primary goals of the Alliance were to accelerate economic growth, raise living standards, and encourage social reforms. Responding to the need for internal security, the president dramatically shifted the focus of American military strategy in Latin America away from hemispheric defense to internal defense against Castro-type guerrilla warfare.

While Kennedy and other American leaders sincerely wanted to use America's power as a liberalizing force in underdeveloped countries, they were pragmatic when it came to protecting American corporate interests. Although repulsive to their ideals, repressive dictators were consistently supported when American business interests were threatened by instability. A case in point is the Dominican Republic. Rafael Trujillo had ruled the Dominican Republic with a bloody vengeance for thirty years before his assassination in 1961. During most of his tyrannical reign, he received support from the American government in exchange for a good investment climate. However, shortly before Trujillo's death, he lost favor with the United States because of his political and economic excesses (at the time of his death his family owned about 80 percent of the Dominican economy).

Afraid that Trujillo's abuses might give rise to another Castro-type movement, the United States did nothing to prevent his assassination. In fact, it was welcomed by many American observers. After Trujillo's death Kennedy hoped to turn the Dominican Republic into a showcase of development made possible by the Alliance for Progress. That was the ideal, but Kennedy was also pragmatic. Reflecting on the different forms of government possible in the Dominican Republic, he made it clear that supporting a repressive dictator was acceptable if other options failed. "There are three possibilities in descending order of preference," Kennedy told Arthur M. Schlesinger, Jr., "a decent democratic regime, a continuation of the Trujillo regime or a Castro regime. We ought to aim at the first, but we really can't renounce the second until we are sure that we can avoid the third."[16]

For four years after the death of Trujillo, the United States sought to build a coalition government around moderate candidates who would avoid the excesses of the right (which would make conditions ripe for a Castro-type rebellion) and the left (which would seriously challenge American corporate interests). In 1965 President Lyndon B. Johnson sent the United States Marines to restore order, thus showing the failure of American policy. The pragmatists won out. "Many Americans, having invested $250 million in the Dominican Republic," Senator George Smathers told Congress, "believe that Generalísimo Trujillo was the best guarantee of American interests in the country . . . . Open intervention must now be considered to protect their property and to prevent a communist coup. . . . "[17] Again American leaders justified intervention by the United States by skillfully blaming instability on the communists rather than on repression, violence, misutilization of resources, poverty, and human degradation.

Richard Barnet, a former national security advisor for the Kennedy and Johnson administrations, describes the situation as stability returned to the Dominican Republic:

> . . . the Dominican Republic received the highest per-capita aid of any country in Latin America. . . . The administration established an enormous embassy in Santo Domingo . . . [with] a U.S. counterpart . . . for every major Dominican government official. Private U.S. investment in housing and tourism began to flow into the island once more. The shooting had scarcely stopped before new Hilton Hotels, Holiday Inns, and housing projects sponsored by IBEC, a Rockefeller-family company, were being planned. The South Puerto Rican Sugar Company, now merged with Gulf and Western Industries, decided to diversify and use some of its beachfront property for a new tourist center. Once again U.S. business sensed that "stability" was returning to the island and the danger of a Dominican Castro was receding into the shadows. With the evidence at hand that the United States was prepared to occupy the island to prevent a revolution, U.S. business took increased confidence, and private investment, supported in many cases by low-interest AID development loans, increased dramatically.[18]

In the Dominican Republic there is one physician for every 1,947 people, life expectancy is 58 years, and the infant mortality rate is an astonishing 98 per thousand. There is one teacher for every 85 school-age children, only 68 percent of the adult population is literate, and 54 percent of school-age children attend school. In Chapter

3 we discussed who benefits and who is victimized by the developmental priorities of the Dominican free-enterprise economy, and we do not intend to be repetitious here. However, the radical difference between the well-being of the Cuban people and the poverty of most Dominicans is especially significant because both nations rely heavily on sugar exports to earn foreign exchange.

There are three basic reasons why hunger and poverty remain severe problems in the Dominican Republic while they have been largely overcome in Cuba. First, the price received for Cuban sugar exports has remained relatively stable because of long-term contracts with the Soviet Union. Cuba therefore has been able to plan its developmental course with the reasonable assurance that its export earnings won't fluctuate severely because of price fluctuations in the international market. The foreign-exchange earnings of the Dominican Republic, on the other hand, have been uncertain and have fluctuated wildly.

Second, although Cuba has been forced into a heavy reliance on the Soviet Union, it has received substantial economic assistance without economic strings. The Dominican Republic for its part has received aid from the United States, but much of this aid is conditional on providing American corporations with a good investment climate. This creates dependency and fosters underdevelopment.

Finally, and this is most important, in Cuba the profits from sugar exports are returned to the workers in the form of wages, or are reinvested in the Cuban economy to meet the basic needs of the people. Wealth is evenly distributed and production is socially planned. What's more, Cuba has begun to diversify its agricultural economy. It may be expected to do so even more if it determines that dependence on sugar is a cause of economic vulnerability. In the Dominican Republic, as we saw in Chapter 3, the profits accrue to private individuals and groups who make investment decisions on the basis of personal profitability rather than on social need. The results are that José Juan is dying not far from a luxury hotel, and that 75 percent of the Dominican people are poorly nourished while more and more land is diverted to sugar production.

The relative well-being of the Cuban people was possible because American military policy failed in its efforts to maintain a good investment climate. Conversely, what American corporate and government leaders regarded as successful military operations in the Dominican Republic, Guatemala, and other free-enterprise economies reinforced poverty and inequality. Between 1946 and 1976 American military assistance to the Dominican Republic totaled $245.4 million. In addition, between 1961 and 1973 American assistance to the police forces under the Public Safety Program totaled more than $4 million.[19] Both the poverty of José Juan and the profits of Gulf & Western Industries are linked to American military policy.

The New Realism

After the United States' intervention in the Dominican Republic, the American government announced a new policy regarding its relationship to military dictatorships and military takeovers. Kennedy's idealism had given way to economic realism. According to Thomas Mann, Assistant Secretary of State for Latin American affairs, the United States could not put itself in a "doctrinaire strait jacket of automatic application of sanctions to every unconstitutional regime in the hemisphere." Shortly after the Marines landed in the Dominican Republic, the House of Representatives passed a resolution, 315 to 52, which legitimized the unilateral use of force on foreign territory by any nation that considers itself threatened by "international communism, directly or indirectly."[20]

Kennedy's idealism failed because the United States was pursuing two conflicting strategies. It was attempting to promote and protect American corporate interests, and at the same time to modernize and reform the economies and governments of underdeveloped countries. Once it became clear that these were inherently contradictory concepts, the idealistic goals of the Alliance for Progress were abandoned in favor of economic goals. Ironically, it was Senator Edward M. Kennedy who in 1970 graphically stated the failure of the Alliance his brother had initiated:

> ... their [Latin American countries'] economic growth per capita is less than before the Alliance for Progress began; in the previous eight years U.S. business has repatriated $8.3 billion in private profits, more than three times the total of new investments; the land remains in the hands of a few; one-third of the rural labor force is unemployed and *13 constitutional governments have been overthrown since the Alliance was launched.*[21]

The Alliance for Progress was predicated on the notion that development was essential if social unrest, which threatened American corporate interests, was to be averted in Latin America. Secretary of Defense Robert S. McNamara realized that underdevelopment and stagnation were the principle causes of instability and revolution. In his book *The Essence of Security* McNamara writes:

> Security is development, and without development there can be no security. A developing nation that does not, in fact,

develop, simply cannot remain secure for the simple reason that its own citizenry cannot shed its human nature. If security implies anything, it implies a minimal measure of order and stability. Without internal development of at least a minimal degree, order and stability are impossible . . . because human nature cannot be frustrated indefinitely.[22]

Within McNamara's own system of logic it is understandable that the United States has increasingly been forced to support repressive governments and even armed intervention in order to protect American corporate interests *in underdeveloped countries*. The failure of poor nations to bring about even minimal development within the international free-enterprise system has forced the United States to protect its economic interests by adopting an increasingly counter-revolutionary posture that is weighted in favor of violence and repression. "Our primary objective in Latin America," McNamara told Congress in 1967, "is to aid, where necessary, in . . . development of indigenous military and paramilitary forces capable of providing, in conjunction with the police and other security forces, the needed domestic security."[23]

The official justification for giving military support to repressive governments is that internal security is essential for development. However, as we stated in Chapter 3, development in poor nations does not refer to a process by which the basic needs of the entire population are met but to a process by which foreign corporations and domestic elites enrich themselves at the expense of the overall population. The fact that poverty, hunger, inequality and the violation of human rights are characteristics shared by many poor countries with free-enterprise economies testifies to the failure of what Austin Kiplinger has referred to as "American democratic imperialism."

American Military Assistance and Sales: Tools of American Foreign Policy

In Chapter 2 we quoted a 1957 Senate report on the purpose of American technical assistance to the effect that "technical assistance is only one of a number of instruments available to the United States to carry out its foreign policy and to promote its national interests abroad." P.L. 480, which we discussed in detail, is cited as one such instrument that served as a tool of neocolonialism. Another tool of American foreign policy mentioned in the report is American military assistance. Between 1946 and 1976 the United States provided countries around the world more than $49 billion in grants under the Military Assistance Program (MAP).[24]

Grants under MAP have fostered a good investment climate by enabling poor countries to conduct counterinsurgency programs designed to hold their impoverished people in check. In addition to providing military equipment, MAP funds have financed American military training programs for Third-World military officers. Between 1950 and 1976 more than 483,000 foreign officers and enlisted personnel, including 72,500 Latin Americans, were trained under MAP in the United States and at an American training school in Panama. Others received United States-sponsored in-country training.[25]

The United States-trained foreign officers, who are exposed to pro-American attitudes and assumptions, are more likely to purchase American military equipment, thus insuring continued American influence in their countries. A good example of how training programs serve American interests is provided by Albert L. Morgan, former chairperson of the House Foreign Affairs Committee. After a political coup in Brazil, he stated:

> Every critic of foreign aid is confronted with the fact that the armed forces of Brazil threw out the Goulart government and that U.S. military aid was a major factor in giving these forces an indoctrination in the principles of democracy and a pro-U.S. orientation. Many of these officers were trained in the United States under the AID program.[26]

Often training programs are justified on the basis of insuring American national defense. It is probably more accurate, however, that these programs are defending American economic interests, not our borders. A 1970 House Foreign Affairs Committee Study on MAP training programs concludes:

> The majority of issues which must be addressed about MAP training are political and economic in nature, rather than strictly military. This emphasis reflects our strong convictions that military assistance programs are primarily an instrument of American foreign policy and only secondarily of defense.[27]

Although the United States has shown a willingness to send American troops to foreign shores in defense of American economic interests, this is not a preferred strategy. Military assistance and sales to elites in poor countries are meant to insure a stable investment climate without committing American soldiers. One reason the Vietnam War encountered such stiff opposition in the United States was that the heavy loss of American lives was unacceptable to the majority of the American people. Vietnamization—President Nixon's plan to "end" the war—was a strategy to withdraw American troops and at the same time to continue supplying South Vietnam with the materials and training necessary to fight the war. Nixon generalized and formalized this strategy in the Nixon Doctrine. Secretary of Defense Melvin Laird described the Nixon administration's defense posture to Congress in 1970:

> The basic policy of decreasing direct U.S. military involvement cannot be successful unless we provide our friends and allies, whether through grant aid or credit sales, with the material assistance necessary to assure the most effective possible contribution by the manpower they are willing and able to commit to their own and the common defense. . . . In the majority of cases, this means indigenous manpower organized into properly equipped and well-trained armed forces with the help of material, training, technology and specialized skills furnished by the United States through the Military Assistance Program or as Foreign Military Sales.[28]

As a result of the Nixon Doctrine, the United States greatly accelerated sales of sophisticated weapons to underdeveloped countries. For example, in 1969 *total* U.S. arms sales were less than $1 billion, but between 1970 and 1976 the value of American arms exported to *underdeveloped countries alone* totaled $25.5 billion.[29] The trend toward increased arms sales to poor countries is likely to continue as the United States seeks to protect its global economic interests while committing American troops only in extreme situations.

Summary

After World War II, the national purpose of the United States was foreign expansion. Like Jeroboam centuries before, the United States capitalized on the weakness of its war-torn neighbors. As the United States expanded and established its economic interests throughout the globe, it could no longer limit defense considerations to its national borders. American military assistance and intervention served as tools of American foreign policy, which complemented various economic aid programs and insured the integration of poor countries into the international free-enterprise system. While tactics sometimes changed, the goal was nearly always the same: to insure a good investment climate, including access to the markets, resources, and cheap labor of the underdeveloped countries.

The United States pursued its foreign economic expansion in a spirit of missionary obligation. The American Century was to be different from the British Century. American imperialism was to be democratic. What was good for American corporations, it was thought, would be good for the United States and the world. For millions of hungry people living in poor countries with free-enterprise economies the promise of democratic imperialism is as empty as their stomachs. The multinational corporations and elites of the poor countries that benefit from American military policy do not regard American military spending as a mistaken priority. But what provides them with a stable investment climate may well be a death warrant for the world's poor.

American military assistance and paramilitary operations have made Guatemala safe for United Fruit (United Brands) and other United States-based corporations. But agrarian reform, which is essential for increased food production and a more equitable distribution of wealth, has been thwarted. While the land is owned or controlled by a small group of people who produce cash crops and cattle for export, 80 percent of the pediatric beds in Guatemalan hospitals are filled with children suffering from malnutrition.[30]

Shortly after the United States Marines enforced stability in the Dominican Republic, the cane cutters union was destroyed, and Gulf & Western Industries purchased the South Puerto Rico Sugar Company. Today Gulf & Western operates the world's largest sugar mill. It profits from investments in luxury hotels for tourists and runs an industrial free zone. Meanwhile, José Juan is dying along with 10 percent of all Dominican children who never reach their first birthday.

Between 1950 and 1976 approximately 8,657 Brazilian officers and military personnel were trained in American military schools, being thus indoctrinated with pro-American values. Brazil, which is a haven for American corporate investors, received between 1946 and 1976 $654.5 million in American military assistance. But Brazil is not a haven for the majority of Brazilians whose basic political and economic rights are consistently violated, including the right to a living wage and adequate diet. Although Brazil is the world's second largest agricultural exporter, 40 percent of the Brazilian people are undernourished.

Numerous South Korean workers, including women and children, who produce shoes, textiles, and electronic parts for subsidiaries of United States-based corporations, used to produce food for local consumption. But the importation of American food products under P.L. 480 undermined domestic producers. The result is a chronic food dependency; soon South Korea will import 50 percent of its food. Between 1946 and 1976 the United States provided more than $8.7 billion to the South Korean government under its military assistance program. And between 1950 and 1976 almost 34,000 South Korean officers and enlisted personnel were trained in American military schools.

In the Philippines as much as 80 percent of the rural people, many of whom were once landowners, are tenant farmers today. Large investments in banana and pineapple plantations by local elites and foreign corporations such as Del Monte and Dole lead to high profits for the investors while the caloric intake of the average Filipino has been reduced to approximately the same level as that of the people of Bangladesh. Such injustice in the countryside invariably leads to social unrest. For this reason the United States has developed counterinsurgency programs is such areas. In 1973 Secretary of Defense Eliot L. Richardson told the Senate Armed Services Committee:

> The U.S. Security Assistance Program to the Philippines has as one of its major objectives the improvement of the Philippine Armed Forces capability to cope with insurgency problems. To this end we are providing military assistance suitable for this role. This includes aircraft, rifles, trucks, communications gear, helicopters, patrol boats and landing craft, and other weapons. The goal is to improve mobility, communications, and firepower—all vital elements in the conduct of counterinsurgency operations.[31]

Under the martial law regime of President Ferdinand Marcos, American corporations enjoy a variety of investment incentives, including cheap labor. An advertisement from the Philippines Bureau of National and Foreign Information that appeared on July 28, 1974, in the *New York Times* states:

> Recent Presidential decrees have simplified conciliation and arbitrations of labor disputes (both strikes and lockouts are prohibited), lifted work restrictions on Sundays and holidays, liberalized the employment of women and children, and expanded the scope of the apprenticeship program. Labor costs for the foreign company . . . could work out from 35–50 percent lower than they would be in either Hong Kong or Singapore.

A good investment climate both flows from and needs military support. Between 1946 and 1976 the United States provided the

Philippines more than $877 million in military assistance, and from 1950 to 1976 more than 16,000 Filipino officers and enlisted personnel received training in American military schools.

We could provide numerous examples from Chile, Thailand, Nicaragua, and other countries where American military policies have served to create a favorable investment climate while undermining the position of the poor. What we hope to have demonstrated in this section is that concern for hungry people necessarily leads to a concern about the role of American military policy in a hungry world.

Chapter 5

THE IMPACT OF AMERICAN MILITARY SPENDING AT HOME AND ABROAD

American military *policies* aggravate or cause hunger in ways that are highly visible. For example, it is relatively easy to make the connection between hunger in Guatemala and American military policies that undermine land reform and prevent the poor from having access to land and other resources needed to produce food for local consumption. It is much more difficult to see the linkages between high levels of American military *spending* and hunger abroad. Totally apart from whether or not the weapons produced are used, the large amounts of money the United States devotes to the military sector aggravates hunger. Here we will try to demonstrate how this is so, though the connection might not appear obvious.

Ever since World War II, proponents of military spending have argued that the government-financed production of weapons is good for the American economy. Unfortunately, the long-term effects of relying on military spending to stimulate the economy have been disastrous. Military spending accelerates inflation, creates relatively few jobs, and undermines the competitive position of American industry. Many economic problems facing the United States today can be traced to excessive military expenditures. It is here that hunger enters the picture. *The United States is increasingly relying upon food power to counteract difficulties brought on by a "permanent war economy."* The result is further victimization of the poor.

In this chapter I will spend some time describing the arguments that proponents of high military expenditures offer to justify their position, and I will rebut their arguments. I will do so because I firmly believe that unless we fully understand that military spending

75

is not good for our economy, and unless we understand exactly who is benefiting from the perpetuation of this myth, the United States will utilize food power in ways that undermine the security of the American people while victimizing the world's poor.

War and the Prosperity Myth

World War II brought the United States out of a depression. On the eve of the war 17.2 percent of the American workforce was unemployed. By 1944 unemployment had dropped to 1.7 percent. Between 1939 and 1945 the number of employed Americans increased by 7 million, and the armed forces, which absorbed a sizeable segment of the employable population, were enlarged from 370,000 to 11,400,000 persons. During the same period government orders for goods and services soared from $11 billion to $117 billion, and the market increase in civilian personal consumption rose 25 percent—from $137 to $171 billion.[1]

During the war government spending in the military sector brought full employment and prosperity. But there was an overriding fear that the war-induced economic boom would be short-lived. "In all groups," the *New York Times* reported in March 1946, "there is the gnawing fear that after several years of high prosperity the U.S. may run into something even graver than the depression of the thirties." This widespread anxiety was induced by the problem of how to maintain full employment during peacetime when 20 million defense workers and 10 million service people would be available for employment in the civilian economy. A major difficulty was how to find markets for the goods produced in the civilian sector. Without markets full employment was impossible.

The United States government pursued two strategies, both of which over the long term have had a significant impact on hungry people, in an effort to prevent the country from sliding back into the Great Depression. First, it undertook a policy of foreign expansion. "We cannot expect domestic prosperity without a constantly expanded trade with other nations," Dean G. Acheson stated in 1943. "To keep prosperity, levels of employment, production and income . . . we shall have to find increasing markets for our production and increasing investment outlets for our capital."[2] Secretary of Commerce Henry Wallace echoed Acheson's concern. "Private enterprise in the U.S. can survive," he said, "only if it expands and grows." He then went on to refer to the underdeveloped countries as "this unlimited new frontier of opportunities."[3] As previously noted, the United States through P.L. 480 and other aid programs, and through an aggressive military policy, took steps to expand foreign markets and thus avert domestic political and economic problems.

The second government strategy to ward off a depression was to stimulate the economy through military spending. After the war the United States government continued to finance employment in the military sector rather than try to recycle all defense workers and soldiers into the civilian economy. Such high military spending during peacetime, which was unprecedented, was justified on both economic and ideological grounds. The economic boom accompanying World War II convinced many economists that military spending was good for the economy. In their view, cuts in the defense budget contributed to a recession. For example, a 20 percent reduction in national security expenditures after the Korean War was thought by many to be the principal cause of the 1953–54 recession. The $2 billion cut in the defense budget of 1957 contributed to the recession in that year, and led the National Planning Association to argue that the defense budget could be increased by $22 billion. Meanwhile, the Committee on Economic Development announced that defense spending could safely rise to 15 percent of the Gross National Product.[4]

One consequence of using military spending as an economic stimulant was that military production was no longer necessarily linked with the defense needs of the country. There was, however, an ideological justification for high levels of military spending during peacetime: the Cold War. "Business won't go to pot," the editors of *U.S. News and World Report* wrote in 1950, "so long as war is a threat, so long as every alarm can step up spending-lending for defense at home and aid abroad. Cold War is almost a guarantee against a bad depression."[5] Exaggeration of the Soviet threat was and continues to be a boom to military contractors. George F. Kennan, former American ambassador to the Soviet Union, wrote in 1956:

> The image of a Stalinist Russia poised and yearning to attack the West, and deterred only by our possession of atomic weapons, was largely a creation of the Western imagination, against which some of us who were familiar with Russian matters tried in vain, over the course of years, to make our voices heard.[6]

A year later General Douglas MacArthur told the stockholders of Sperry Rand Corporation:

> Our government has kept us in a perpetual state of fear—kept us in a continual stampede of patriotic fervour—with a cry of a grave national emergency. Always there has been some terrible evil at home or some monstrous foreign power that was going to gobble us up if we did not blindly rally behind it by furnishing

the exhorbitant funds demanded. Yet, in retrospect, these disasters seem never to have happened, seem never to have been quite real.

High military spending seemed an almost perfect way to stimulate the American economy and avoid a depression. It was apparently good for the economy, could be justified to the American people on the basis of their desire to feel secure against "formidable enemies," and, as we shall see, it was highly beneficial to a variety of powerful groups.

Getting a Piece of the Action

"In the councils of government," President Dwight D. Eisenhower stated in his farewell speech to the nation in 1961, "we must guard against the acquisition of unwarranted influence, whether sought or unsought, by the military-industrial complex. The potential for the disastrous rise of misplaced power exists and will persist." The American government's willingness to use military spending to stimulate the domestic economy had by the end of Eisenhower's presidency given rise to a military industrial complex: a loose collaboration of military officers, industrial managers, and legislators, all of whom had a vested interest in continued high levels of military spending.

Legislators hoping to create jobs in their districts were eager to obtain military contracts. In 1959, for example, Congressman Ken Hechler demanded more defense activity for his state:

> I am firmly against the kind of logrolling which would subject our defense program to narrowly sectional or selfish pulling and hauling. But I am getting pretty hot under the collar about the way my state of West Virginia is short-changed in Army, Navy, and Air Force installations. . . . I am going to stand up on my hind legs and roar until West Virginia gets the fair treatment she deserves.[7]

Military officers from the various branches of the forces benefited from high defense budgets. With each increase in military spending they acquired new weapons systems, more personnel, greater prestige, and increased power. At the end of World War II the Pentagon employed five legislative agents. By 1967 it employed 339 lobbyists to plead its case, inform legislators about contracts in their areas, process inquiries about military personnel in the armed services, and perform a variety of other tasks. In 1967 the largest private lobbying force was the Postal Clerks Union, which spent $277,524. That same year the Department of Defense had more than $4 million budgeted for that purpose, in addition to the lobbying done on its behalf by defense contractors and associations.[8] According to Sydney Lens, by 1970:

> The Pentagon own[ed] 29 million acres of land—almost the size of New York State—plus another 9.7 million acres under the control of the Army Civil Works division, valued, all-told, at $47.7 billion. It is custodian of $100 billion worth of weaponry and $55.6 billion in supplies and plant equipment. Its true wealth undoubtedly ranges from $300 to $400 billion, or about six to eight times the annual after-tax profits of *all* American corporations.[9]

American corporations, for their part, were eager to get a piece of the military action. Between 1959 and 1962 manufacturing firms outside the defense sector purchased 137 companies in the defense sector. By 1966 ninety-three of the top five hundred manufacturing firms had diversified into the defense sector from a traditional non-defense base.[10] Today the largest corporations in the country dominate the lucrative defense business. Here is a list of the top fifty defense contractors (fiscal year 1976) arranged according to rank, the monetary value of their contracts, and their rank in terms of the *Fortune* 500 list of the largest American industrial corporations (fiscal year 1977):[11]

Rank	Company	Contract (millions of $)	Ind. Rank
1.	McDonnell-Douglas	$2,464.6	64
2.	Lockheed Corporation	1,509.8	71
3.	Northrop Corporation	1,480.2	153
4.	General Electric Company	1,347.0	9
5.	United Technologies Corporation	1,233.1	34
6.	Boeing Company	1,176.3	49
7.	General Dynamics Corporation	1,073.0	85
8.	Grumman Corporation	982.0	161
9.	Litton Industries	978.2	69
10.	Rockwell International Corporation	966.0	31
11.	Hughes Air Corporation	910.9	?
12.	Raytheon Company	784.4	89
13.	Tenneco Corporation	767.8	19

14. Sperry Rand Corporation	505.5	75
15. Westinghouse Electric Corporation	482.4	26
16. Chrysler Corporation	468.5	10
17. American Telephone and Telegraph Company	447.0	?
18. FMC Corporation	417.8	103
19. Honeywell	385.7	82
20. Textron	371.7	90
21. General Motors Corporation	345.2	1
22. RCA Corporation	330.4	30
23. LTV Corporation	315.8	43
24. Todd Shipyards Corporation	314.0	?
25. Teledyne	296.3	112
26. TRW	291.5	76
27. Ford Motor Company	285.4	3
28. Standard Oil Company of California	280.9	6
29. International Telephone and Telegraph (ITT)	260.0	11
30. International Business Machines (IBM)	255.9	7
31. Congoleum Corporation	250.3	453
32. Martin Marietta Corporation	248.7	177
33. Exxon Corporation	244.8	2
34. Amerada Hess Corporation	243.6	45
35. Mobil Oil Corporation	240.7	4
36. Fairchild Industries	226.8	455
37. Harsco Corporation	198.8	?
38. Singer Company	191.4	109
39. GTE Corporation	189.8	?
40. Bendix Corporation	161.8	73
41. Texas Instruments	156.8	124
42. Morrison-Knudsen	154.8	?
43. Texaco	145.9	5
44. Pacific Resources	140.0	459
45. R. J. Reynolds	134.0	41
46. American Motors	122.5	110
47. Control Data	121.7	170
48. Guam Oil & Refining	120.1	?
49. Goodyear	119.4	22
50. General Tire and Rubber	116.4	122

The top hundred defense contractors for fiscal year 1976 received $42 billion in prime contract awards. Many of America's largest and most powerful corporations have a vested interest in protecting their piece of the military pie. All but seven of the top twenty-five defense contractors are among the top hundred industrial corporations in America. For the largest corporations defense contracts are a steady source of profits. The Council on Economic Priorities released its first analysis of the Department of Defense's annual listing of contractors in 1972. It found that the fifty-five companies listed among the hundred top contractors in fiscal year 1971 had been included on that list for the previous ten years. All these companies are still among the top contractors.[12]

According to Senator Fulbright, not only the largest American corporations have self-interested reasons for supporting a permanent war economy, although they certainly reap a majority of the profits. Approximately 22,000 prime contractors and 100,000 subcontractors depend on the Pentagon for some share of their business, and nearly 10 percent of the American workforce is dependent upon military spending for its livelihood. "Millions of Americans whose only interest is in making a decent living have acquired a vested interest in an economy geared to war," says Senator Fulbright. "Every new weapons system or military installation soon acquires a constituency. . . . "[13]

Profits on military contracts are higher than for civilian industries. In a comparison between large defense firms doing three-fourths of their business with the government and industrial firms of comparable size selling their products on the commercial market, Professor Murray Weidenbaum found that the former earned 17.5 percent on their investment between 1962 to 1965, while the latter realized only 10.6 percent.[14] According to a 1970 General Accounting Office report, an analysis of 146 defense contracts showed pretax profit on total capital investments of 28.3 percent, or roughly twice the normal average for manufacturing profits.[15]

In 1970 the Senate Subcommittee on Executive Reorganization and Government Research did a survey of 118 industries with significant military contracts; this survey focused on the industries preparations for conversion to peacetime uses. The findings, summarized by Senator Abraham A. Ribicoff, showed an unwillingness by "private" industry to make changes that might endanger the generous profits available from military contracts:

> In general, the response indicated that private industry is not interested in initiating any major attempts at meeting critical public needs. Most industries have no plans or projects designed to apply their resources to civilian problems. Furthermore, they indicated an unwillingness to initiate such actions without a firm commitment from the government that their efforts will quickly reap the financial rewards to which they are accustomed.[16]

If military spending were good for the U.S. economy, as its proponents claim, there would be little harm in a few excess profits earned by corporate giants. Unfortunately, this is not the case.

The Unintended Consequences of Military Spending

Cancer patients often undergo extensive chemotherapy in an effort to stop the growth of tumors. Many of the chemicals used are extremely potent, and their use is generally confined to relatively short periods of time. For some people chemotherapy treatment is successful and results in a cure. However, in some cases the long-term effects of these powerful drugs are unknown or perhaps damaging. The United States has utilized military spending as a sort of chemotherapy to treat an ailing economy. Unfortunately, the dose of military spending has been massive and ongoing. According to its proponents, military spending is good for the U.S. economy. But a war economy, which on a short-term basis (World War II) appeared to be a boom, has shown itself to be a bust in the long term.

Since World War II the United States has spent $2,000 billion on the military! Nearly half of all the scientists and engineers in the country are employed at present in the defense sector. This enormous long-term commitment of money and human talent to military priorities has three unintended consequences. First, military spending accelerates inflation. Workers in military industries receive wages and consume goods and services in the civilian marketplace without producing socially useful products. This results in escalating prices as more dollars (wages earned in the military sector) compete for a limited amount of consumer goods and services. Also the United States government finances excessive military production through deficit spending. For example, between 1974 and 1976 the government spent $175 billion more than it took in through taxes. Deficit spending spurs inflation that amounts to a hidden tax on all Americans; it especially strikes the low- and middle-income groups that can least afford it.

A second unintended consequence of military spending is unemployment. One of the bitter ironies of the permanent war economy is that military spending, which was supposed to relieve unemployment by creating jobs, is an inefficient job creator. Dollar for dollar, more jobs are created outside the military sector because military operations require high levels of technology and capital investment, and because military corporations have higher costs and profit margins. In other words, military production is generally capital-intensive rather than labor-intensive. In 1972 Representative Les Aspin submitted to the *Congressional Record* the following estimate of jobs created within and outside the military sector per billion dollars expended:[17]

Jobs corps (includes training)	151,000
Public service jobs	132,000
Teaching	100,000
Accelerated public works	87,500
Nurses	77,000
Public housing	75,900
Sewer construction	75,700
Private housing	66,500
Hospital construction	56,900
School construction	49,900
Defense	35,000
NASA space shuttle	10,000

Aspin's figures demonstrate that expenditures outside the military sector produce far more jobs than those within. The former also have the added benefit of producing goods and services essential for meeting basic human needs. Only expenditures for NASA have a poorer record in creating jobs than defense spending.

A third unintended consequence of military spending is the progressive deterioration of the American competitive position in world markets. In 1964 the Congressional Committee on Government Research issued a report indicating that over the long haul military spending and priorities might undermine the competitive future of American industry:

In the world of our probable future, our ability as a nation to compete will depend to a great extent on the efficacy of today's research into our grave social and economic problems. . . . In the sense of mission-oriented programs, *we are spending greatly on defense, space, and nuclear missions and virtually nothing on the mission of our competitive future;* . . . apart from strictly economic problems many of our social problems have become costly. In comparison to the dollars spent on the space program we can well afford some additional pennies for research into these and many other areas.

The Committee's report continues:

It is critical that the government avoid policies or procedures which lead to inefficient deployment or stockpiling of trained personnel. Manpower cost is as important as fiscal cost in consideration of major programs. But this has not been a significant criterion in major program choices to date. The huge technical programs of NASA, DOD, and AEC have absorbed large numbers of engineers and scientists. Yet no one at the time of decision has reckoned their worth on these programs as opposed to their alternate use in teaching, private industry, or other government programs.[18]

Today the Committee's report looks much like true yet unheeded prophecy. In 1967 the international Organization for Economic Cooperation and Development reported that the United States had 700,000 scientists, engineers, and technicians working in research and development. But military activities accounted for 63 percent of their work.[19] From the end of World War II to 1972, federal spending for research and development (R & D) totaled $200 billion, 80 percent of which was devoted to defense, space, and the Atomic Energy Commission.[20] In 1976 alone R & D spending of the federal government totaled $13.4 billion. And as we mentioned previously, the United States has spent since World War II $2,000 billion for military purposes.

The nation has invested so heavily, both in terms of money and skilled personnel, in technologies of war that it can no longer compete in technologies of peace. As a consequence more and more of the goods consumed by Americans as well as the equipment in use in our factories are imported.

> By the late 1960's, imports were taking over large and growing portions of U.S. domestic markets of a spreading variety of manufactured goods and components, including relatively sophisticated goods. By 1968 and 1969, the U.S. had become a net importer of steel, autos, trucks and parts, as well as such products as clothing, footwear, and glass. In consumer electrical goods, imports took over major parts of the U.S. domestic market. Even in electrical and nonelectrical machinery, during the 1960's imports increased more rapidly than exports— posing serious potential problems for the 1970's.[21]

There are two reasons why imports are taking over a greater share of the American market. Both are related to American military spending and policy. First, growth that results from military spending is nonproductive, that is, it produces no economically useful goods for society—either for consumption or for future production. The emphasis on nonproductive growth has undermined the capacity of civilian industries to compete in the world marketplace.

Second, the period of unprecedented use of human resources and capital for nonproductive military equipment was accompanied by a massive export of capital by United States-based global corporations, which increased their direct foreign investments from $32 billion in 1960 to $71 billion in 1969.[22] Earlier we documented how an aggressive foreign policy, including military sales, assistance, and intervention, enabled United States-based corporations to expand their operations abroad. The overriding belief was that what was good for American corporations was good for the United States and the world. We have already discussed the impact of foreign expansion on the world's poor; now we can get a glimpse of its impact on American workers. The long-term effect of shifting production facilities abroad is to set in motion a substitution process that displaces exports from the United States. Nathan Spero of the United Electrical Workers Union described this process in 1971:

> Following investment made abroad by the U.S. firm, the first effect of setting up a foreign subsidiary is to substitute for the export from the U.S. to the foreign country. The second step . . . is where a U.S. company that has been exporting from the U.S. to a third country has its foreign subsidiary take over that export now serving the third country. The result is, then, two sources of displacement. The third effect is that the foreign subsidiary begins to take over the U.S. domestic market of the multinational company.[23]

While the overall industrial capacity of the United States has seriously deteriorated over the past several decades, and millions of workers have seen their jobs exported to foreign countries, many United States-based corporations are doing quite well. Not only do they earn large profits from military contracts but they also have a well-integrated and cozy relationship with their foreign subsidiaries. An article entitled "A Labor View of Foreign Investment and Trade Issues," which was part of a 1970 governmental study of American trade and investment policy, notes:

> At least 25 percent of U.S. exports are now intra-corporate transactions between U.S. based multinationals and their subsidiaries and probably about a quarter or more of U.S. imports are similar intra-corporate transactions. Moreover, an additional, significant portion of what is reported as U.S. trade— perhaps another 25 percent—is between U.S. based multinationals and firms in foreign countries, with whom they have license, patent or other joint-venture affiliations.[24]

By 1970 the United States was harvesting the bitter fruits of thirty years of a continuous war economy and blind capitulation to the interests of large United States-based multinational corporations. Balance-of-payments problems had worsened to the point that they threatened our trade relations with Europe and Japan. The balance of payments measures the flow of goods and services among countries as well as other financial flows, including military and economic assistance and foreign investment. After World War II dollars backed by gold acted as the world's basic currency. Any foreign country holding dollars was free to exchange them in the United States for gold. By 1970, however, the United States had printed and spent so many dollars abroad—purchasing foreign goods, setting up subsidiaries of United States-based corporations, and financing military and paramilitary operations to insure a good investment climate—that the United States no longer had enough gold to back the dollars held by foreigners. As a consequence, the Nixon administration in 1970 refused to redeem foreign-held dollars for gold. A graphic illustration of our waning economic power was that in 1971 dollar holdings abroad exceeded three times the United States Treasury's gold reserves, which had declined from $24 billion in 1950 to $9–$10 billion in 1973.[25] That same year (1971) the United States experienced its first trade deficit of the century (a trade deficit indicates that the value of American imports from foreign countries is greater than the value of American exports to foreign countries. This situation is referred to as a negative balance of trade).

The Government Response:
Recommendations of the Williams Commission

Faced with a serious and worsening economic crisis, the Nixon Administration appointed a commission on American trade and investment policy in May 1970. The Williams Commission—named after Albert Williams, the chairman of IBM who chaired it—began its report to the President on this rather somber note:

> There are unmistakable signs in the U.S. of a developing crisis of confidence in the system. The crisis is reflected in: mounting pressures in the U.S. for import restrictions as foreign-made textiles, clothing, shoes, steel, electronic products and autos penetrate our market; growing demands for retaliation against foreign measures which place American agricultural and other products at a disadvantage in markets abroad; . . . a growing

concern in this country that . . . foreign countries have found other ways, besides tariffs, of impeding our access to their markets abroad; labor's contention that our corporations, through their operations abroad, are "exporting jobs" by giving away the competitive advantage the U.S. should derive from its superior technology; a sense of frustration with our persistant balance of payments deficit; . . . an increasing concern that the foreign economic policy of our government has given insufficient weight to our economic interests and too much weight to our foreign political relations.[26]

"The crisis of confidence can be traced to some major developments both here and abroad," the Commission continued. "Foremost among these, without doubt, is the increased pressure of imports in the U.S. market."[27] Also, "foreign concern about our trade policy has been reinforced by our inability to reduce our balance of payments deficit. The steady outflow of dollars . . . has made it more difficult to control inflation in other countries." This, according to the Commission, was unacceptable to these countries, which believed "the U.S. was spending and investing abroad beyond its means, and they were being called upon to finance the difference."[28]

"At the conclusion of World War II," the Williams Commission noted, "the U.S. emerged alone among the major industrial countries, with its production capacity and technological base not only intact, but strengthened. We did not have to worry about our competitive position in the world. Today . . . the European Community and Japan have become major centers of economic power and strong competitors in world markets."[29] The Commission was aware that American military spending and policy had contributed to the declining competitive position of the United States:

Our situation changed for the worse as our trade balance deteriorated by $5 billion between 1964 and 1969. . . . Of major importance was our failure to contain the inflationary pressures induced by accelerated government expenditures, including those accompanying the war in Vietnam, without timely and commensurate increases in taxation.[30]

"Indeed the Commission was impressed," the report continues, "with the fact that many of the economic problems we face today grow out of the overseas responsibilities the U.S. has assumed as the major power of the non-Communist world"[31]—i.e., as the majority stockholder in the corporation known as the world. Also the Commission recognized that "U.S. Government support for research and development today is concentrated in military fields having only relatively modest civilian fallout," and it recommended "a much higher level of government support for research and development directed specifically to industrial objectives, as is found in other countries."[32]

In the midst of an economic crisis the Commission stressed the importance of expanding American exports:

> In recent years . . . a number of major changes in world trade have heightened rather than diminished the importance of exports to the U.S.: the increasing competitive world marketplace, the high rate of import growth in the U.S. and the growth of the U.S.-controlled overseas production.[33]

The Commission forcefully stated that "the U.S. must launch a vigorous export drive for the 1970's."[34] The general conclusion of the Commission was that the competitive strength of the American economy was in high-technology goods and agriculture. It was these two sectors that would determine whether the United States could regain some ot its waning economic power. In trying to meet the challenge of increased competition from Japan and Europe, "the pattern of our trade was changing," the Commission noted. "Our exports shifted increasingly to high-technology capital goods, and we imported more consumer goods."[35] Today, "technologically based products are the United States' principal assets in increasing its exports and meeting import competition."[36]

The Williams Commission also placed great emphasis on increasing American agricultural exports. "Exports of farm products are crucial to our agricultural industry and to our overall economy," the study noted.[37] Of particular interest to the Commission was removal of trade barriers erected by Japan and western Europe to protect their agricultural producers:

> U.S. agriculture has been greatly affected by restrictions on and distortions of agricultural trade. Endowed with plentiful good land and highly efficient technology and organization, we have a productive capacity far in excess of our domestic needs. Only on the basis of large and growing exports can we use our resources efficiently and thereby exploit our comparative advantage in agriculture.[38]

The study, which was completed during a period of oversupply on the world market, was actually concerned that American food exports might decline. Nevertheless, the Williams Commission stressed the critical importance of expanding agricultural exports and assigned as a high priority goal for American policy makers increased sales to western Europe, Japan, communist, and underdeveloped countries.

> Reduced markets for U.S. agriculture would also affect nonfarm sectors of the economy. In the agribusiness sector sharp reductions in purchases of the equipment, fertilizers, seeds and pesticides used in crop production could be expected. In summary, the economic health of U.S. agriculture is likely to become increasingly dependent on world markets. Furthermore, we have the capacity to export more if foreign markets are opened to us. *We believe that our national interest demands agricultural policies that will permit and promote expansion of . . . U.S. exports . . .*[39]

Food Power: The American Response to a Worsening Crisis

The Nixon Administration, which was concerned about the declining competitive position of American industry and the worldwide decline of American power, did not receive good news from the Williams Commission. But there was worse news to come. Shortly after the Williams Commission had released its report, other evidence surfaced indicating that the economic problems facing the United States were even graver than reported. The 1971 trade deficit of $2.2 billion dollars had by 1972 tripled to more than $6.6 billion; *and the deficit had occurred largely in the area of high-technology items* (chemicals, nonelectrical machinery, electrical apparatus, and transport equipment), which the Williams Commission had regarded as "the United States principal assets in increasing its exports."

In 1960 the U.S. imported $807 million in chemicals; ten years later it imported $1.45 billion, a 79.6 percent increase. In nonelectrical machinery the 1960 import bill was $438 million; by 1970 that figure had jumped to $3.1 billion, a 608.2 percent increase. In the area of electrical apparatuses, the import bill jumped from $286 million in 1960 to $2.27 billion in 1970, a 694.4 percent increase. And in the area of transport equipment, the import bill jumped from $742 million in 1960 to $5.79 billion in 1970, a 681.3 percent increase.[40] Economist Michael Boretsky of the Department of Commerce analyzed the deterioration in the American trade position in 1971, and concluded that it was likely to continue, given the following developments:

1. A gradually growing deficit in trade with minerals, fuels, and the like (e.g., from $1.7 billion in 1957 to $3.3 billion in 1969).

2. A dramatically growing deficit in trade with non-technology-intensive manufactured products (from a surplus of about $1.1 billion in 1957 to a deficit of $5.6 billion in 1969).

3. A rapidly deteriorating trade situation in the technology-intensive manufactured products, the only commodity groups still yielding sizable surpluses, with imports persistently growing at a rate about 2.5 times as fast as exports and about 3.2 times as fast as the growth of the GNP (in current prices).

4. A rapidly deteriorating trade situation with nearly all the developed world and a dramatic deterioration with Japan and Canada.

The principal causes of this deterioration have been:

1. The gradual loss of industrial and technological superiority by U.S. industry (narrowing the gap).

2. Weak international price competitiveness of U.S. industry.

3. Inadequate natural resources in the United States relative to the economy's needs.[41]

When the 1972 trade deficit revealed a further weakening in what the Williams Commission had presumed to be an area of strength, an already serious situation became desperate. Two "solutions" soon emerged to the impending crisis: a massive campaign to sell weapons abroad and food sales to a world experiencing shortages the United States had helped create.

There are several reasons why exporting weapons to earn foreign exchange became a cornerstone of American policy. First, after more than thirty years of a permanent war economy, weapons are a high-technology item in which the United States holds a competitive advantage. Second, as we described earlier in this chapter, arms sales are consistent with the Nixon Doctrine that committed the United States to protecting its global economic interests by upgrading the military establishments of foreign countries rather than by committing American troops. Third, in 1973 the Organization of Petroleum Exporting Countries (OPEC) drastically increased the price of oil. This sent more dollars abroad, thus aggravating the American trade deficit. Arms sales to OPEC countries were one way of recycling petrodollars. Finally, an increase of weapons sales was acceptable to the military-industrial complex, which had a vested interest in maintaining a permanent war economy. The bitter irony, of course, is that military spending was largely responsible in the first place for undermining the American economy and putting our trade balance in the red. Yet arms sales are being utilized today as a means of improving our balance-of-trade position. These four reasons together with the desperate economic crisis confronting the United States today explain why our arms sales increased from $945 million in fiscal year 1970 to more than $11.5 billion in 1974,[42] and why they have continued at a level of more than $10 billion for each succeding year.

Because of the unexpected deterioration of American high-technology exports, the Williams Commission's recommendation that the United States make every effort to expand agricultural exports took on added significance. Poor weather presented the United States with a golden opportunity. In 1972 poor weather contributed to production setbacks in the U.S.S.R., China, India, Australia, Sahelian Africa, and Southeast Asia. This development, coupled with a decline in the world fish catch, gave a clear indication of a worsening world food situation. "The weight of the gathering evidence was hard to mistake," writes Hal Sheets in an article entitled "Big Money in Hunger:" "There would be unprecedented demands—much of them humanitarian—on the U.S. grain supply, with consequences reaching far into the future." There was little or no evidence that his information was misunderstood. It was understood but ignored for the sake of different and "higher stakes."[43]

In early 1972 Henry A. Kissinger sent a letter to the U.S. Department of Agriculture (USDA) asking for plans to increase agricultural exports. Apparently Kissinger and the Department gave serious consideration to the recommendation of the Williams Commission that the United States should expand trade with communist countries as a means of increasing agricultural exports. What emerged from Kissinger's initiative and USDA's planning was the Russian Wheat Deal.

In 1972, with images of world food shortages on the horizon, the USDA withheld 62 million acres of farmland from production, and paid farmers $4 billion not to farm. That same year American grain companies sold the Soviet Union a quarter of the American wheat crop and other grains. The Russian Wheat Deal served several important functions for a nation desperately seeking to expand its revenues through agricultural exports. It improved our balance of trade and opened a large and potentially long-term market for American agricultural exports. "The opening of trade with China and Russia," a chairman of a major grain corporation said in an article entitled "Can Agriculture Save the Dollar?" "is the greatest thing of the century. It has taken the farm economy out of jail."[44] The wheat deal also strengthened détente, but most important, it depleted American grain reserves and led to a tripling of prices on the world market. According to USDA figures, wheat prices increased from $60 per ton in the second quarter of 1972 to $210 per ton in the first quarter of 1974, a 250 percent increase. During the same period, the price of rice rose over 300 percent from $132 to $570 per ton.[45]

For the world's dominant food-producing nation, the world food crisis was an opportunity, not a tragedy. In 1969 revenues from agricultural exports were $5.9 billion, of which 17 percent was related to concessional sales under P.L. 480. In 1974 they were $21.9 billion, of which only 3 percent was concessional. Steep price rises for domestic consumers (food prices rose approximately 14 percent in both 1973 and 1974), and malnutrition for millions of poor people throughout the world were apparently inconsequential in light of the demands of the economic crisis. "Our primary concern is commercial exports . . . ," Assistant Secretary of Agriculture Richard Bell said in an interview, "We can't subordinate our commercial exports to needy people."[46] Or as Senator George McGovern wrote recently:

> The import cost of cereals to the poorer nations more than tripled from $3 billion in 1971 to $10 billion in 1974. . . . The United States provided more than four fifths of all food aid between 1965 and 1972. But the primary purpose was the disposal of surplus. As this surplus was depleted and commercial demand expanded, food assistance was reduced. As drought struck and food shipments slowed, developing countries did not even have promises to eat. And for the United States food aid was no longer a promise to keep.[47]

In a world of hunger and want, food is a vehicle for both political and economic power. In August 1974 the Central Intelligence Agency's Office of Political Research completed a study entitled *Potential Implications of Trends in World Population, Food Production and Climate*. This study projected unprecedented power for the United States in world affairs because in a hungry world food is power. Although the study speculated about what would happen if predictions about a cooling trend in the earth's climate were accurate, the study was prompted by immediate world food shortages and underscored both present and future possibilities of food power. "The U.S. *now* provides nearly three-fourths of the world's net grain exports, and its role is almost certain to grow over the next several decades," the study noted. "The world's increasing dependence on American surpluses portends an increase in U.S. power and influence, especially vis-à-vis the food-deficit poor countries."[48] Twenty years of American food aid had apparently born the fruit of dependency.

"Twenty years ago, North America exported mainly to Western Europe; most other regions were basically self-sufficient," the study continued. "*Now*, the whole world has become dependent on North America for grain."[49]

These are not speculative statements. They are statements about present opportunities which will undoubtedly expand in the future. With or without normal weather, the study notes, "the U.S. is almost certain to increase its dominance of the world's grain trade over the next couple of decades." This, the study continued, "will provide the U.S. with additional levers of influence."[50] The report goes on to make the following prediction:

> In bad years . . . Washington would acquire virtual life and death power over the fate of the multitudes of the needy. In a cooler and therefore hungrier world, the U.S. near monopoly position as food exporter would have enormous, though not easily definable, impact on international relations. It could give the U.S. a measure of power it has never had before—possibly an economic and political dominance greater than that of the immediate post-World War II years.[51]

American leaders certainly did not confine food power to the future. Three months after completion of the Central Intelligence Agency's study, Secretary of Agriculture Earl Butz stated: "Food is a weapon. It is now one of the principal tools in our negotiating kit."[52] On another occasion Butz remarked: "The single most important way we have of communicating with two-thirds of the people in the world is food."[53] *Business Week* in an article entitled "U.S. Food Power: Ultimate Weapon in World Politics?" noted:

> The deployment of American Food Power is the focus of a serious policy debate now under way in Washington. Nearly everyone agrees that in a world of hunger and overpopulation, the U.S. can apply its tremendous agricultural capacity *as a lever on foreign countries to adopt policies beneficial to this nation.*

The article continued:

> In a world of growing scarcity, it remains to be seen how far the U.S. will go in linking food resources with industrial commodity needs. Many links could be established. In the case of 21 important minerals, the U.S. is 60% to 100% dependent upon foreign suppliers—some of which are large importers of U.S. food.[54]

In the same article a "high-level State Department official " is quoted as saying, "We have the food, and the hell with the rest of the world." But it is more likely that *Business Week* captured the essence of American food power when it suggested that food was a lever by which the United States could pressure dependent countries to adopt policies that might not be in the best interests of the majority of their people but would be beneficial to American corporate interests. To speak about food as a weapon might in a certain sense overdramatize a basic American policy. Food power is only one tool, although an important one, among several foreign-policy tools which are employed together in the service of our nation's bottom-line commitment: to stay the number one nation.

To sum up briefly our argument to this point, military spending, which according to its proponents is good for the American economy, has had several unintended consequences, including aggravating inflation and unemployment and undermining the American economy. We have not meant to suggest that the solution to all social and economic problems plaguing the United States as well as the solution to world hunger problems is simply to restore the competitive position of American industry in world markets. Earlier we documented those who benefit and those who are victimized by the international free-enterprise system. We have sought to demonstrate that military spending adversely effects the American economy, and that increasingly the United States relies on food power to overcome its economic difficulties. This results in the further victimization of the poor.

When the world food crisis intensified during the beginning and middle of the 1970s, the United States was in the middle of a desperate political and economic crisis. The nation was on the verge of defeat in Vietnam where the war had cost countless lives and billions of dollars. Any loss of this kind, President Nixon had warned earlier, would expose the United States to the world as a "pitiful, helpless giant." The nation's preoccupation with war and war production had resulted in a serious deterioration both in its balance of payments and in its trade. OPEC's decision to boost oil prices in 1973 further aggravated the problem of payments.

Food power and the sales of weapons were siezed on as solutions to the crisis by American policymakers. But while increased sales of food and arms may provide temporary relief for ailing trade-balance sheets, they in no way constitute solutions to fundamental economic problems. In 1977, despite arms and agricultural exports of more than $34 billion, the American trade deficit was $26.7 billion, an increase of more than 1,200 percent over the nation's first deficit of $2.2 billion in 1971.

Between 1976 and 1978 good weather and bountiful harvests throughout much of the world took world hunger off the front pages of our newspapers. The less dramatic, ongoing, and painful reality of malnutrition is less newsworthy than a "crisis" situation. But food dependency has increased each day and, given the developmental priorities of many poor countries within the international free-enterprise system, the next world food crisis is just around the corner. We live in a country whose political and economic power is waning, a country that will not give up its privileged position without a bitter struggle. Because of its yearly trade deficits of $27 billion, the United States, as the Central Intelligence Agency's study indicates, will probably lean on food power even more heavily during the next crisis.

The Meaning of Security

Each year about the time of budget appropriations in Washington, D.C., there is rumor of a missile gap, a submarine gap, or some other kind of megatonnage gap that implies that the United States has fallen further behind the Russians. Our security, we are told, is endangered, and we must tighten our belts and turn over several billion dollars more to the military for this or that weapons system. After more than thirty years of the Cold War, it has been deeply imprinted into our collective psyche that the way to insure the security of the United States is to increase its defense budget and to develop new weapons. However, after years of a permanent war economy and capitulation to the interests and ideology of the military-industrial complex, we have reached a curious impass: *today in this country the national security establishment and the powerful corporate interests it represents now constitute the gravest threat to our national security.*

Increasing arms sales to foreign countries that oppress their people but provide a good investment climate can only lead to further injustice, violence, and repression. If supporting U.S. economic interests involves supporting injustice, it is possible that we may be drawn into other Vietnam-type conflicts. It is certain that exploiting hunger and utilizing food as a political and economic weapon will not bring security to the American people nor to any other people. In the Central Intelligence Agency's study one discerns a delicate balance between the desired goal of power and influence resulting from food power and the potential risks to the United States as the world's major food exporter. "As custodian of the bulk of the world's exportable grain," the study pointed out, "the U.S. might regain the primacy in world affairs it held in the immediate post-World War II era." But the study continued, "nuclear blackmail" on the part of countries with a food deficit "is not inconceivable."[55]

Injustice and violence often have a way of turning on those who oppress others. In the words of Proverbs 1:10–11, 13–19:

> My friend, if sinners entice you, do not consent.
> If they say, "Come with us, let us lie in wait for blood,
> let us wantonly ambush the innocent; . . .
> we shall find all precious goods,
> we shall fill our houses with spoil;
> throw in your lot among us,
> we will all have one purse"—
> my friend, do not walk in the way with them,
> hold back your foot from their paths;
> for their feet run to evil,
> and they make haste to shed blood.
> For in vain is a net spread
> in the sight of any bird;
> *but these people lie in wait for their own blood,*
> *they set an ambush for their own lives.*
> *Such are the ways of all who get gain by violence;*
> *it takes away the life of its possessors* [emphasis added].*

The Strongholds of Israel

The prosperity in Amos's Israel, as we previously discussed, was based on foreign expansion and exploitation of the poor. The wealthy in Israel were both economically and militarily secure. Often they built strongholds—two-story mansions built so as to be defensible—which were part of the defense system of the city. These strongholds protected their unjust wealth and were a vivid demonstration that the people looked to themselves, and not to God, for their security. Amos announces the charge and judgement:

> "They do not know how to do right," says the Lord,
> "those who store up violence and robbery
> in their strongholds."
> Therefore thus says the Lord God:
> "An adversary shall surround the land,
> and bring down your defenses from you,
> and your strongholds shall be plundered" (Amos 3:10–11).

The prosperity of the upper classes in Israel is plunder, and their reliance on a military defense system to protect their unjust wealth undermines their security whose true foundation is justice and trust in God.

The wealthy in Israel find Amos's criticism incomprehensible because during the reign of Jeroboam they are experiencing unprecedented prosperity. In fact, they quickly point out that Israel is the greatest of the nations (Amos 6:2), a boast reminiscent of former President Lyndon B. Johnson. They lie upon beds of ivory, eat lambs from the flock, sing songs, drink wine in bowls, and anoint themselves with the finest oils (Amos 6:4–6); they are also well protected in their strongholds. To this Amos responds:

> The Lord God has sworn . . .
> (says the Lord, the God of Hosts):
> "I abhor the pride of Jacob,
> and hate your strongholds;
> and I will deliver up the city
> and all that is in it (Amos 6:8).*

For the affluent social classes in Israel, the national destiny is no longer linked to justice and fidelity to God. Prosperity is the unjust fruit of their own hands, and defense is a matter of their strength alone. To view this as a foundation for security is, according to Amos, absurd:

> Do horses run upon rocks?
> Does one plow the sea with oxen?
> But you have turned justice into poison
> and the fruit of righteousness into wormwood . . . (Amos 6:12).

Today we might offer a different translation:

> Do trains run upon rocks?
> Does one plow the sea with tractors?
> But you exploit the poor and use food as a weapon,
> you build a nuclear bomb every eight hours,
> and sell arms to dictators.
> You have turned justice into poison
> and the fruit of righteousness into hunger and starvation.

According to Amos, national security founded on injustice leads to destruction. The prophet Hosea whose ministry followed closely that of Amos condemns economic injustice and religious apostasy, and warns that reliance upon military power for security will not protect Israel from the coming judgment. Hosea began his ministry during the prosperous years of Jeroboam II, but prosperity quickly gave way to devastation and tragedy. In the fourteen years after the death of Jeroboam, four Israelite kings were assassinated, and Israel was reduced to a vassal state of Assyria. Throughout the crises of the period, Israel's leaders attempted unsuccessfully to provide the nation with security through foreign alliances.

> Israel is swallowed up;
> already they are among the nations
> as a useless vessel.
> For they have gone up to Assyria,
> a wild ass wandering alone;
> Ephraim has hired lovers.
> Though they hire allies among the nations,
> I will soon gather them up.
> And they shall cease for a little while
> from anointing king and princes (Hosea 8:8–10).

Foreign alliances and military power could not substitute for allegiance to God:

> For Israel has forgotten its Maker,
> and built palaces;
> and Judah has multiplied fortified cities;
> but I will send a fire upon their cities,
> and it shall devour their strongholds (Hosea 8:14).*

Summary

Let us reflect on what we've discussed in this chapter. Each American has a right to basic human security. We need jobs that provide us and our families with adequate income to meet our basic needs for food, clothing, housing, education, recreation, and health care. We need jobs that contribute to our social well-being and offer us some opportunity for personal growth and fulfillment. And we need to be free of fear of nuclear disaster, environmental catastrophe, and the dangers of crime in our neighborhoods and streets. But the basis of human security is justice. We cannot expect to be safe in our neighborhoods if we tolerate poverty and social inequality, nor can we expect to be free of fear of a nuclear destruction if we utilize food as a weapon or pursue a foreign policy that impoverishes Third World peoples. Military security can be a valid component of human security, but it cannot be its guarantor in the face of global injustice.

American military leaders and leaders of our government and corporations have taken actions in the name of national security that, in fact, have secured benefits for a privileged few while making life less secure for most of us. The production of new weapons systems will not enhance our security. The United States possesses more than thirty thousand nuclear warheads—enough firepower to destroy every city in the Soviet Union thirty-six times or to kill every person on earth twelve times over. The Soviet Union can destroy every American city eleven times. Still the United States produces a new nuclear weapon every eight hours. An escalating arms race brings us less security, not more. As sons and daughters of God we know that our security is ultimately linked to faith and justice. If our confidence in weapons systems makes us indifferent to injustice, we are likely to be insensitive to the word of God in our time. If this happens, our faith in weapons is ultimately a faith against God.

> Sow for yourselves righteousness,
> reap the fruit of steadfast love;
> break up your fallow ground,
> for it is the time to seek the Lord,
> that the Lord may come and rain salvation upon you.
> You have plowed iniquity,
> you have reaped injustice,
> you have eaten the fruit of lies.
> Because you have trusted in your chariots
> and in the multitude of your warriors,
> therefore the tumult of war shall arise among your people,
> and all your fortresses shall be destroyed . . .
> (Hosea 10:12–14).*

A few years after the prophetic ministry of Hosea, the prophet Micah rose up and spoke the word of God to Israel's southern neighbor, Judah. He denounced injustice (Micah 3:9–11), and proclaimed a beautiful vision that is a practical necessity for our world today:

> It shall come to pass in the latter days
> that the mountain of the house of the Lord
> shall be established as the highest of the mountains,
> and shall be raised up above the hills;
> and people shall flow to it,
> and many nations shall come, and say:
> "Come, let us go up to the mountain of the Lord,
> to the house of the God of Jacob;
> that the Lord may teach us the ways

and we may walk in the Lord's paths."
For out of Zion shall go forth the law,
and the word of the Lord from Jerusalem.
The Lord shall judge between many peoples,
and shall decide for strong nations afar off;
and they shall beat their swords into plowshares,
and their spears into pruning hooks;
nation shall not lift up sword against nation,
neither shall they learn war any more;
but they shall all sit under their own vines
and under their own fig trees,
and none shall make them afraid;
for the mouth of the Lord of hosts has spoken (Micah 4:1–4).*

Micah's vision of human security is possible, and more and more people are recognizing that it is also necessary. It will be achieved because people will demand that instruments of destruction be transformed into hospital equipment, houses, public-transit systems, and other socially useful products. It will be achieved because the voices of the world's hungry clamoring for justice will be louder and more compelling than the voices of the military-industrial complex. And it will be achieved because the Lord of history opens us to the possibility of authentic security based on justice:

For all the peoples walk each in the name of its god,
but we will walk in the name of the Lord our God
for ever and ever (Micah 4:5).

Chapter 6

IS OVERPOPULATION
THE BIGGEST PROBLEM?

How the hell are we supposed to be "Good Samaritans" when these hungry countries are overpopulated? If we don't help, people are going to starve. But if we do help, more people will starve later.

My husband and I have decided not to have any children. With so many hungry people in the world, we feel it would be irresponsible. With a shortage of resources, we're trying to simplify our life-styles, get by with less, you know.

You can talk about multinational corporations if you want, but why don't you talk about the real cause of hunger? These countries are overpopulated. Until they stop having so many babies they will never develop.

I have heard these statements and numerous others like them during speaking engagements and seminars on hunger and in personal conversations with Christians. My experience as an organizer is that most Americans, including most American Christians, believe overpopulation is the principal cause of world hunger. For some, overpopulation poses a serious moral dilemma and leaves them feeling powerless. For others it forces difficult personal and family choices. And for others still it serves as a trump card capable of taking any trick in a card game: if the political and economic causes of hunger are discussed, overpopulation is thrown in like a smoke bomb to cloud over sensitive issues.

As a college student I was firmly convinced that overpopulation was the greatest problem facing humankind. I read *The Population*

Bomb by Paul Ehrlich and *Famine 1975* by William and Paul Paddock, and was certain that millions of people would die and that the ecosystem would be undermined unless steps were taken to halt population growth. A year or two later I traveled to India where I witnessed poverty of a magnitude that defied my imagination. One day as I walked through the streets of Calcutta feeling guilty and powerless, I decided to buy bananas and distribute them to children. One child whose arms had been cut off above the elbow ran up to me. He looked at me intensely, and I put a banana under his arm pit. His face grew more stern, and his brown eyes cut to the center of my conscience and my heart. So I took another banana and put it under his other stumplike arm. At that moment his face broke into a smile, and he ran away into the street and disappeared.

I felt better about myself for just a moment as the child's smile radiated hope to this guilt-ridden American. But I continued walking, and there were many children in need and my money was limited. After a while my heart that had been opened by the suffering of children began to harden. I could not deal with their suffering or with the inadequacy of my response. So I stopped feeling and caring, or at least I tried to. As I emotionally distanced myself from those who suffered, I began blaming the poor for their poverty. Somehow, I reasoned, it was their fault that they suffered. My background in overpopulation theory perfectly met my need to rationalize away any sense of accountability. These people were poor because there were too many of them.

But somehow I wasn't able to feel comfortable with the solution of not caring. Something stirred inside me—ethical murmurs that reminded me that the essence of Christian faith is love and not detachment. Gradually I began to see that in addition to the massive poverty, there was great wealth in India. The wealth of the rich and the misery of the poor existed side by side. It was awareness of this inequality that planted a seed that eventually sprouted into questions about the validity of the overpopulation theory.

This chapter examines both *why* overpopulation is commonly cited and accepted as the principal cause of world hunger, and *whether* it is, in fact, the principal cause.

Nonpolitical Population Control?

One of these days, as you sort through your mail, you may discover a letter of appeal from one of many organizations committed to slowing population growth in poor countries. I recently received an appeal from the Pathfinder Fund. What immediately caught my attention was the organization's claim to be *nonpolitical.*

The Pathfinder Fund, a non-profit, non-political organization, is working in 49 developing countries helping reduce birth rates and helping establish a balance between numbers of people and available resources.[1]

Population control is a very sensitive issue. When a population agency like the Pathfinder Fund claims to be nonpolitical, this claim must be closely scrutinized. Here are several statements from the Pathfinder Fund appeal, an evaluation of the political assumptions implicit in each statement, and a statement that poses alternative political assumptions:

1. "Surging population growth is wiping out the gains of economic development, . . . condemning entire nations to poverty, ignorance and disease."

Unstated political assumptions. Surging population growth *causes* underdevelopment. Nations are condemned to poverty because the economic gains of development do not keep pace with rapidly growing populations. Whether the development strategies of poor nations are capital- or labor-intensive, give priority to agriculture or industry, stress production of luxury items or production for basic needs, is not important in assessing why countries are underdeveloped and why their populations are growing rapidly.

Alternative political assumptions. While rapid population growth puts strains on economic development, it is a *consequence* of underdevelopment. To understand both surging population growth and underdevelopment, it is necessary to examine the developmental strategies and priorities of nations.

2. "Everywhere that excessive population growth is exacting a high and tragic price, robbing people of the gains of development, condemning them to a brink-of-death existence, the Pathfinder Fund is working to limit births."

Unstated political assumptions. Excessive population growth causes underdevelopment. Therefore, the solution to problems of underdevelopment is population control.

Alternative political assumptions. Because rapid population growth is a consequence of underdevelopment, efforts to limit births will be generally unsuccessful unless linked to comprehensive development strategies aimed at meeting the basic needs for food, clothing, housing, health care, education, and employment of a nation's overall population.

3. "Urban concentration [is] vivid evidence of the population explosion. . . . Landless peasants pour in—coagulating in slums— seeking work, a decent dwelling, a school for their children. They find only misery. . . . Every major city in the Third World . . . is col-

lapsing under the weight of too many people—too many clamoring for food and jobs and homes that don't exist."

Unstated political assumptions. Urban areas are overpopulated because rural areas are overpopulated. There isn't enough land for exploding populations to farm. Therefore people flee to the cities where they find not jobs but misery. Factors such as concentrated land ownership, types of agricultural and industrial commodities produced and under what conditions are not important in determining why people flee the countryside and why unemployment is high in urban centers.

Alternative political assumptions. Urban concentration may indicate that a nation's population is growing rapidly but it may also indicate that agricultural production is organized in a manner that displaces labor. To explain why there are few job opportunities in rural and urban areas and why populations are growing rapidly it is necessary to examine the developmental priorities.

4. "Eight out of ten families in Asia, Africa and Latin America are unaware of modern methods of fertility."

Unstated political assumptions. People in underdeveloped countries have large families because they are ignorant. If they knew how to limit the size of their families, they would clearly choose to do so.

Alternative political assumptions. While there is a large unmet need for birth control in many underdeveloped countries, it is also true that many couples have large families quite intentionally. Large families are often necessary for economic survival. Until changes in a nation's economic and social structures make having small families viable, birth control for many poor people is tantamount to economic suicide.

5. "I want to be a Pathfinder. I want to help find new ways of slowing population growth that threatens to engulf our world."

Unstated political assumptions. The greatest threat to citizens of the United States and the world is rapid population growth. If you are concerned about hunger or poverty or about world survival, the best thing you can do is to support family-planning programs.

Alternative political assumptions. The greatest threat to citizens of the United States and the world is unjust political and economic structures that cause the underdevelopment of which hunger and rapid population growth are symptoms. If you are concerned about hunger, poverty, or world survival, the best thing you can do is first to understand and then to try to overcome the political and economic causes of underdevelopment.

A brief look at the Pathfinder Fund Appeal uncovers numerous political biases which, as we shall see, have ominous political and social implications. Both the Pathfinder Fund's statements and the alternatives presented are political. The question we shall deal with in this chapter is which group of political assumptions most accurately reflects the world situation.

The Trial

Imagine that you are the member of a jury that must decide one of the most important cases in modern history. The defendant is overpopulation, which is charged with causing world hunger and poverty. As we enter the courtroom, the prosecuting attorney is making an opening statement.

Prosecuting Attorney: "Your Honor and ladies and gentlemen of the jury, as we begin this trial, we do so with the sobering reality that a quarter of the world's people are poorly nourished. More than fifteen thousand people die each day of hunger or hunger-related diseases. What's more, 40 to 50 percent of the population of poor countries is now under age fifteen. If present growth rates continue, the world's population will probably double in thirty-five years. Instead of 4 billion people to feed, house, and clothe, there will be 8 billion. 'By the end of this century . . . we'll be scraping the planet to keep up with the minimal demands of the mounting flood of people."[2]

"The seriousness of the immediate food and population crisis is well known. Television news reports bring into our living rooms pictures of starving children and endless lines of people waiting for food handouts on which their survival depends. Major newspapers throughout the country portray a serious and worsening situation with headlines such as 'The Next Crisis: Universal Famine'; 'Experts Ask Action to Avoid Millions of Deaths in Food Crisis'; 'Grim Reaping: This Year the Whole World is Short of Grain'; 'One Billion Face Not Deprivation but Death'; and 'Population Bomb and Food Shortage: World Losing Fight for Vital Balance."[3]

"During this trial we will demonstrate beyond the shadow of a doubt that world hunger is caused by overpopulation. This conclusion should not be surprising. In 1798 English clergyman and political economist Thomas Malthus warned that the 'power of population is definitely greater than the power in the earth to produce subsistence for man. . . . Population is always and everywhere, in some measure, pressing against the available food supply.' Since Malthus wrote those words, the world's population has more than quadrupled. Many of the distinguished persons who will testify on behalf of the prosecution issued warnings that overpopulation would precipitate a world food crisis, but their warnings fell on deaf ears. It is the duty of this jury to find the defendant guilty as charged, thereby demonstrating that we have ears to hear, and that we are capable of responding to the population crisis that threatens to engulf our planet."

Witnesses for the Prosecution

In this section we place in the mouth of a hypothetical prosecutor questions that might realistically be asked of population and food experts. We shall then record likely responses of these experts, based on their writings to which we shall provide references for the benefit of the reader. The first witness is Dr. Paul Ehrlich, a well-known American ecologist and overpopulation theorist.

Prosecutor: "Dr. Ehrlich, over the past several years you have traveled around the country with the zeal of a crusader promoting population control and issuing dire warnings of mass starvation due to overpopulation. Would you describe for us here this morning when you first became convinced of the seriousness of the population problem?"

Dr. Ehrlich: "Certainly. It was one stinking hot night in Delhi. As our taxi crawled through the city, we entered a crowded slum area. The temperature was well over 100, and the air was a haze of dust and smoke. The streets seemed alive with people. People eating, people washing, people sleeping. People visiting, arguing, and screaming. People thrusting their hands through the taxi window, begging. People defecating and urinating. People clinging to buses. People herding animals. People, people, people, people. As we moved slowly through the mob, hand horn squawking, the dust, noise, heat, and cooking fires gave the scene a hellish aspect. Would we ever get to our hotel? All three of us were, frankly, frightened. . . . Since that night I've known the feel of overpopulation."[4]

Prosecutor: "In light of the massive food crisis of the '70's, many people are proclaiming that Thomas Malthus was a true prophet. For example, John Knowles, president of the Rockefeller Foundation, said recently, 'Malthus has already been proven correct.'[5] I think it is fair to say, and there are many people who would agree with me, that you also are a true prophet. Would you please read for the benefit of the jury a paragraph from the prologue to your provocative book *The Population Bomb*, which was published back in 1968. It is a terrifying though amazing example of foresight that has long been ignored in this country and throughout the world."

Dr. Ehrlich: "The prologue began with these words: 'The battle to feed all of humanity is over. In the 1970's the world will undergo famines—hundreds of millions of people are going to starve to death in spite of any crash program embarked upon now. At this late date nothing can prevent substantial increase in the world death rate. . . . We must have population control at home . . . we must use our political power to push other countries into programs which combine agricultural development and population control. And while this is being done we must take action to reverse the deterioration of our environment before population pressure permanently ruins our planet. The birthrate must be brought into balance with the death rate or mankind will breed itself into oblivion. We can no longer afford merely to treat the symptoms of the cancer of population growth; the cancer itself must be cut out. Population control is the only answer.' "[6]

Prosecutor: "No further questions."

At this time the prosecution calls its next witness, Mr. Asa Singh, a part-time farm laborer who is a watchman at the high school in the village of Manupur, India. With the court's permission the prosecutor provides the following background to the jury.

"Mr. Singh is from the village of Manupur, one of several villages selected as sites for the first major field study of birth control in India. This study is known as the Khanna Study after the market town where its field headquarters were located. It was conducted from 1954 to 1960, with a follow-up study in the summer of 1969. Manupur and other villages were selected for the field study because they are in the state of Punjab. When the study began, Punjab had a population density 20 percent higher than that of the rest of India with a birthrate the same as India as a whole.[7] In other words they were selected because they are located in one of the most overpopulated areas in India."

"The field study, which was financed by the Rockefeller Foundation and the Indian government, grew out of a report on the population problem prepared in 1953 by the Harvard School of Public Health. The report indicated that recent advances in the field of public health had led to a spectacular drop in the death rate in many underdeveloped countries. While these advances were welcome, they had precipitated a population crisis. 'Should the present trends of population growth in several parts of the world continue unchanged for a matter of ten or even fewer years,' the report warned, 'disastrous famine is inevitable and civil unrest likely.' Faced with this impending disaster, the report recommended that the population problem be given the same priority as 'the great plagues of yesterday."[8]

"The Khanna Study, it was hoped, would serve as a model project for reducing the birth rate in underdeveloped countries. By introducing birth control devices and conducting extensive educational campaigns at the village level it was thought that birthrates could be significantly reduced. Unfortunately, the follow-up study in 1969 revealed that the experiment was a complete failure. Birthrates in the test villages remained at high levels and were comparable to those of India as a whole. We have brought Mr. Singh here this morning to explain the pathetic reason for the project's failure."

Prosecutor: "Mr. Singh, did you and your wife use the birth control tablets that were provided to you without charge?"

Mr. Singh: "Certainly, we did. You can read it in their books. We didn't use them for the first few months. Then they explained to us all the advantages of using those tablets. You know, we villagers are illiterate. Well, after that, from 1957 to 1960, we never failed."

Prosecutor: "Mr. Singh, do you have a son who was born in late 1958 or early 1959?"

Mr. Singh: "Well . . . yes."

Prosecutor: "Will you please explain to the jury how it is possible that your wife, while using the foam tablets all the time, could have conceived a son during the same period?"

Mr. Singh's face assumes a distant look, he scratches his beard, and reluctantly ponders the question.

Mr. Singh: "Babuji, someday you'll understand. It is sometimes better to lie. It stops you from hurting people, does you no harm, and might even help them."

Prosecutor: "So you didn't use the contraceptives?"

Mr. Singh: "That's right, we didn't. And there were others like us."

Prosecutor: "What did you and the others do with the birth-control devices?"

Mr. Singh: "Most of us threw the tablets away. But my brother made a sculpture out of his. He finds some use for everything."[9]

Prosecutor: "Ladies and gentlemen of the jury, we cannot let our sympathies for the ignorance of Mr. Singh and millions of other poor souls throughout the world stand in the way of a just verdict: overpopulation causes hunger, and ignorance breeds overpopulation. No further questions."

At this point the prosecutor calls his next witness, James P. Brown, a member of the editorial board of the *New York Times*.

Prosecutor: "Mr. Brown, there was a great deal of pessimism among food experts in the 1960's. Dr. Ehrlich, who testified earlier, was not a lone prophet. William and Paul Paddock published a book in 1968 entitled *Famine 1975*, which warned that world population growth was outstripping food production and that an international food crisis was probable by the middle of the decade. Yet isn't it true that their book met with skepticism, particularly after the start of the Green Revolution?"

Mr. Brown: "Yes, the Paddocks' dire prediction did encounter heavy resistance, and the skepticism . . . was reinforced in subsequent years by the encouraging results of the so-called Green Revolution when farmers in many lands adopted new 'miracle seeds' developed at about the time the Paddocks were writing their book. Optimism rose steadily as the new seeds sharply increased acreage yields in such perennially hungry countries as India. . . ."[10]

Prosecutor: "This new-found optimism seemed to reach its height in 1970 when Dr. Norman Borlaug, director of the International Maize and Wheat Improvement Center in Mexico and the 'father' of the Green Revolution, was awarded the Nobel Peace Prize. When the chairperson of the prize committee announced his selection, she said: 'Dr. Borlaug, through his improvement of wheat and rice plants, has created a technological breakthrough which makes it possible to abolish hunger in developing countries in the course of a few years.'[11] What happened to this optimism?"

Mr. Brown: "It was shattered by that old bugaboo of farmers throughout history—bad weather—which struck savagely. A drought of unprecedented severity sharply reduced crops over wide areas of the globe."

Prosecutor: "Is the present world food crisis evidence that the Green Revolution is a failure?"

Mr. Brown: "No. The problem of food shortages does not arise primarily from failure of the Green Revolution, although it is evident that much more can and must be done to extend the benefits of the new food technology. The basic problem, as the Paddocks foresaw, is that population growth has kept pace with, if not exceeded, increases in food production in those areas of the world where the Malthusian food/population squeeze has always been most acute. India, for example, has made quite spectacular strides in agricultural production over the last two and a half decades. . . . The trouble is that during the same period India's population has risen, not quite proportionately, but still dramatically."

Prosecutor: "So population growth is the culprit and not the shortcomings of the Green Revolution?"

Mr. Brown: "That's correct. There are simply too many people to feed."

Prosecutor: "I would like to point out to the jury that Dr. Borlaug was himself aware that population growth could cancel out the gains of the Green Revolution. Just two months before being selected for the Nobel Peace Prize he warned: 'The world's population problem is a monster which, unless tamed, will one day wipe us from the earth's surface.'[12] Mr. Brown, has India been indifferent to its population problem?"

Mr. Brown: "No. The Indian government was one of the first among developing nations to launch a serious official family-planning effort. Small-family propaganda, the pill, the loop, sterilization—the whole arsenal of birth-control weapons has been promoted with zeal by Indian family planners for years. But nothing seems to have worked. . . ."

Prosecutor: "Mr. Brown, in your view what is the solution to the world food crisis?"

Mr. Brown: "The deepening crisis . . . can be alleviated only through greatly intensified international efforts to solve the population problem."

Prosecutor: "Thank you. No further questions."

At this time the prosecutor calls his final witness, Lester R. Brown, president and senior researcher for Worldwatch Institute, a research organization that analyzes global problems.

Prosecutor: "Mr. Brown, you are perhaps the most highly respected and most often quoted American hunger analyst. What is your assessment of the prospects for the developing countries to improve the diets of their people?"

Mr. Brown: "Given the growing scarcity of the basic inputs of land, water, energy, and fertilizer, it is becoming more unlikely that the less developed countries will be able to improve diets significantly in the foreseeable future unless they can quickly reduce birth rates. Indeed, it appears very possible that per capita food production will even decline in the years ahead. If the population growth rate of a country continues to be high for an extended period, the descendants of the present population will be doomed to unbelievably miserable conditions of existence. The demand for food will outrun all available indigenous supplies of land and water, creating severe and chronic scarcity."[13]

Prosecutor: "Then high birthrates are clouding the food and overall economic picture of developing countries?"

Mr. Brown: "That's correct. . . . Rapid population growth intensifies almost every important problem with which humanity wrestles. Although the food dimension of the population threat remains paramount, population growth also contributes to ecological, economic, and social stresses. It fans inflation by creating resource scarcities. It raises unemployment by increasing the number of job-seekers faster than jobs are created. Where it outstrips economic growth, it pushes down living standards. It undermines efforts to spread literacy, to improve health services, and to provide housing. . . . Population growth in some situations acts as a double-edged sword, simultaneously increasing demands and reducing supplies."[14]

Prosecutor: "Mr. Brown, when the Green Revolution made head-

lines several years ago you were one of its chief proponents. At the
time you seemed to suggest that it would solve the world food crisis,
but more recently you referred to the Green Revolution as 'an opportunity lost.' Would you explain this shift in your perspective?"

Mr. Brown: "Yes. Today it is clear that the Green Revolution does
not represent a solution to the food problem; rather, it has been a
means of buying time—perhaps an additional fifteen years—during
which to find some way to apply the brakes to population growth.
. . . Almost a decade has now passed since the launching of the
Green Revolution, but there are few success stories in family-
planning programs. It is now, quite frankly, futile to rely solely on
the new agricultural technologies to 'solve' the population problem. . . ."[15]

Prosecutor: "Then programs to reduce birthrates are essential?"

Mr. Brown: "Yes, but I think the goal must go beyond reducing
birthrates. We must pursue with a new urgency the goal of population stabilization."[16]

Prosecutor: "Is there any reason to be optimistic about achieving
the goal of population stabilization, or is the situation hopeless?"

Mr. Brown: "The situation isn't hopeless but it certainly is serious.
On the optimistic side, China, from 1970 to 1975, reduced its crude
birthrate from 32 per thousand of total population to 19 per thousand.
This is the most rapid decline ever recorded for a five year span. On
the pessimistic side, few Latin American countries have reduced
birthrates, and India's intensive family-planning efforts have
proved largely unsuccessful. In fact, in India in 1976 the government
sanctioned, 'as a last resort,' the use of compulsory sterilization."[17]

Prosecutor: "No further questions."

The Verdict and Sentencing

The prosecution seems to have an open-and-shut case. We have
the confession of Mr. Singh that he and others willfully reject birth
control, even when freely offered, plus the testimony of highly
respected writers, ecologists, and hunger analysts. It isn't surprising
then that the verdict on this trial, as we mentioned at the beginning,
seems to be in: the defendant is guilty as charged; overpopulation
causes hunger. With a verdict comes a sentence, and it is here that we
can begin to get a sense of the human stakes of focusing on overpopulation as the cause of hunger.

Thomas Malthus, the founder of the overpopulation theory, believed that Europe was overpopulated and that the poor had only
themselves to blame for their misery. He recommended that the role
of the State was to "leave the poor to their fate, at most making death

easy for them." Well-known ethicist Garrett Hardin offers a similar solution today:

> How can we help a foreign country to escape over-population? Clearly the worst thing we can do is send food. . . . Atomic bombs would be kinder. For a few moments the misery would be acute, but it would soon come to an end for most of the people, leaving a very few survivors to suffer thereafter.[18]

Hardin justifies such brutality on the basis of "lifeboat ethics."

> Each rich nation amounts to a lifeboat full of comparatively rich people. The poor of the world are in other, much more crowded lifeboats. Continuously, so to speak, the poor fall out of their lifeboats and swim for a while, hoping to be admitted to a rich lifeboat, or in some other way to benefit from the "goodies" on board.

According to Hardin, we cannot risk the safety of all the passengers by helping others in need. "What happens if you share space in a lifeboat?" he asks. "The boat is swamped, and everyone drowns. Complete justice, complete catastrophe."

There has also been a recent revival and reinterpretation of the ethics of triage. Triage is a term of French origin, which during World War I referred to a procedure for sorting persons wounded in battle into three groups: those likely to die no matter what was done for them; those who would recover if left untreated; and a third group that could survive only if cared for immediately. The main conclusion of those who apply triage to the world food crisis is that some nations are basket cases, and that it is unethical to provide them with food relief if this relief promotes a further population growth.

An additional option in the sentence would be compulsory sterilization. For overpopulation theorists like Lester R. Brown, compulsory sterilization is a regrettable, though seemingly unavoidable, step in the struggle to limit births. Voluntary family-planning programs, in India and presumably in other underdeveloped countries, are not working. Therefore, compulsory sterilization must be adopted as a "last resort."

Malthus, Hardin, triage ethicists, and Brown all present the American people with a moral dilemma whose political consequences limit our choices to two seemingly unethical options. We can summarize the choices posed by their analyses and the solutions they offer as follows:

Malthus: If the State keeps the poor alive, it will encourage poverty and overpopulation. Consequently, the role of the State is mercy killing, i.e., making death easy for the poor.

Hardin: Overpopulated nations are basket cases which, if helped, will destroy competent, viable nations. Consequently, the role of the State is "nuclear mercy killing."

Triage ethicists: Some nations are beyond hope. To send relief would only lead to more births and eventually more deaths. Consequently, the role of the State is "ethical neglect."

Brown: To support voluntary family-planning programs that don't work would result in continued high birthrates and aggravate poverty. Consequently, the role of the State is to do what it has to do to limit births, i.e., compulsory sterilization.

My own sense of moral paralysis resulted from the lack of meaningful choices offered by traditional overpopulation theorists. This led me first to question *my* values; finally it led me to question *their* presuppositions. Are my values, which are concerned with the dignity of the human person, out of touch with reality? And are my concerns for poor and hungry people perversions? Or are my values a genuine expression of concern for others that is being perverted by the liberal framework of overpopulation theorists? Perhaps those liberal economists and ethicists, who developed the framework within which my values can or cannot find meaningful expression, need to be challenged.

Returning to the trial and the recommended solutions or "verdicts," all of which struck me as harsh and unethical, I find that the testimony of the prosecution witnesses has failed to answer some key questions. Their statements, in fact, are riddled with inconsistencies. Let me point out just a few of the inconsistencies that will be dealt with more extensively in the next chapter:

1. Paul Ehrlich seemed to be frightened by the poverty in Delhi, not necessarily by the numbers of the people. When I visited India, I was struck by the tremendous discrepancy between the wealth and power of the rich and the misery of the poor. Before translating one's fear of poverty into an overpopulation theory it would seem important to probe the causes of that poverty. China has a much larger population than India, including twice as many people per acre of farmland. Yet experts agree that China has eliminated hunger, is meeting the basic needs of its people, and is well on its way to reducing the birthrate. It would be interesting to know whether Ehrlich would have been afraid had he been in Peking instead of Delhi, and whether he regards China as being overpopulated.

2. James P. Brown stated that the world food crisis was caused by "a drought of unprecedented severity." But then he added that it was caused by overpopulation. Which is it?

3. Several prosecution witnesses indicated that India has aggressively pursued population-control programs but that none of them has been successful. None of the prosecution witnesses indicated *why* population programs are failing.

4. The prosecution simply assumes that Mr. Singh rejected birth control because he is ignorant. Yet many experts recognize that parents who are poor often have children because their offspring are an economic necessity.

5. Lester R. Brown indicated that China has achieved the most rapid decline in its birthrate ever recorded for a five-year span. India, on the other hand, despite extensive family-planning efforts, has had little success in reducing birth rates. What accounts for this difference?

6. Lester R. Brown referred to India's decision to adopt compulsory sterilization as a "last resort" strategy. Has India really exhausted all other reasonable options?

Let us consider these and other related matters in the following chapter.

Chapter 7

POPULATION CONTROL
IN THE THIRD WORLD

If we are going to uncover the root cause of the "population problem," we must make critical distinctions between overpopulation, surplus population, and rapid population growth. By carefully defining and discussing these terms, we hope to demonstrate that overpopulation is not the cause of world hunger, nor is population control in itself the solution.

Overpopulation, understood correctly, assumes a proper utilization of a nation's resources. It refers to a situation in which the number of people outstrips the nation's ability to transform available resources into products needed to meet the basic needs of its entire population. For example, if a country sets for itself the developmental goals of meeting the basic needs of its whole population for housing, clothing, health care, employment, transportation, and education, if it organizes its productive resources in an effort to reach these goals, and if it then fails, it can properly be considered as overpopulated. On the other hand, if a country establishes developmental goals that neglect the basic needs of its overall population and only serve the interests of an affluent minority, it cannot properly be considered overpopulated. Instead, such a nation has misused its resources.

The traditional view is that many hungry countries are overpopulated, and that overpopulation causes hunger. In our view no nation today suffers from overpopulation, although many people suffer in nations that are misusing their resources. If the resources of each and every country were being developed by and for the material advancement of all the people, there is no country on the earth that could not adequately feed, house, clothe, employ, and educate even the poorest of its citizens.

Surplus population is a by-product of the misuse of resources by

115

not developing them by and for the material advancement of the entire population. It consists of the people in a nation who are economically superfluous; therefore, such people are unemployed or underemployed within the context of a particular organization of production. Commonly referred to as "overpopulation," surplus population consists of society's so-called marginal people—those who are not needed to extract wealth for foreign corporations and for local industrial or agricultural elites. Surplus population is made up of millions of peasants struggling to eke out a subsistence on land too steep to farm while prime agricultural land is controlled by foreign corporations and large landowners growing crops for export. Surplus population also includes persons seasonally employed to produce carnations, fruits, or vegetables for the international market. Also included are idle urban dwellers who scrounge out a daily subsistence without hope of finding meaningful employment, or workers who yesterday were employed but who today are surplus because machines can perform their tasks more profitably and without "union hassles."

Traditional overpopulation theorists rarely talk about surplus population. If they do, they refer to surplus in the sense of "too many." In our view surplus population must be understood in relation to the organization of a country's productive resources. For example, if these productive resources are owned or controlled by a small group which uses the agricultural sector to earn foreign exchange for private consumption, and the industrial sector to produce luxury consumer goods, we will probably discover a large surplus population. On the other hand, if productive resources could be mobilized to meet the basic needs of that nation's overall population, we would probably find there little or no surplus population because all the people would be participating in and sharing the benefits of development.

Rapid population growth refers to the fact that world population, in particular the population of poor countries, is increasing at a fast pace. For example, the fact that the world's population may double in thirty-five years is an indication of rapid population growth. We agree with traditional theorists that a rapid population growth is a *very serious problem*. Indeed, continued high rates of population growth threaten the well-being of all the world's people. But to state this danger, as the prosecution witnesses and the Pathfinder Fund have done, is not enough. It is urgent that we understand *why* the population of the poor countries is growing so rapidly. We must undertake solutions that are economically and ethically responsible. It is over causes and solutions that we part company with the traditional theorists.

A Brief Historical Background of the Problem

Overpopulation and rapid population growth are so often associated with today's poor countries that we tend to forget that the population explosion began in Europe where improved public health advances dramatically lowered death rates while birthrates remained high. Rapid population growth in Europe substantially changed the racial make-up of the world's population: in 1800 about 22 percent of the human race was Caucasian; by 1930 that figure was approximately 35 percent.

At the time that public health advances were introduced, Europe was involved in the economic transition from feudalism to capitalism. This transition displaced many subsistence workers. Problems associated with rapid population growth were aggravated, therefore, by an increasing number of surplus laborers. We noted previously that surplus population must be understood in relation to the organization of productive resources. Under one set of economic conditions there may be little or no surplus population, while under a different set of conditions there may be a great many surplus laborers. This can best be illustrated by considering Europe's overpopulation crisis.

During the feudal period the people of Europe were spread throughout the countryside, and many of them produced food for their own consumption. For this highly dispersed population there was no talk of overpopulation. As the economy changed, so also did the situation of the peasants. For example, when new markets in Flanders made sheep raising highly profitable, the feudal lords evicted large numbers of tenants. The dispossessed peasants were forced into cities to seek work in factories. Like today's peasants of the poor countries described by the Pathfinder Fund, the European peasants found only misery and congestion in slums. Suddenly the cities of Europe were crowded with peasants who had formerly been self-sustaining. In the emerging capitalist economy these peasants became unwittingly a surplus population.

The overall increase in the number of Europeans, together with a large surplus population, posed significant problems for Europe. This prompted Thomas Malthus to construct his theory of how overpopulation outstrips available food supplies. Speaking against the Poor Laws in England—the eighteenth-century equivalent of our welfare system—Malthus stated in 1798 that the poor had only themselves to blame for their misery, which was the direct consequence of their "irrational propensity to proliferate." He added that "since population is constantly tending to overtake the means of subsistence, charity is folly, a public encouragement of poverty. The State can therefore do nothing but leave the poor to their fate, at most making death easy for them."

Europe averted the tragedy of overpopulation predicted by Malthus. The potentially explosive situation of a rapid population growth and a surplus population was diffused by a number of factors. First, this development occurred during the Industrial Revolution so that some of the increased population of displaced peasants found employment in the cities where factories needed cheap, unskilled workers. Second, it occurred during a period of colonial expansion so that the population stresses that developed found outlets in new lands, including North America. Third, the public health advances were introduced into Europe gradually so that the death rates receded gradually. As a result, the population increase was also gradual. Finally, as Europe developed throughout the nineteenth and twentieth centuries, surplus laborers became a productive workforce. As the basic needs of the population were met, parents became less dependent on their offspring for security. They desired and had fewer children.

The Demographic Transition

The process whereby societies move from a stage of high rates of births and deaths to one of low rates is known as the demographic transition. Initially all such nations experience a high birthrate, but their population remains stable because the rate of deaths is also high. As improved public health measures and increased production improve living conditions, the death rate declines while the birthrate remains high. This results in a rapid increase in the population. In other words, it is an improved standard of living that precipitates an increase in the rate of population growth. However, when the standard of living continues to increase and the benefits of development reach the overall population, the population begins to level off.

The case of Sweden is illustrative. In 1800 Sweden had a high birthrate of about 33 per 1,000, but the population was in balance because the death rate was equally high. As medical advances and increased agricultural and industrial production improved living conditions, the death rate receded to about 20 per thousand by the mid-nineteenth century. Because the birthrate remained high during this period, there was a large excess of births over deaths and the population grew rapidly. But as living conditions continued to improve, the birthrate dropped so that by the mid-twentieth century it was about 14 per 1,000 with a death rate of about 10 per 1,000.[1]

Development then is the key factor in the demographic transition. The process begins with a population in balance, a high rate of births and deaths, and a low standard of living. Along with economic development the country moves toward a population which is larger but once more in balance; the rate of births and deaths is low, and there is a high standard of living. Europe and other developed regions have made this transition or are well along in it. Developing or underdeveloped countries are attempting to make the same transition, but they have traveled varying distances through it and face special problems.

The Crisis in Underdeveloped Nations

If development is the key factor in the demographic transition, it should not be surprising that most countries referred to as "developing" or "underdeveloped" are experiencing a rapid population growth. Various health measures were introduced rapidly into such poor countries, significantly reducing the death rate. Unfortunately, these countries have not repeated the developmental experience of Europe whereby birthrates declined as the standard of living continued to improve. Therefore, in most poor countries birthrates remain high while the population grows rapidly.

For people concerned with population issues, it would seem that there are two critical questions: (1) why is Europe developed? and, (2) why are undeveloped nations experiencing a rapid population growth? In numerous discussion groups with Christians I have commonly heard the following answers: Europe is developed because it organized its economic production efficiently and limited its population growth. At the same time the underdeveloped countries are poor because they are overpopulated, inefficient, and lacking in modern technology. These views are reinforced by most overpopulation theorists.

We believe that there is an alternative answer for both questions: colonialism! It is not a coincidence or a historical accident that the *countries that held colonies are today developed and have populations that are either stable or growing slowly while the countries that were once colonies are today underdeveloped and have rapidly growing populations.*

Colonial expansion, which served as a buffer for Europe's population growth and surplus population, was stimulated primarily by economic motives. Cecil Rhodes, the millionaire British capitalist and statesman, believed it was necessary to engage in exploitation abroad in order to solve domestic problems. In 1895 he remarked:

I was in the East End of London [a working-class quarter]
yesterday and attended a meeting of the unemployed. I lis-
tened to the wild speeches, which were just a cry for "bread!
bread!" and on my way home I pondered over the scene and I
became more than ever convinced of the importance of imperialism. . . . My cherished idea is a solution for the social
problem, i.e. in order to save the 40,000,000 inhabitants of the
United Kingdom from a bloody civil war, we colonial statesmen
must acquire new markets for the goods produced in the factories and mines. The Empire, as I have always said, is a bread
and butter question. If you want to avoid civil war , you must
become imperialists.[2]

It is safe to say that "colonial statesmen" were not primarily concerned with the well-being of the colonies. As most junior-high
history books state rather benignly, a colony existed for the benefit of
the "mother" country. It is not surprising, therefore, that while
imperial colonialism enriched the Europeans, helped to solve
Europe's population problem, and diffused the class struggle—what
Rhodes called civil war—it also plundered the peoples of the colonies.

The colonial period exacerbated unjust economic relationships
that are the root cause of the poverty, hunger, surplus population,
and rapid population growth that plague underdeveloped countries
today. The entire economic infrastructure—systems of transportation, communication, and commerce—was designed to aid the development of the colonial power. Colonies, according to the
nineteenth-century political economist John Stuart Mill, were
"agricultural establishments" whose purpose was to supply the
"larger community to which they belong," places "where England
finds it convenient to carry on the production of sugar, coffee, and a
few other tropical commodities."[3] The imperialism of the British
Empire may have been a bread-and-butter issue, as Cecil Rhodes
claimed, but it clearly undermined the food systems of the colonies.

At the same time as the agricultural priorities within the colonies
were distorted, their industries were greatly restricted. Because the
colonies were economic appendages of the colonial power, they
were not allowed to industrialize. Their role was to supply first
European and later American industries with raw materials and to
purchase finished goods manufactured in the colonizing nation.

Colonialism, therefore, helped Europe's development but served
to underdevelop colonies in Asia, Africa, and Latin America. When
public health improvements were introduced into the colonies,

their population began to soar almost without warning. Because agriculture served primarily the interests of the foreign powers, and because industry had either a small basis or none at all, the colonial peoples poured into the cities well ahead of the industrial demand. The new city-dwellers were a surplus population in view of the distorted economy's ability to absorb new workers. Most important, the wealth produced in the colonies was largely diverted to the colonizing nations. If that wealth had been used to raise living standards in the colonies, it might have led to a stable population. Instead, it was used to raise living standards in Europe and to contribute to a stable population in the colonizing nations. *Colonialism, therefore, was both an economic and a demographic parasite!*

Poor countries today face serious problems as they struggle to develop and to limit their population growth. They do not have areas of the world to colonize so that the colonies might serve as buffers for an increasing population or as appendages for economic development. Instead, they have a colonial heritage of exploitation within the international free-enterprise system. Their distorted economies, which foster poverty, hunger, rapid population growth, and a surplus population, are the darker side of western economic development.

Solutions

As we discussed in chapter 6, the Pathfinder Fund and witnesses for the prosecution regarded overpopulation as the cause of hunger and underdevelopment and offered population control as the solution. An alternative analysis suggested that the poor countries are not really overpopulated, but that because of distorted economic priorities they face the problems of a surplus population and a rapid population growth. It is difficult to get past blaming overpopulation for world hunger because it seems to match the facts: there is a real crisis of food and population in many poor countries. In addition, it is politically and economically expedient to blame overpopulation and offer population control as the solution. It is easier to blame the poor for their poverty than to examine structural causes indicating that development and underdevelopment are one and the same historical process, not two separate realities. While rapid population growth is a very serious problem, population control programs must not be viewed as substitutes for fundamental social changes that are needed if problems of hunger, poverty, surplus population, and rapid population growth are to be overcome.

India and China: Different Approaches
to Population Control and Development

India and China are large countries with long histories of foreign domination, underdevelopment, and famine. Both experienced a rapid population growth; both achieved independence or liberation about the same time. India was until 1947 a colony of Great Britain. In 1949 China ended exploitation at the hands of a number of western powers. After independence India and China both faced serious political, economic, and social problems, including a high birthrate and a large surplus population relative to their "colonial" economy. India's birthrate in 1951 was approximately 41 per 1,000, and its population increased from 350 million in 1950 to about 613 million in 1975; China's birthrate in 1954 was approximately 43 per 1,000, and its population increased from 588 million in 1954 to about 837 million in 1974. Both countries regard rapid population growth as a serious problem; both have extensive family-planning programs.

Although the postindependence problems faced by India and China were similar, and both made extensive efforts to limit population growth, their development and demographic situation in the 1970s is radically different. Between 1970 and 1975 India's birthrate averaged about 39.9 per 1,000 while China during the same period reduced its birthrate from 32 per 1,000 to approximately 19 per 1,000. The difference in their situation with regard to food is equally striking. In 1974, in the midst of the world food crisis, Norman Borlaug warned that without massive international aid between 10 and 50 million people might starve to death in India.[4] The same year, after a trip to China, Senator Mike Mansfield told the Senate Foreign Relations Committee that "China has solved the food problem. In all sections of the country, grain reserves are being built up." He went on to say that "the basic needs of the Chinese people for food, clothing, and shelter are being met. Food and clothing are plentiful and low priced. The people appear healthy and well-fed."[5]

Why is India's birthrate high and its food situation precarious while China's birthrate is rapidly declining and its food situation appears secure? By briefly discussing differences in the two countries' agricultural and industrial policies, and in their birth-control programs, we shall try to answer this question.

Agriculture, Industry, and Birth Control in India

In view of India's problems of hunger, surplus population, and rapid population growth, we might expect the Indian developmental planners to regard labor-intensive agriculture as their highest developmental priority. By doing so, food production could be increased, surplus labor absorbed, and population growth rates slowed as the overall population began to benefit from the development. Surprisingly, these developmental planners did not regard agriculture as a high priority. In 1973 a member of India's Planning Commission resigned in anger over slashes in outlays for agricultural development. Another Indian economist, Prem Shankar Jha, wrote in the *Times of India:*

> The main needs of any poor country are obvious—food, clothing, shelter, health and gainful employment. . . . One only has to turn the pages of the successive plan documents to notice the stepmotherly treatment which the planners have given to these basic goals. . . . The share of agriculture in successive plans has dwindled from 31.4 per cent in the first plan (1951–56) to 20.7 per cent in the fourth (1969–74). It has been slashed further in the annual plan for 1974–75.[6]

The low priority given to agriculture only partly explains India's food and population problems. An even greater problem is inequality in the agricultural sector. An estimated 50 percent of the land is owned by 8 percent of the people, and 70 percent of India's farmers have less than one acre.[7] Absentee landlords and moneylenders are powerful groups in the countryside. Landless peasants pay high rents, borrow money at exorbitant interest, and receive pitifully low wages. Given the present organization of agricultural production, millions of peasants are a surplus population.

Structural changes in land ownership and use that could transform a surplus population into productive labor are politically sensitive; for this reason the Indian government has avoided them. As a consequence millions of the rural poor have migrated to cities. What's more, as India modernized its agricultural system, it did so with the highly energy-intensive technology of the Green Revolution, which increased dependency on foreign imports, further concentrated land ownership, and displaced more peasants who were unable to afford the new technology or who were evicted by landlords eager to expand their acreage. The Green Revolution increased food production without an accompanying social transformation; it aggravated inequalities, created more surplus laborers, and further encouraged migration to urban centers.

India's agricultural production is organized in a manner that serves the interests of a small group of people at the expense of the vast majority. For this reason it tends to aggravate rather than solve

India's food and population problems. The same is true for industry. India's industrial progress since independence is impressive but not geared to meeting the basic needs of the people. The goals of industrialization are import substitution and export promotion.

India has long been a country of great contrasts where the conspicuous consumption of the wealthy existed alongside the misery of the masses. For a long time the luxury goods consumed by the rich were imported. Paying for these imports was costly and strained the Indian economy. Import substitution is an effort to establish certain domestic, consumer-goods industries that cater to high-income groups, thereby cutting down the need to import luxury goods. The result is a widening gap in consumption between a small affluent class and a large low-income group.

Distorted industrial priorities have diverted resources from the production of socially necessary goods to that of nonessential goods. Another problem is that many of the new consumer-goods industries are capital- rather than labor-intensive, and therefore do not absorb surplus labor. At the same time the traditional sector of small-scale and cottage industries that utilizes locally available resources and skills, and generates more employment per unit of capital investment, is in a state of crisis as India shifts to a so-called modern economy.

Import substitution is not India's only distorted industrial priority. Efforts to expand exports also victimize the poor. Indian economist Samuel L. Parmar noted that India often exports essential commodities that are in short supply domestically. This pushes their domestic prices beyond the reach of low-income consumers. "Export promotion of this kind," according to Parmar, deprives "the needy in a poor country in order to add to the range of goods available in a rich country—a case of the weak subsidizing the strong." In addition, most export industries are capital-intensive so that their role in alleviating unemployment and underemployment is marginal. Even more serious is the fact that they weaken efforts to develop technology appropriate to the needs of the Indian economy.[8]

It is in the context of massive inequalities brought on by distorted agricultural and industrial priorities that India has focused on overpopulation as the cause of underdevelopment as well as on birth control as the solution. The same economic planners who ignored the basic needs of the Indian people in their developmental plans impressed upon the political leadership the virtual impossibility of raising living standards if population growth continued unabated. India's political leadership under Indira Gandhi took these warnings so seriously that it sanctioned compulsory sterilization, which according to Lester R. Brown is a strategy of "last resort."

It is clear, however, that *compulsory sterilization is not a strategy of last resort; it is a last-ditch effort to reduce population growth without changing unjust political and economic structures.* Overpopulation theorist Dudley Kirk acknowledges the failure of many birth control programs, but remains optimistic:

> Given the favorable attitudes found in surveys, *family planning may be easier to implement than major advances in education, or the economy, which require large structural and institutional change in the society as a whole.*[9]

For political conservatives optimism about successful birth-control programs without social change is the ultimate self-protecting ideology. Mahmood Mamdani investigated the reasons why the Khanna Study cited earlier failed in its efforts to convince villagers to use birth control. He noted that while villagers may have shown favorable attitudes when surveyed by investigators, they, like Asa Singh, threw their birth-control tablets away. Why? Mamdani claimed that birth control contradicts their vital interests. To practice contraception is to willfully court economic disaster.[10]

For many poor people in India and other underdeveloped countries, large families are an economic necessity. A peasant with a small piece of land cannot afford to hire laborers; it is much cheaper to have children. Small children can carry water, gather firewood, or watch cattle. Parents blessed with many sons have a large labor force to earn income for the family. What's more, in the absence of authentic development, sons provide the only effective form of social security. According to nutritionist Alan Berg, studies indicate that given current infant and adult death rates in India, a couple must bear 6.3 children to be 95 percent certain that one son will be surviving at the father's sixty-fifth birthday. The average number of births in India per couple is 6.5.[11]

Birth-control programs in India are failing because India has adopted two conflicting strategies. It has sought to reduce its rate of population growth at the same time as it pursued a developmental strategy that ignores the basic needs of its overall population, fosters rapid population growth, and creates a large surplus population. What we can learn from the failure of India's population program is that population control isn't a substitute for social justice. Unless birth-control programs are linked to fundamental economic changes aimed at meeting the basic needs of a nation's overall population, they are likely to fail, become increasingly brutal, and serve the interests of economic elites.

Agriculture, Industry, and Birth Control in China

Today China is meeting the basic needs of its people, and is radically reducing its birth rate. This is a remarkable achievement given the problems facing the country thirty years ago. According to a Joint Economic report to the United States Congress:

> When the Communists under Mao Tse-tung came into power on October 1, 1949, the Chinese economy lay battered and broken from decades of war, flood, famine, and disease. Rail lines were cut. Factories were idle from lack of raw materials. Fields lay fallow, and dikes and irrigation canals over large areas were in disrepair. Tens of millions of people were destitute, many near death from starvation. Runaway inflation had rendered money useless as a medium of exchange.[12]

Faced with a battered economy, hunger, a surplus population, and rapid population growth, we might expect China's developmental planners to radically alter social and economic institutions. This is indeed the case. Land reform was implemented immediately after the liberation; the power of the landlords and moneylenders was broken, and the land was distributed to the peasants. Millions of peasants who had been a surplus population were given an opportunity for productive employment.

Redistribution of land was the beginning of an evolutionary process in Chinese agriculture and the consciousness of the peasants. For the long-exploited peasants the eviction of landlords and their own return to the land must have seemed as marvelous as the words spoken by Jesus to the paralytic: "I say to you, rise, take up your bed and go home" (Luke 5:24). For both, their changed condition offered new possibilities.

When it became clear in China that small private plots were uneconomical and inhibited cooperation, mutual-aid teams were formed. These evolved into simple cooperatives, which became advanced cooperatives that further evolved into the communes that are today the mainstay of Chinese agriculture. It is not our intention to describe this evolution in detail. The point we wish to make is that the institutional changes needed to transform a surplus population into a productive labor force have been implemented in China while avoided in India.

In the early 1960s agriculture was assigned the highest development priority in China's national planning. Agriculture was designed to serve three complementary goals: to increase food production, maximize employment possibilities, and evenly distribute the benefits of production. Food production increased dramatically in China. The creative and cooperative energies of the peasants literally transformed the Chinese countryside. Trees were planted, deserts reclaimed, valleys leveled, hills terraced, and irrigation and flood control works built. New seed varieties, intensive cropping patterns, and irrigation made it possible to produce two or three crops per year on land that used to produce only one. Local initiative, skills, and resources were utilized to encourage self-reliance. Food produced was distributed equitably among the members of communes. The surplus was sold to the State at fixed prices. The State then distributed food to the cities where a rationing system insured equal distribution. In contrast to India and other countries, there was no food inflation, no hoarding, no speculation, no profiteering, and no hunger.

There has also been no unemployment in China. Both agriculture and industry were organized to make an optimal use of China's large labor supply. Agriculture has been labor-intensive. While the current national thrust has been on mechanization, the emphasis was on small-scale technology to enhance the productivity of labor rather than displace it. Instead of producing luxury consumer items for an affluent class, industry was designed to serve the needs of agriculture and to absorb labor. For example, factories have often been located in rural areas where they provided communes with farm implements and other essentials. This enhanced regional self-reliance, provided additional rural employment, and militated against the need of the peasants to migrate to urban areas.

China is no longer marked by great contrasts between the rich and the poor that are common to many underdeveloped countries. By strategically organizing agricultural and industrial production China adequately feeds, clothes, houses, educates, and employs its people. It is in this context that the success of China's family-planning programs should be evaluated.

The Chinese government has made a full range of contraceptive methods available: the pill, IUD, condom, diaphragm, and male or female sterilization. All are commonly used. When contraception fails, abortion is available upon request, apparently without social stigma. The Chinese government like the government in India also carries out extensive education programs that encourage late marriages and extoll the benefits of small families. What's more, in China birth-control programs are succeeding. Why? We offer four suggestions.

First, despite rhetoric to the contrary, rapid population growth is regarded as a serious problem. But while recognizing the need to reduce population growth, China does not view its population as an obstacle to development. People are precious. Since the liberation people have been viewed as a valuable resource that can be tapped for development *provided the productive forces of society are organized to maximize their productive potential.* Laborers who are surplus in India are productive in China. While India and many other underdeveloped countries focus on their population problem and blame overpopulation for their underdevelopment, China has sought to reduce its population growth as part of a comprehensive developmental strategy aimed at meeting the basic needs of its people.

Second, the basic needs of the Chinese people are being met. This reduces their dependency on children for security. You will recall that development is the key factor in the demographic transition. As improved living standards change the lives of a nation's people, the people become less dependent on their offspring for security. As a result they desire and have fewer children. Conversely, in the absence of improved living standards large families are often an economic necessity because sons provide the only effective means of social security. In China children are no longer the basis for old-age security. When men retire at the age of sixty and women at the age of fifty-five, they receive 70 percent of their previous wages.

Third, the changing role of women as fully productive members of society has greatly altered the birthrate in China. It is widely recognized that women can be men's equals only if they are freed from endless childbearing.

Finally, in China there is a great deal of social pressure for couples to have no more than two or three children, regardless of their personal preference. This should not be surprising. In India there is also social pressure for small families. The difference—and it is a significant one—is that in India the pressure is exerted by the upper classes who promote birth control as a substitute for social change. Given the present economic priorities, they in effect are asking the peasants to commit economic suicide. For while small families may be in the interest of the nation, they contradict the vital interests of many villagers. In China the pressure is exerted by one's peers who recognize that small families serve the interests of the nation and the immediate mutual interests of members of communes.

China's development and demographic experience differ radically from those of India. Once considered a basket case, China was refused assistance by the International Red Cross during a severe famine in the 1930s. The reason was that the Red Cross had been designed to meet national emergencies while famine was a chronic state of affairs in China. Today China is far from being a basket case.

Unlike India, it is meeting the basic needs of its population and radically reducing the birthrate. China's experience indicates that overpopulation is not the cause of world hunger. Hunger and a rapid population growth are consequences of distorted economic priorities.

Motives of American Birth-Control Assistance to Underdeveloped Countries

Through government aid programs and private foundations, the United States has been an avid promoter and large supplier of birth control to underdeveloped countries. Both the government and foundations have accepted the view that overpopulation is the cause of hunger and underdevelopment; both of them view population control as the key solution. Because the United States government regarded population control as a sensitive issue, private foundations got the birth-control ball rolling.

In 1952, under the sponsorship of the National Academy of Science, the late John D. Rockefeller III convened a conference of population experts and established the Population Council. The Council served a variety of functions, including studying the impact of rapid population growth on underdeveloped nations, designing birth-control programs for use overseas, and encouraging individuals and other organizations concerned about population problems to begin discussions with the leaders of poor nations about birth control. In 1958 the Council had a budget of $18.3 million, most of which was provided by the Rockefeller Foundation, the Ford Foundation, and the Mellon family. Its charter members included Secretary of Commerce and Labor Lewis L. Strauss, Caryl P. Haskins of the Council on Foreign Relations, and General Dwight D. Eisenhower.[13]

We have previously noted that the Khanna Study was financed in part by the Rockefeller Foundation. The Ford Foundation also actively promoted birth control in India and elsewhere. Once these and other programs were off the ground, the United States Agency for International Development (USAID) began offering birth control as part of its aid program. From its inception in 1965 through fiscal year 1976, the population program of USAID spent more than $835 million. USAID, for example, is the largest source of funds for the Pathfinder Fund and other similar groups.

There needn't necessarily be anything evil or pernicious about the United States offering birth-control assistance to poor countries. After all, as long as birth control is linked to a developmental strategy aimed at meeting the basic needs of a nation's people, it is an important component in reducing birthrates and improving the quality of life. Unfortunately, the developmental models encouraged by American foreign policy and corporations are precisely those favoring the consumption of luxury goods by elite social classes while effectively impoverishing the majority of people in poor countries. In other words, consciously or unconsciously, birth-control programs promoted by the American government and foundations have served as substitutes for social justice. This fact led Josué de Castro, a Brazilian sociologist, demographer, and former president of the Food and Agriculture Organization of the United Nations, to conclude:

> The United States imposes birth control, not to help the poor countries—no one believes anymore in its "disinterested" aid programs—but because that is its strategic defense policy. We must realize that the pill is North America's best guarantee of continuing a dominant minority. . . . If ever the Third World achieves normal development, Washington's "Roman Empire" will disappear.[14]

A statement made in 1977 by the director of the United States Office of Population, Dr. R. T. Ravenholt, confirmed de Castro's views. Ravenholt was quoted in the *St. Louis Post Dispatch* as saying that the United States was "seeking to provide the means by which one quarter of the [world's] fertile women can be sterilized." Population control, according to Ravenholt, was needed to maintain *"the normal operation of U.S. commercial interests around the world"* (emphasis added). "Without our trying to help these countries with their economic and social development," he continued, "the world would rebel against the strong U.S. commercial presence. . . . The self-interest thing is a compelling element."[15] In addition, de Castro may have been more accurate than even he realized when he referred to birth control and the "strategic defense policy" of the U.S. In February 1978, at a major population and food-policy conference sponsored by the Population/Food Fund, several keynote speakers indicated that rapid population growth is a primary threat to American national security, and that the Defense Department should administer American population programs![16]

We demonstrated earlier that hunger and rapid population growth have roots in distorted economic priorities by which underdeveloped colonies aided in the development and demographic transition of Europe. Political independence did not bring an end to the economic exploitation of the majority of people in poor countries. Instead, distorted economic priorities have continued. While people in Europe and the United States and elites in poor countries may benefit, the situation of poor majorities worsens. It is within this context that foundations and the American government promote birth control. Seeking to limit populations is less threatening to American corporate interests than changes in economic priorities and structures. The United States depends heavily on the resources, raw materials, and cheap labor of underdeveloped countries, which also serve as markets for our agricultural and industrial surpluses. If poor countries were to adopt a self-reliant developmental strategy and use their resources to meet the basic needs of their people it would pose serious problems for American-based corporations that have grown fat during the age of American "democratic imperialism."

It is important for Americans concerned about world hunger and poverty to take de Castro's perspective seriously. There is a grave danger that American Christians will become the unwitting allies of groups who are seizing on population control as a solution to underdevelopment, thereby blaming the poor and condemning them to poverty. Our close association with such groups may result in their making use of our naiveté to help them exploit poor people in underdeveloped countries.

Chapter 8

HUNGER AND THE CRISIS OF AMERICAN VALUES

There is a tendency among people in this country to locate the world food crisis "out there." It has penetrated our consciousness but remains distant from our lives. Some American policymakers see the crisis as something affecting only other countries, and view it as an opportunity to recover American power and prestige. Many American Christians spend hours raising funds for famine relief abroad but little or no time dealing with the crisis at home. In fact, discussions about "agripower" and "food weapons," repeated references to the United States as the world's "breadbasket," and the availability of "cheap food" in our supermarkets lull us into a false sense of power and security.

In chapters 8 and 9 we shall describe the enormous crisis of values that underlies the world food crisis. The developmental goals of nations reflect basic value choices, which in turn are reflected in economic priorities that often lead to hunger and inequality, and to the destruction of cultures. Placing the world food crisis in a value context must in no way obscure the fact that for the most part it is corporations and economic elites that determine economic priorities and developmental goals. By and large, the values of the well-to-do are dominant, and the wealthy are the ones who dictate policies, define problems, and outline solutions. We shall try to demonstrate that the world food crisis, including the crisis in American agriculture, cannot be solved without a fundamental shift in values, economic priorities, and distribution of decision-making power.

132

The Crisis at Home: The Shift from Agriculture to Agribusiness

Foreign Expansion and the Changing Social Fabric

The successful policy of foreign expansion of Jeroboam II brought prosperity to Israel, but not without substantial social costs and human suffering. Inequality between social classes, poverty and powerlessness, the undermining of small farmers, increased urbanization, and the centralization of power among those engaged in commerce were all part of a changing social fabric. The social costs that fueled prosperity were visible and obvious to Amos, but were nearly invisible to the wealthy in Israel whose values were conditioned by their affluence. As the rich drank wine from the vineyards of the poor, ate lambs from their flocks, anointed themselves with fine oils, and rested on beds of ivory (Amos 6:4–6), they found their social and economic system to be the pinnacle of efficiency. They were the "notable people of the first of nations" (Amos 6:1).* But negative social costs, such as the exploitation of the poor, were not factored into their efficiency equation. Consciously or unconsciously the upper classes valued wealth, profits, and power more than social justice and equality.

Not surprisingly, American foreign expansion and prosperity after World War II also involved uncounted social costs. Previously we discussed the impact of American economic expansion on poor people abroad. Here we are concerned about the domestic social costs. The values fostered by foreign expansion were not conducive to recognizing and setting limits. Through an aggressive foreign policy the United States secured access to an enormous share of the world's resources, and our economy has been built in large measure with artificially cheap raw materials and minerals. This helps explain the nation's commitment to unlimited growth and its propensity to waste energy and raw materials. "During the last thirty years," President Kennedy told Congress in his message on conservation in 1962, "this nation has consumed more minerals than all the peoples of the world had previously used." Eleven years later, as the United States entered the era of the energy crisis, President Nixon told the Seafarers International Union:

> There are only 7 percent of the people of the world living in the United States, and we use thirty percent of all the energy. That isn't bad; that is good. That means we are the richest, strongest people in the world, and that we have the highest

standard of living in the world. That is why we need so much energy, and may it always be that way.[1]

The values implicit in Nixon's statement are hardly those of a conservationist. Our expansionist mentality, which is an outgrowth of an economic system requiring growth and mass consumption, militates against conservation. As a consequence we fail in any meaningful sense to recognize both the limits and value of the human scale, and the importance of working within the confines of soil, water, and our energy resources. Alongside the outward signs of prosperity—huge tractors and mechanical harvesters thundering across America's farmland, surplus production and booming agricultural exports, abundance of automobiles, trucks, and other consumer goods, gigantic skyscrapers and luxury high-rise apartments—there are indications of a deep spiritual and social crisis in both rural and urban America. Inequality, the elimination of millions of family farms, the use of food as a weapon, soil erosion and environmental pollution, urban sprawl and decay, and the centralization of power are all evidence of a changing social fabric. Perhaps most important, prosperity, mass consumption, and the large centralized enterprises on which they are based have not brought us personal fulfillment, happiness, spiritual rootedness, or social equality and justice.

What is not fully understood is that our rural and urban problems are deeply connected, and that the crisis of the United States is a crisis of American culture. In 1935 there were approximately 6.8 million farms throughout the countryside; today less than 2.7 million remain. Farms continue to fold at the rate of between a thousand and fifteen hundred per week. A small farm economy has been sacrificed to other values. As we shall try to demonstrate, eliminating family farms has reshaped both rural and urban America and has actually undermined the food security of the American people.

Displaced farmers and their families for the most part migrate to urban areas in search of jobs. Between 1920 and 1960, more than 25 million people left our farms for our towns and cities. In 1910 more than 54 percent of the American population lived in rural areas. The process of rural displacement and subsequent urbanization has taken place at such a rapid pace that today 75 percent of our population lives on 2 percent of our land.

Urban areas have not coped well with the influx of rural migrants. "America's large, old cities are facing a hidden and largely ignored problem under their streets, . . ." the *New York Times* recently reported, "an uncharted maze of aging water mains, sewer lines and other subterranean facilities that have deteriorated to the point where they threaten public safety." Many cities, according to the *Times*, are sitting on a "time bomb."[2] But the most visible time bomb is above and not beneath the streets. Unemployment, overcrowding, poor housing, inadequate health care and transportation facilities all testify to the problems facing America's cities. Similar to Amos's Israel, our cities have distinct sections: one with large luxurious houses and apartments; the other marked by poverty, burnt-out buildings, overcrowding, and dilapidated housing. To this should be added a third section, closely linked to the first: an area dominated by the headquarters and branches of multinational corporations and banks whose sights are focused well beyond the poverty of their own cities to the world of international trade, investment, and profit.

Getting the Farmers off the Farms

The relationship between rural and urban problems can be explained in the context of the value crisis implicit in the shift from agri*culture* to agri*business*. In 1947, six years after *Life* Magazine published Henry R. Luce's editorial outlining the American Century, it carried another full-page editorial discribing a farm program for the United States. The solution to our farm problem, according to *Life*, was the elimination of 3,800,000 family farms. Just two years earlier, a committee report of the Agriculture Department Chamber of Commerce had indicated that small farm units were "economic and social liabilities."[3] Committee members included representatives of Armour & Company, General Electric Company, Pillsbury Company, Carnation Company, and Ralston Purina Company. These spokespersons for big business and big agriculture recommended that between one-half and two-thirds of all farms be eliminated even though "these farms are definitely of the family type and apparently constitute a substantial portion of that type which is supposed to be the backbone of the nation. . . ."

A major problem, according to the committee, was that the small farmers who preferred farm life "to any other" were not good consumers.

> Often there has been developed little desire for the variety of material things associated with a higher standard of living, if their attainment must be at the cost of that freedom which comes from self-employment and a leisurely mode of life. Very often the ambition, the energy, and the managerial ability, as well as the capital and experience necessary for larger-scale production, are lacking.

One might have thought it possible for a Department of Agriculture, with land-grant colleges throughout the country and extension agents in nearly every agricultural county, to assist these family farmers. It is at least conceivable that maintaining a way of life and increasing production and income are compatible goals. However, there were two reasons why the "farm problem" in this country was defined (not by small farmers of course) as too many farmers and why American agricultural policy broke the backs of the small farmers instead of regarding them as the backbone of the nation: the need of agricultural input corporations (the machinery, pesticide, and fertilizer companies) to sell their wares, and the need for a nation beginning the American Century to provide its industrial plants with cheap laborers. As the Chamber of Commerce report stated:

> If nonagricultural industry continues active and in need of manpower, and if the mechanization of agriculture goes further, a considerable portion of the younger generation reared on these low-producing units may leave them for the cities and other industries. As a consequence, many low-producing units may be consolidated with other farms to form more economical operating units. . . . Thus, many farms of this character will disappear in the course of time.

In 1962 a similar government study indicated that "although the exodus from agriculture in the past decade or longer has been large by almost any standards, it has not been large enough."[4] This study, which was entitled "An Adaptive Program for Agriculture," was conducted by the Research and Policy Committee of the Committee for Economic Development. The Committee's membership included representatives of Ford Motor Company, Standard Oil Company of New Jersey, H. J. Heinz Company, American Telephone and Telegraph, American Can Company, Northwest Bancorporation, Connecticut General Life Insurance Company, General Motors Corporation, Scott Paper Company, and IBM. The committee offered "statements on National Policy as an aid to a clearer understanding of the steps to be taken in achieving sustained growth of the American economy." The committee made the following comments:

> Net migration out of agriculture has been going on for 40 years, and at a rapid rate. Nevertheless, the movement of people from agriculture has not been fast enough to take full advantage of the opportunity that improving farm technology and increasing capital create for raising the living standards of the American people, including, of course, farmers.

While the stated goal of the committee was prosperity for all Americans, including the relatively few large farmers who presumably were to remain on the land, the concepts implicit in the study were clear: the values, lives, and communities of the small farmers on the land were of less worth than the technological innovations and opportunities for capital investment on the part of corporations and banks. The small farmers should be forced to "adapt" to the needs of a corporate-dominated economy that cannot survive without growth. This means that they must leave. Interestingly, the committee also recommended that wages for nonfarm laborers be kept low in order to raise nonfarm production and employment.

There was no input on the part of small farmers into the committee's report. Had there been, it is doubtful that small farmers would have agreed that the way to "attack the farm problem at the root" was to reduce the "farm labor force on the order of one third in a period of not more than five years." Nor is it likely that they would have concurred with the committee's recommendation that children of farm families be educated in order to get "a large number of people out of agriculture before they are committed to it as a career." The committee presumed that no one who was educated would forsake the values of the American Century in favor of small-scale agriculture.

Corporate Domination of Rural America

Since World War II the American farm has rapidly evolved into a factory. Many farm families have been forced off the land into cities. The remaining farms have been consolidated into large-scale units capable of providing corporations with markets for their energy and capital-intensive farm inputs. Several years ago Secretary of Agriculture Earl Butz told farmers to get big or get out. Evidence indicates that farmers are doing one or the other, and at a rapid pace. According to USDA figures, 4 percent of all American farms in 1974—those earning $100,000 or more yearly—earned 35 percent of the total farm income. At the same time 25 percent of all farms received only 2.4 percent of the net income from farming.[5] *Time* magazine's issue of 6 November 1978 reported that the number of farms grossing $100,000 a year or more increased from 23,000 in 1960 to 162,000 in 1977. These large farms, according to *Time*, were "swallowing up the lands" of their less fortunate neighbors. "Though these very large operations still constitute only 6% of all farms, they take in 53% of all farm cash sales receipts, almost double their share as recently as 1967."[6]

Each year USDA publishes a *Fact Book of U.S. Agriculture*. In a section entitled "Agriculture's Efficiency Increases," the report boasted in 1976 that "one farmworker now supplies enough food and fiber for 56 people. Only 10 years ago, he was producing enough for 29." What accounted for this rapid increase in productivity per worker, according to the *Fact Book*, was the "substitution of machinery for labor."[7] Or as another USDA publication noted, "Farmers have substituted mechanical power and machinery for labor inputs, and agricultural chemicals for land." Since 1965 the "use of mechanical power and machinery increased 21 percent, while agricultural chemicals' use nearly doubled."[8]

USDA assumed that replacing farm labor with energy-intensive inputs was efficient, and that we should applaud the displacement of the farmers. Over the past thirty years the use of chemical pesticides has increased fourteenfold, from 50 million pounds a year to 700 million pounds. According to the *Fact Book*, between 1964 and 1974 the use of chemical fertilizers increased more than 85 percent. Average horsepower per tractor on farms also increased dramatically. In 1969 the average horsepower was 42; in 1973, 44 percent of the wheel tractors sold to farms were rated at 90 horsepower or more, compared with only 4 percent in 1963.[9] Yet given the fact that energy prices are rising rapidly and are likely to continue to do so in the future, there seems to be a justification for some concern about the policy of replacing people with machines and chemicals.

It should not be surprising that the cost of farming has escalated with increased use of energy-intensive inputs. According to USDA, the "prices paid by farmers have more than doubled during the past decade." Farm indebtedness is now over $100 billion, more than eight times the 1950 level![10] The high cost of farming, which by and large has outstripped gains in the income of the farmers, has further accelerated the decline in the number of family farms.

The definition in the *Fact Book* of efficiency—that is, that only one farmworker supply enough food and fiber for 56 people—is not the only instance of questionable logic on the part of the USDA. In the same publication we find the following statement:

> The Nation's food and fiber needs are now being met by only a small portion of the total work force of the Nation, thus freeing much of the manpower needed to provide other goods and services that contribute to our high standard of living.[11]

Statements about freeing "manpower" are highly misleading. The shift from agriculture to agribusiness has not reduced the amount of labor needed to produce the nation's food supply. It has more accurately *shifted labor from family farms to the agroindustrial sector,*

and shifted profits from small farmers and local communities into
the coffers of corporate giants.

Fifty years ago rural and urban areas were intimately connected.
Millions of small farms dotted the countryside. Farm families were
basically self-sufficient in food, and produced a surplus for nearby
towns and cities. Most food consumed by city people was produced
within a fifty-mile radius. The marketing arrangements were simple
and efficient: the food products went from the farm to the whole-
saler, retailer, or directly to the consumer. Very few of these products
underwent significant processing or packaging. Food was nutritious
and fresh, prices were determined by the cost of production, not by
packaging, advertising, convenience, and long-distance transportation. Agriculture's work force was primarily made up of farmers.

The situation today is radically different. We can get a sense both
of the high corporate stakes in shifting from agri*culture* to highly
capital- and energy-intensive agri*business* and the misleading nature of USDA's claim that the nation's food and fiber needs are being
met by a small portion of the total work force by quoting from the
Fact Book itself. Under section headings "The Nation's Agricultural
Industry" and "The Marketing Network" the study noted:

> *Agriculture is the Nation's biggest industry.* Its assets, totaling
> $531 billion, amount to about three-fifths of the capital assets of
> all manufacturing corporations in the United States. *It is also*
> *the Nation's largest employer.* Between 14 and 17 million
> people work in some phase of agriculture—from growing food
> and fiber to selling it at the supermarket. . . . The Nation's
> agriculture is based on fewer than 3 million farms. . . .
>
> Between the farm and the dinner table agriculture requires
> the services of 8 to 10 million people to store, transport, process,
> and merchandise the output of the Nation's farms. . . . Another
> two million people provide the seeds, fertilizers, and other
> supplies farmers use for production and family living. That
> adds up to approximately *one out of every five jobs in private*
> *enterprise.*

The study continued:

> The American farmer is linked to you by a complex food mar-
> keting system. Last year [1975] we spent more than $154 billion
> on U.S. farm-produced foods. *About $100 billion of that was to*
> *get the food from the farm to your table. The food was assem-*
> *bled, inspected, graded, stored, processed, packaged, whole-*
> *saled, and retailed*—over 400 million tons of it. To reach you,

this food traveled across 201,000 miles of railroads, 3.2 million miles of intercity highways, and 26,000 miles of improved waterways.

The foods that poured into your supermarket came in *6,000 to 8,000 different forms*—many of which did not even exist 5 years ago and may very well not exist 5 years from now. That's because Americans demand newer and better foods with more built-in conveniences. Consumers like food in attractive packages that preserve the quality. *Packaging and transportation cost $20 billion last year.* . . . The food marketing system is developing a computerized checkout, inventory, and ordering system that may further streamline food retailing and help to simplify shopping.[12]

I seriously question whether USDA's description of the *agricultural industry* represents an improvement in the quality of life or a "freeing of manpower." Ironically, millions of people who were forced to leave rural America are now employed in the nation's biggest industry: agribusiness. Many who once nurtured and were nurtured by the soil now help transport food several thousand miles, fill it with chemicals to prevent spoilage, package it to make it look appealing (even though most of the nutrients have been processed out), or process it into one of the six thousand to eight thousand food forms available to American consumers. (How do you like eating an I.T.T. Hostess Sno-Ball, which is 42 percent sugar, or King Vitamin cereal, which is 50 percent sugar?) Still others produce the giant tractors that roam the countryside, and the chemical fertilizers and pesticides that are the basis of the nation's energy-intensive agribusiness.

The shift from agriculture to agribusiness is accompanied by oligopoly power. According to Jim Hightower, there are 32,000 food manufacturing firms in the United States. Fifty of them account for about three-fourths of the industry's profits. A handful of giants, such as Beatrice Foods, Proctor & Gamble Company, Unilever, Consolidated Foods Corporation, American Brands, United Brands, American Home Products Corporation, CPC International, and Standard Brands, are among the companies that own most of the processed, heavily advertised grocery brands. Eighty-nine percent of the soft-drink sales are controlled by Coca-Cola, Pepsico, Royal Crown, and Seven-Up. Borden, National Dairy, and Carnation control 60 to 70 percent of the dairy products. Three national firms produce 50 percent of the beer sold in the country. Kellogg's, General Mills, General Foods (Post), and Quaker account for 91 percent of breakfast cereal sales. The four top vegetable canners sell 60 percent of the fruit cocktail, 57 percent of the apple sauce, 82 percent of the canned figs, 52 percent of the canned sweet corn, 58 percent of the tomato paste and vegetable juice, 53 percent of the canned peas, and 72 percent of the tomato sauce. Six multinational grain companies now handle 90 percent of all the grain shipped in the entire world. Cargill and Continental alone split half of this market.[13] A study completed in 1979 by Corporate Data Exchange, Inc. (CDE) confirms the trend toward increased concentration in the food industry. The *CDE Stock Ownership Directory: Agribusiness* profiles 222 companies that form the backbone of the U.S. food system, identifying their top stockholders, investment banks, legal counsels, and accountants. Of the $250 billion revenues detailed by the directory, nearly three-fourths is accounted for by only seventy-three companies. This concentration is even higher within certain sectors. For example, fifteen companies account for 60 percent of all farm inputs, forty-nine companies account for 68 percent of food processing, and forty-four companies control over 77 percent of wholesale and retail revenues.[14] Certainly the merchants in Amos's Israel would have been proud of such monopoly power (see Amos 8:4–7).

Significantly, the shift from agriculture to agribusiness has not improved the diet of the American people. Since World War II the nation's consumption of staple foods has declined significantly while the consumption of fabricated foods has increased dramatically. Per capita consumption of dairy products has declined 21 percent, of vegetables 23 percent, and of fruit 25 percent. At the same time, per capita consumption of soft drinks went up 80 percent, of pastries 70 percent, and of various "munchie" foods like potato chips 85 percent. USDA studies indicate a decline in the overall quality of our diet. In 1955, 60 percent of a group surveyed by the Department of Agriculture had an adequate diet; in 1965 a similar survey indicated that this was so for only 50 percent. Many researchers believe that the rising incidence of many diseases and physical ailments, including heart disease, diabetes, hypertension, some forms of cancer, obesity, and tooth decay, are linked to our declining national diet.[15]

Small farmers and their families have not been forced to leave their land, culture, and communities because their labor could be better utilized to produce goods that would enhance "the quality of life." Instead, they were sacrificed on the altar of corporate values and profits. Today the final nails are being driven into the coffin of small-scale agriculture in the United States. Its end is both necessary and inevitable in the viewpoint of the corporate giants that dominate agribusiness. "What is needed," according to Rudolph A. Peterson, former president of the Bank of America, "is a program which will enable the small and uneconomic farmer—the one who is unwilling or unable to bring his farm to the commercial level of expansion or merger—to take his land out of production with dignity."[16] But the demise of small-scale agriculture is not inevitable. Small farms are regarded as "social and economic liabilities" because they have stood in the way of corporate agribusiness.

In 1974, Ted Owens, an official with the Agency for International Development, wrote in a *Washington Post* article that small farms in other parts of the world outproduce giant American farms on a per-acre basis. The reason, according to Owens, is that the farm-support systems in those countries *adapt to farmers* and not vice versa. This is a wholly different approach from the one taken by the "Adaptive Program for Agriculture," which we discussed earlier in this chapter. Under the Adaptive Program, corporate giants design programs to meet their own needs for capital investments, cheap labor, and the marketing of technological products. "The improbable feature of small farm systems to Americans," Owens writes, "is the use of small-sized farm machinery and tools to supplement human effort, not replace it, to increase the amount of work farmers can do rather than drive them off the land."[17]

United States government-sponsored agricultural research has adapted agriculture to the needs of agribusiness and not of the small farmers. "When we ask what agricultural research has done for this group of farmers," a former director of USDA's Office of Science and Education said in a 1969 speech, "the answer comes back: 'Very little.' In fact, the overall impact of agricultural research has threatened their survival."[18]

Wendell Berry, a small farmer and the author of *The Unsettling of America: Culture & Agriculture*, writes:

> That one American farmer can now feed himself and fifty-six other people may be, within the narrow view of the specialist, a triumph of economics and technology; by no stretch of reason can it be considered a triumph of agriculture or of culture. It has been made possible by the substitution of energy for knowledge, of methodology for care, of technology for morality. This "accomplishment" is not primarily the work of farmers—who have been, by and large, its victims—but of a collaboration of corporations, university specialists, and government agencies. It is therefore an agricultural development not motivated by agricultural aims or disciplines, but by the ambitions of merchants, industrialists, bureaucrats, and academic careerists. We should not be surprised to find that its effect on both the farmland and the farm people has been ruinous.

Berry continues:

> If agriculture is acknowledged to have anything to do with
> culture, then its study has to include people. But the agriculture
> experts ruled people out when they made their discipline a
> specialty—or rather, when they sorted it into a collection of
> specialties—and moved it into its own "college" in the univer-
> sity. . . . They appear to have concluded that agriculture is
> purely a commercial concern; its purpose is to provide as much
> food as quickly and cheaply and with as few man-hours as
> possible and to be a market for machines and chemicals. It is,
> after all, "agribusiness"—not the land or the farming people—
> that now benefits most from agricultural research. . . .[19]

The High Costs of "Cheap Food"

"The New U.S. Farmer," according to a recent cover story in *Time*,
is typified by Pat Benedict, a Minnesotan who farms 3,500 acres of
wheat and sugar beets.[20] Benedict owns half a million dollars' worth
of machinery, which according to *Time* "requires a football-field-
sized yard just to park it." A partial inventory includes "four 15-ton
trucks, three pickup trucks, seven tractors, three center-pivot ir-
rigators and three wheat combines that cost $30,000 each, yet are
used only about two weeks a year." His farm over the years has
"absorbed three others; in three cases, he razed and burned the
houses, uprooted graceful shade trees and returned all the land to
crops." The article further notes: "Tenant farmers these days are no
longer the classic Southern sharecroppers, who have almost disappeared, but are often expanding agriculturalists like Benedict who
own land too."

Benedict, who farms with the aid of a computer, is according to
Time:

> . . . archetypal of the farmers who make U.S. agriculture the
> nation's most efficient and productive industry and by far the
> biggest force in holding down the trade deficit. Revolutionary
> changes are sweeping the croplands, making agriculture an
> increasingly *capital intensive, high technology, mass-
> production business. As a result, U.S. farmers are dividing into
> two distinct classes.* Small farmers, who do not have the techni-
> cal expertise, are rapidly leaving the land. Large farmers, like
> Benedict, who know how to use credit and the latest in agricul-
> tural science, are gaining an ever greater share of the market
> (emphasis added).

The large farmer, according to *Time*, is the only real farmer. "Some 70% of the 2.7 million farms left in the U.S.," the article states, "gross $20,000 or less each year, and *the people who work them should not be classed as farmers at all*" (emphasis added).

Time acknowledges that there are some problems related to the "technological innovation that has made U.S. agriculture the productivity wonder of the world." The greatest problems are "whether farmers can keep up with it and scrape up the money to use it." The article notes with amazement that scientists at the University of California at Davis are taking the "lowly tomato" and making it "square" with "a tough flat-sided skin that is ideal for both picking by machine and packing for shipment without bruising." They quote one researcher as saying "I don't think we'll ever be satisfied until we've got a tomato that can be grown on the moon and whistles *Yankee Doodle Dandy*." Speaking as one American, I would prefer a tomato with taste rather than one that sings. "Some of the strawberries that Americans buy and eat are cloned," the article adds with astonishment. The problem is that "some people cannot discover any taste at all in cloned strawberries," nor in much of the other agribusiness-produced food. As the article points out:

> To be sure, epicures complain rightly that the bland taste of American fruits and vegetables cannot compare with the flavor of much produce delivered to European tables. In the U.S., food must be refrigerated, preserved and shipped across continental distances, and the varieties suitable to mechanical planting and harvesting often are not as tasty as those cultivated lovingly by hand. . . . But agricultural mass production has a benefit more important to most people: it keeps costs down.

Food may not taste good, but according to *Time* it is cheap. Even according to a narrow definition of food costs, i.e., the prices paid for food at the supermarket, the article's assertion that agribusiness keeps food prices down is questionable. *Time* itself notes that "zooming costs of processing and distribution have created a strange paradox. Higher farm prices instantly bring increases at the grocery checkout, *but retail food prices can also go on rising while farm prices drop suddenly*." This, of course, is evidence of the power of the oligopoly, which we mentioned earlier. In addition, *Time* claims that "food accounts for only 23% of all private spending by Americans," but this is an average figure that is highly misleading. For the 26 million Americans who live below the poverty line and for millions of others whose incomes do not keep pace with inflation, the rising food prices of recent years have made it difficult or impossible to maintain good nutritional health.

There are other problems related to our "cheap food" policy. Numerous costs, including social decay, environmental pollution, soil erosion, and regional food dependency, are not factored into the prices of agribusiness food for domestic consumption and export. In 1944 anthropologist Walter Goldschmidt conducted a study of two farm communities, which gave a good indication of some of the uncounted social costs of corporate-dominated agriculture. In his study, which was published by the United States Senate in 1946, Goldschmidt evaluated community life in the two California towns of Arvin and Dinuba, which were alike in basic economic factors but different in the size of their farms. His goal was to determine the impact of farm size on local communities. Comparing the community surrounded by large farms (Arvin) to the small-farm community (Dinuba), he discovered that the small-farm community had twice as many businesses; 61 percent more retail trade; 20 percent more people and a higher standard of living; more independent entrepreneurs; more schools, parks, newspapers, civic organizations, and churches; better physical facilities for community living such as paved roads, sidewalks, garbage-and-sewage disposal and other public services; more institutions for democratic decision-making, and a much broader participation in these activities by its citizenry. The development of corporate agriculture "has like so many other events of the period," Goldschmidt commented, "been assumed to be natural, inevitable and progressive, and little attention has been paid to the costs that have been incurred. I do not mean the costs of money; *I mean the costs in the traditions of our society and its rural institutions. . . .*"[21]

On completion of the study Goldschmidt was ordered by the Bureau of Agricultural Economics to discontinue his work. However, several other studies confirmed his findings. A 1977 California study expanded Goldschmidt's work by examining 136 towns. It concluded that small-farm regions had more towns and that small-farm communities were more viable and support more services. Another study in South Dakota showed that every time six family farmers left the land, one small business closed down.

Another measure of social costs rarely considered in measuring American agricultural "efficiency" and "cheap food" policy are the counterparts to rural migration: the uprooting of rural people, their culture, and their values, as well as urban decay. The 1945 Agriculture Department Chamber of Commerce study cited earlier noted that "in all sections of the country" there were "low value producers" who constituted "economic and social liabilities." These producers were *"unskilled in any other occupation and ill-adapted to urban life"* (emphasis added). The study made it clear that people in the South (presumably black tenants and farmers) would be most seriously affected by policies to get small farmers out of agriculture.

This indeed has been the case. In 1910 over 15 million acres were owned by blacks. By 1950 this figure had declined to 12.5 million and has been decreasing steadily since 1954. The annual rate of black farmland loss now stands at approximately 500,000 acres, or roughly 9,000 acres per week. In 1920, 925,000 blacks operated farms in this country. Ninety percent were in the South. As of 1964, according to estimates from the Emergency Land Fund and the National Association of Landowners, only 52,000 black-operated farms remained.[22] Estimates suggest there are less than 40,000 black landowners in America today. Between 1940 and 1970, 4.5 million blacks—poor and uneducated—migrated North in search of jobs. Many, as the Chamber of Commerce study realized, were ill adapted to urban life. Their rural values, skills, and occupations had been undermined. Some found jobs, but many others remained unemployed. They were, in the terminology of a previous chapter, a *surplus population* relative to the organization of economic production in both rural and urban areas.

The social costs of this economically forced migration surfaced in the middle and later part of the 1960s. Watts exploded in 1965; Detroit and Newark in 1967; and in 1968, following the murder of Martin Luther King, Jr., Washington, D.C., and dozens of other American cities caught fire. In large measure the designers of our food and farm policies are responsible for the human tragedies common to many of our cities. The price we pay for the "cheap food" of our agribusiness-dominated food system in no way factors in the human costs of rural displacement, nor the costs of food stamps, welfare and unemployment insurance, breakdowns in health and hospital care, overtaxed transportation systems, rising police and penal costs, pollution, and breakdowns in school systems.

Other uncounted costs linked to America's "cheap food" policies are pollution from the run-off of chemical fertilizers and pesticides, and soil erosion. Agriculture requires energy to produce the food and fiber we need to sustain life. The functional purpose of agriculture, as biologist Barry Commoner has forcefully argued, is to harness or capture solar energy.[23] "Organic matter is the fuel that drives the great cycles of the ecosystem which support not only agriculture but all life," Commoner writes. "Solar energy, trapped by living plants, produces that fuel." Since World War II, however, the source of the energy that fuels agricultural production has drastically changed. The postwar "agricultural revolution" has substituted nonrenewable fossil fuels (gas, oil, chemical fertilizers and pesticides) for solar energy.

Traditional agriculture was a highly diversified system. Each farm produced a variety of crops and animals. The cattle were fed grasses from the farm, and animal waste, a valuable organic fertilizer, returned nutrients to the soil. Farmers grew crops in a yearly sequence, beginning with those that green up in the spring through a summer crop, and ending with one that remains green late into the fall. This, according to Commoner, "maximizes the capture of solar energy and the production of the organic matter that drives the soil cycles." It also helps to prevent soil erosion. Farmers also rotated crops with nitrogen-fixing legumes, thus naturally enhancing the fertility of the soil. Crop rotation also reduced pests and thus the need for pesticides.

Commoner describes the shift from solar to fossil-fuel energy that accompanied the so-called agricultural revolution:

> The storybook farm, with its menagerie of animals personally attended by the farmer and his family amid checkered fields of corn, oats, hay, and clover and a garden of fruits and vegetables, is long gone. Nearly all the horses have disappeared, their place before the plow taken by tractors, . . . many now riding on seven foot-wheels and carrying an air-conditioned cab. Most of the cattle have been banished to feed-lots. . . . The chickens are no longer in the barnyard, scrambling about for food and laying eggs in nests of their own making; now they are congregated in long buildings, confined in rows of cages, their food and water delivered and their eggs and waste removed by endless belts.
>
> Now the once variegated fields are uniformly covered with a single crop. The corn no longer dries in the sun, but is harvested as moist grain which is fed into gas-burning drying ovens and trucked to feed companies that supply the penned cattle and the caged chickens. Where once the animals' manure made the fields fertile, now it has become feed-lot waste. Instead the crops are nourished by purchased chemicals. Other chemicals are used to kill weeds and insect pests, no longer kept in check by shifting crops from field to field. The farm land . . . is now more often bare ground, green for only a few summer months, when the single crop that is mandated by the market is rapidly grown, harvested, and turned into cash. And most of the people have left. . . .

He concludes:

> Given what we know about the natural cycles that maintain the fertility of the soil, and particularly their dependence upon energy, a system of agriculture that used solar energy effi-

ciently would be based on a sequence of crops that are green for the longest possible yearly period, that are in a rotation which includes legumes, and that are mixed with animal production. This is, of course, the pattern of traditional agriculture. *But this pattern has been largely destroyed by the post-war changes in agricultural production* [emphasis added].

According to USDA's *Fact Book*, "the general farm which produces a half-dozen products is rapidly fading."[24] Under the heading "Specialization" the study notes:

Continuing advances in production technology and changes in market demands are the major forces leading to increased specialization in farm production. Eggs, chickens, and turkeys, once sideline enterprises on millions of farms, are now produced primarily by a relatively few farms, often raising nothing else. . . . About two-thirds of the production of fed beef now comes from specialized feedlots. . . . Fruits, such as citrus, grapes, and apples, and vegetables for canning and freezing are produced chiefly by specialized farms on a substantial scale.

Energy inputs, including chemical fertilizers and pesticides, have substituted for diversity, human scale, and caring. Healthy soil, the foundation of long-term food security, is no longer considered an important resource. "The three basic 'inputs' for agricultural production," the *Fact Book* states, "are land, labor, and capital. Land is no longer the major production tool. The productivity of the land now depends upon the skill and knowledge with which capital is applied—the use of mechanical power and machinery, fertilizer, lime, better seed, [and] pest control chemicals. . . ."[25] According to one expert, whom *Time* refers to as "the ruler of a family agribusiness empire big enough to make him a prairie Rockefeller," crop rotation is a thing of the past. *"Insecticides and herbicides have done away with the need to rotate crops in order to keep pests from infesting the soil.* No longer must a farmer periodically allow his best land to lie fallow, or plant it with unprofitable crops."[26]

U.S. agriculture is suffering from a massive chemical overdose. Like drug addicts who must increase their intake in order to remain functional, our nation's farms are using more and more chemical fertilizers and pesticides just to maintain their present yields. And while drugs may allow addicts to function over a short period of time, they are not a substitute for health, nor are chemicals a substitute for healthy soil. An article in the *Washington Post* describes the problem in the following terms:

The nagging problem with monocultures, as a special USDA task force has warned, is that this creates an environment favorable to damaging pest populations . . . . While only 1 percent of the corn crop was treated with insecticides in 1951 USDA statistics show, up to 70 percent of the corn in some major corn belt states gets routine doses today.[27]

Thirty years ago farmers were using 50 million pounds of agricultural pesticides, and they suffered a 7 percent preharvest loss. Today farmers apply more than 700 million pounds and have a 13 percent preharvest loss. As the *Post* article indicates, pesticides have become a sort of plague:

In major crops, from corn to cotton, from onions to oranges, the pesticide blitz is warping the ecological balance so drastically that super strains of insects and weeds, resistant to poisons and freed from their natural enemies, are proliferating like Andromeda strains out of control.

An entomologist at Louisiana State University noted that vegetable growers in Florida have been spraying their fields 40 times a season. "We have created monsters out of previously unknown pests."[28]

Pollution from the run-off of chemical fertilizers and pesticides is a major unfactored cost in our "cheap food," agribusiness-dominated food system. On a recent trip to Nebraska I talked with farmers who were concerned that chemical run-off was poisoning the state's underground water supply; they felt they were locked into a system that left them powerless to do much about it. They were intrigued to learn that organic producers were getting yields similar to their own, but the Nebraska farmers were unwilling to risk a changeover. Columnist Jack Anderson recently reported that a geological survey of the drinking water in Holt County, Nebraska, disclosed that "40 percent of the tap water contained nitrate levels exceeding federal safety standards. Some wells showed contamination of three times the acceptable amount." Physicians in the area were treating infants for nitrate poisoning.[29]

Another unfactored cost is soil erosion. According to Michael Perelman, 4 billion tons of soil are eroded away in the United States each year! This figure, which was developed before the farmers expanded production to marginal soils in 1973, comes to a total of almost 20 tons of soil erosion per person per year in the United States, *or about 30 pounds of erosion for every pound of food produced for domestic use or foreign export.* The average depth of topsoil in the country has fallen from three feet to six inches.[30] USDA soil-erosion estimates are somewhat lower but still astounding. A recent report on erosion and sedimentation released by Assistant Secretary of Agriculture M. Rupert Cutler indicates that soil is being washed away on the nation's cropland at an average annual rate of nine tons per acre, about three times the "tolerable" rate. Cutler noted that in 1975 American soil losses on cropland were 2.8 billion tons.[31]

Soil erosion is a consequence of the post-World War II agricultural revolution. However, the long-term costs of erosion are not calculated into efficiency equations promoted by USDA or the writers of *Time*. The huge machines that roam the countryside pack the soil, thus aggravating problems of wind erosion. In addition, because the land is covered with crops for only a few months of the year, the soil is at the mercy of the wind. Many farmers are forsaking the lessons of the Dust Bowl of the 1930s. "All across the Midwest," Jack Anderson writes in the column cited earlier, "the soil is being swept away by wind and water." Many farmers, eager to expand acreage under the plow in order to make a profitable use of their gigantic farm equipment, have cut down windbreaks and planted marginal land. According to one USDA soil expert, in Nebraska alone there are more than "200,000 acres of this land [which] should never have been put to the plow." According to Anderson, vital stands of trees planted after the Dust Bowl to break the wind, have been bulldozed down to install giant irrigation systems and cross-slope farming methods to reduce water erosion are often ignored.

The undermining of our land and water resources is bound to accelerate as the United States continues to rely upon food exports as a vehicle of political and economic power. Within our present agro-industrial complex, the policy of exchanging "food for crude" is in fact an unstated policy of exchanging "soil for oil." "Pat Benedict and farmers like him," the writers of *Time* note, "are America's best hope to counter the trade challenge presented by the oilmen of Araby and the energetic manufacturers of Japan." The irony of agripower is that the United States is utilizing food exports to try to prevent its nearly $30 billion trade deficit from worsening, but in doing so, it is undermining our agricultural resources and the food security of the American people. An additional irony is that excessive military expenditures are in large measure responsible for the noncompetitiveness of American producers in the world marketplace. Such military expenditures gave rise to the need for agripower in the first place. Yet the Carter Administration's budget for fiscal year 1979 called for a significant increase in American military spending although it trimmed the Agricultural Conservation Program by almost $100 million, and cut other soil-conservation appropriations by $580 million. In addition it proposed to stop all future small-watershed program starts and planning funds.[32]

One additional ironical twist is that the foreign countries that enjoy a substantial trade surplus with the United States are increasingly using their surplus dollars to purchase American farmland. "Other investment markets have waned," *Business Week* reported in March 1978, "but cheap dollars, political instability overseas, and a long record of rising prices have made U.S. farmland the single hottest area for foreign investors." What we are witnessing," said one Department of Commerce official, "is the biggest, continuing investment in American farmland since the turn of the century."[33] Foreign investment in American agricultural land will only accelerate the trend toward agribusiness and a form of ecologically disastrous farming. The spread of center-pivot irrigation in Nebraska, mentioned earlier, has aggravated erosion and poisoned underground water supplies. This development was partially financed by nonfarm investors, including some who are presumed to be foreigners.[34] There is only one positive side-effect of foreign investment in American agricultural land that I can think of: it may quicken the pace of a growing consciousness that in many ways most of the American people have more in common with José Juan than with the agroindustrial complex of this country.

The values of agribusiness are the values of agripower. Secretary of Agriculture Earl Butz, who openly referred to food as a weapon in 1974, brought with him to USDA a strong agribusiness orientation. While dean of agriculture at Purdue University, he sat on the boards of directors of Ralston Purina Company, J. I. Case Company (Tenneco), International Minerals and Chemicals, Stokely-Van Camp, and Standard Life Insurance Company of Indiana. But the confusion of agri*culture* with agri*business*, and of food with an instrument of war, has and will continue to be costly. As Wendell Berry writes:

> The concept of food-as-weapon is not surprisingly the doctrine of a Department of Agriculture that is being used as an instrument of foreign political and economic speculation. This militarizing of food is the greatest threat so far raised against the farmland and the farm communities of this country. If present attitudes continue, we may expect government policies that will encourage the destruction, by overuse, of farmland. This, of course, has already begun. To answer the official call for more production—evidently to be used to bait or bribe foreign countries—farmers are plowing their waterways and permanent pastures; lands that ought to remain in grass are being planted in row crops. Contour plowing, crop rotation, and other

conservation measures seem to have gone out of favor or fashion in official circles and are practiced less and less on the farm. This exclusive emphasis on production will accelerate the mechanization and chemicalization of farming, increase the price of land, increase overhead and operating costs, and thereby further diminish the farm population. Thus the tendency, if not the intention, of Mr. Butz's confusion of farming and war, is to complete the deliverance of American agriculture into the hands of corporations.[35]

Another uncounted cost of present "cheap food" policies is closely related to those discussed previously: regional food dependency. Earlier we described the vulnerability of poor nations that are subordinating the production of food crops for local people to the production of cash crops for export, thus becoming dependent upon the United States for food. Here we are concerned about regional food dependency within our country. The American food system was built during a period of cheap energy. As the *Time* article underscored, the United States is good at mass-producing food. But *Time* neglects the important fact that it is cheap energy "that has made U.S. agriculture the productivity wonder of the world."[36] Heavy reliance upon fossil fuel-based fertilizers and pesticides, huge tractors, combines, and other farm machinery, transportion networks that move food across continents, energy-intensive processing and packaging all help make the American food system the *least efficient agricultural system in the world measured in terms of energy efficiency.*

As energy prices continue to rise, and as the nation begins paying the true cost of soil erosion and chemical pollution, various regions in the United States will find themselves in a highly vulnerable position. We do not mean to suggest that one state or region will utilize food as a weapon against another. What we do mean to suggest is that our present agricultural system is not sustainable over the long term, and that states and regions that have come to depend on imports from California, Mexico, or the Corn Belt will likely be in trouble.

Massachusetts provides a good illustration of the shifts that have occurred since the postwar "agricultural revolution," and of the potential dangers of relying upon outside suppliers for food. According to the Massachusetts Department of Agriculture's official policy statement, "the number of farms in Massachusetts has declined since World War II from 35,000 to little more than 6,000; the number of farmland acres has plummeted from over 2,000,000 to about 700,000 in the same period. There is no indication now," the policy statement continues, "of any reversal in these alarming trends. In fact, Massachusetts can expect to lose roughly 20,000 acres of farmland or 200 farm businesses per year if no state-wide action is taken to preserve this vital resource."[37]

During the period of "cheap energy and cheap food imports," Massachusetts let its agricultural system decline. As a consequence, the study notes, Massachusetts, "which was once largely self-sufficient . . . now imports 85% of its foodstuffs."[38] "This high degree of dependency," a Governor's Emergency Food Commission report states, "can result in food emergencies whenever the usual pattern of distribution is disrupted." The commission also indicated that Boston has only a week's supply of food on hand at any given time.[39] Meanwhile, a regional conference attended by legislators from several Northeastern states indicated that the police are being trained in major American cities for action in the event of food riots.[40]

According to the Massachusetts policy statement, state residents already "pay from 6–10% more for their food than the national average." High costs are attributed to "the high cost of marketing, including transportation and out-of-state processing and packaging." Given "the costs of energy and serious questions regarding its future availability," the report concludes that "the revitalization of food production in Massachusetts is essential to our future," and recommends policies to conserve and harness agricultural land and water resources and promote local purchase of Massachusetts-grown produce so as "to make Massachusetts more nearly self-sufficient" in food.

Declining farm numbers, reduction in agricultural land base and production, and subsequent food dependency and vulnerability are common to the Northeast as a whole as well as to other parts of the country. Connecticut farms have been reduced from 15,000 in 1949 to 3,800 in 1974. Over the same period acreage devoted to agriculture fell from 1.3 million acres to less than 400,000.[41] Even New York State, where agriculture is regarded as a major "industry," lost millions of acres of farmland after World War II. Since 1940 land in farms within the state declined from about 17 million acres to 10 million. Between 1950 and 1959 withdrawals of land from farm use averaged 280,000 acres per year. The period 1959–69 brought withdrawals averaging 335,000 acres per year.[42] Assemblyman Maurice Hinchey indicated that "90 percent of the food purchased in New York comes from outside the state, much of it from as far away as California and Mexico."[43]

Local co-op people and other food activists have pointed out the inefficiency of the U.S. food system for more than a decade. It is encouraging that their concerns are increasingly being voiced by state officials, at least in certain areas of the country. Still it is discouraging to note that agribusiness and food-power advocates are firmly in control of American agricultural policy. The Department of Agriculture is planning the nation's farm future on the basis of the availability of unlimited energy supplies. The future is regarded as a simple extension of the present.

"Misuse of our natural resources," a USDA publication notes, "could have long-term adverse effects on the Nation's economy and the quality of the environment."[44] A subsequent article entitled "Farmland: Are We Running Out?" describes an apparently serious problem:

> Each year for the past 10 years, like giant hens, cities have pulled nearly three-quarters of a million acres of countryside under their wings. Roads and airports covered another 130,000 acres of rural land, and reservoirs engulfed still another 300,000 acres annually. Together, they gathered up more than a million acres each year that may never again be used for agriculture. Another 2 million acres on the average have gone out of rural land annually since 1959 into what are considered "reversible" uses for recreation and wildlife areas.

The article also notes that "urban areas now claim twice as much land as they did in 1950," and of the approximately 34 million acres expected to go out of farming from 1969 to the year 2000, "22 million would be for urban expansion, including highways and airports." The study indicates that "this would have an *insignificant effect on land available for agricultural production nationally*, but could have *a major impact around the current growth centers*" (emphasis added). Another problem acknowledged by USDA is that "strip mining lays waste to large areas." In addition, "drainage of wetland destroys wildlife habitat." Regarding the impact of strip mining on agriculture, the article says that "although the projected land area for *surface mining won't adversely affect agriculture nationally, it could have significant impact in local areas* and on the water supply" (emphasis added).

USDA also acknowledges that the energy crisis will affect agriculture. "In some areas, agriculture may experience adverse effects from the emerging energy crisis due to the development of coal and oil shale resources." The point being made is a good one: rather than conserve energy, which would involve a fundamental restructuring of an agricultural and industrial economy built during a period of cheap energy, the nation is likely to destroy agricultural land in its quest for more energy. In fact, this is already happening at an alarming rate, as residents of Appalachia can testify.

Curiously absent from USDA's discussion of the energy crisis is any mention that high energy costs (not to mention environmental costs) may make it problematic for vulnerable regions to import food over continental distances. In fact, all the problems acknowledged above by USDA officials are not considered by them to be problems because they assume that the agricultural resources of the *nation* are adequate to meet *national* needs. "We're not in a bind for agricultural land, nor are we expected to be by the year 2000," the study indicates. The reason for this optimistic assessment is that land is no longer the basic resource on which food production depends. Greater productivity, which we previously demonstrated is a result of a massive chemical overdose, has made land obsolete. This explains USDA's tolerance of soil erosion and its lack of concern about the rate at which land around urban centers is being paved over. Our "great productivity increase," the study stated, "stems from more efficient farm organization, improved machinery, increased use of agricultural chemicals such as fertilizers and pesticides, . . . more irrigation, and regional shifts in production." USDA's operating assumptions that energy is permanently cheap and that chemically intensive agriculture is efficient have led it to conclude that regional agriculture is obsolete. These assumptions have resulted in regional food dependency and vulnerability. "Nationwide, the projected 34 million acres going out of land in farms over the next 30 years," the article concludes, "won't have much effect on production. . . . But by region, it's apparent that there will be great impact in some areas, particularly the Northeast. In some parts, little agricultural land will remain."

Summary

Over the past several decades millions of Americans have been uprooted from the soil. We would be naive, I think, to easily dismiss the correlation between this uprootedness and the spiritual and value crisis so much in evidence in our country today. Millions of our children grow up believing that the origin of food is the supermarket. They, and many of us as well, no longer appreciate the delicate interface between creation, soil, and human labor. This interface, which is known as agriculture, has been rapidly replaced by agribusiness. With the onslaught of agribusiness has come violence to ourselves and our soil. Ours is literally a throw-away society, and we throw farmers off the land and replace them with chemicals and machines as easily as we dispose of nonreturnable bottles and cans. Both are signs of progress. As an American Christian who has been raised in the most consumptive and wasteful society in the history of the world, I find the fact that today the "Good News" is a disposable razor by Gillette—an alarmingly accurate symbol of our times. To unveil such a symbol is to call for repentance.

As we do violence to the soil and to one another, we also do violence to creation and thus to our Creator. The biblical principle of jubilee called for a redistribution of wealth-producing resources every fifty years (Lev. 25:10–13), and the sabbatical year provided that every "seventh year there shall be a sabbath of solemn rest for the land, a sabbath to the Lord" (Lev. 25:4). By and large we have ignored this relationship between faith, social justice, and a healthy environment. Ultimately it is God who owns the land (Lev. 25:23). We are stewards, and responsible stewardship is predicated on faith and social justice, which are the basis for human well-being and ecological harmony.

But within our capitalist economy land has become a commodity to be traded, an opportunity for investment, and no longer a public trust. As a consequence rural America is today a colony of corporate America. According to New York State Assemblyman Maurice Hinchey, 5 percent of our farmers now control over half of our farmland. The eight largest oil companies own 65 million acres of land; timber companies control 43 million acres; railroads, 23 million; in Appalachia, nine corporations own 34 percent of the land surface and all but one of these companies are controlled from outside the region.[45] In direct violation of federal reclamation law, corporations in California irrigate hundreds of thousands of acres of farmland with federally subsidized water which was meant to benefit small resident farmers. The top 2 percent of Americans own about 80 percent of privately held corporate stock, 90 percent of privately held corporate bonds, and nearly 100 percent of privately held (mostly tax-free) municipal bonds.[46] It is impossible to conceive of responsible stewardship in the context of this massive inequality in wealth and power, which is an outgrowth of our "free-enterprise" economy.

Strip mining; shopping centers, airports, and highways that sprawl over once-fertile fields; football park-sized fields covered with giant machines; planes dusting crops with chemicals; trucks loaded with produce preparing for cross-country trips; and artificially preserved, processed, and attractively packaged food that line the shelves of our supermarkets, all reflect the values of investors. But there are other costs that make up the darker side of those investments: soil erosion, chemical run-off, nonnutritious food, the victimization of small farmers, rural decay, urban sprawl, regional food dependency, and cultural bankruptcy. Still through it all USDA remains optimistic. "All the evidence indicates that U.S. agriculture can maintain," the *Fact Book* states, the high levels of production of the past few years, "and attain even higher rates, if necessary—during the next 10 to 15 years." Such optimism in the midst of a rapidly emerging social and environmental crisis is the epitome of arrogance.

As human beings we are part of creation and intimately bound to nature. The biblical writers insist that the way God's gift of land is utilized reflects the spiritual and social fabric of the nation. Just land-use was evidence of faithfulness to God, on whose blessing the people depended. Spiritual health was intimately tied to the health of the soil and to the economic health of the community (i.e., social justice). Unjust land-use, on the other hand, was accompanied by spiritual, social, and environmental decay. We cannot expect to do violence to ourselves and our soil without precipitating a social and environmental crisis:

> The earth mourns and withers,
> the world languishes and withers;
> the heavens languish together with the earth.
> The earth lies polluted under its inhabitants;
> for they have transgressed the laws,
> violated the statutes,
> broken the everlasting covenant.
> Therefore a curse devours the earth,
> and its inhabitants suffer for their guilt;
> therefore the inhabitants of the earth are scorched,
> and few people are left.
> The wine mourns, the vine languishes,
> all the merry-hearted sigh.
> The mirth of the timbrels is stilled,
> the noise of the jubilant has ceased,
> the mirth of the lyre is stilled.
> No more do they drink wine with singing;
> strong drink is bitter to those who drink it.
> The city of chaos is broken down,
> every house is shut up so that none can enter.
> There is an outcry in the streets for lack of wine;
> all joy has reached its eventide;
> the gladness of the earth is banished.
> Desolation is left in the city,
> the gates are battered into ruins.
> For thus it shall be in the midst of the earth
> among the nations,
> as when an olive tree is beaten,
> as at the gleaning when the vintage is done (Isa. 24:4–13).*

Chapter 9

SEEKING SOLUTIONS FOR THE WORLD FOOD CRISIS

Corporate, military, and government elites have succeeded in amassing many signs of power. But they have also outlined with a clarity never before realized the poverty of their power. Food power is a sign of weakness easily perceived by many Americans. Agribusiness is an economic, ecological, and cultural nightmare. A consumer society fails to bring us to happiness, spiritual rootedness, or a sense of community. Foreign expansion victimizes the world's poor. All of this is quite simply unacceptable. Many Americans are beginning to realize that they are deeply implicated in the tragedy of the world food crisis, *both as executioners and as victims.* Unknowingly we have participated in a system that oppresses hungry people worldwide while threatening our lives and well-being. Our recognition of this fact may lead us to feel angry about the deterioration in the quality of our lives and the health of our communities. Or it may trigger a reaction of moral outrage at the suffering of the poor brought on by American corporate and governmental policies. It is important for us to recognize that there is a profound connection between our own hurt and the victimization of others. If we take each seriously, the healing of one will assist in the healing of the other. Also it is important to underscore that the only cure for us, as we begin to understand the injustice around us, is to regain our power to act in stopping it.

Ironically, the poverty of power evidenced by our nation's leaders, which breeds in many Americans a deep sense of powerlessness, is beginning to give rise to new signs of hope, a profound sense of the necessity and possibility of human liberation. The lack of vision so apparent in the policies of corporate, military, and governmental elites has outlined with unusual clarity the unity of the struggle among oppressed people in poor countries and in people at home. We are bound together, vulnerable, and in need of change, and we share a common and correct perception that none of us are "surplus persons." There is a growing awareness that real power lies with the people, and that within each of us there is a source of untapped intelligence and creativity which, if collectively harnessed, is capable of human and social transformation.

It is important to keep in mind the value judgments and economic interests that are reflected in any interpretation of a problem or proposed solution. We must ask ourselves who stands to profit, and who stands to lose from a particular interpretation of what is wrong and what needs to be done. If the diagnosis and cure are coming from the wealthy, powerful, and privileged, we can expect further victimization of the poor. We have seen ample evidence of this already: overpopulation is blamed for the world food crisis, and population control programs—which are ineffective substitutes for social change—are offered by the elites as the solution. Big business and big agriculture define the farm problem in the United States as "too many farmers," and outline a solution that eliminates millions of small farms. Poor nations face balance-of-payments problems, and elites embark upon programs to increase agricultural exports, while more of their citizenry go hungry. The military-industrial complex defines the security problem of the United States as insufficient military power, and builds new weapons systems. And the United States tries to solve its balance-of-trade difficulties through food power and weapons sales rather than confront the forces responsible for the deficit.

When the elites diagnose problems and offer solutions, the result is a spiral of violence inflicted on the poor. Solutions will benefit those who at the present time are without power, prestige, and wealth only when they themselves participate in the decision-making process.

Development Through Self-Reliance

The notion of self-reliance runs counter to the modern spirit of unlimited growth and possibility. It recognizes both the value and importance of accepting limits and setting priorities. Not all things are possible, and so decisions must be made to meet certain goals while abandoning or subordinating others. To cite several examples, many poor countries face constraints on their resources and capital that make it impossible to produce automobiles for luxury consumption, and provide adequate mass transportation; build luxury apartments, and construct low-cost housing; produce fine textiles for export, and provide coarse and medium cloth to its overall citizenry; build huge multipurpose dams, and construct small irrigation projects; import capital-intensive technology, and develop labor-intensive technologies suitable to local skills and resources; train medical personnel for modern hospitals concentrated in urban areas, and provide basic health skills appropriate for rural health services and local urban clinics; finance luxury consumption through agricultural exports, and meet the basic food and employment needs of the whole population.

Development necessarily involves critical choices. No country that is establishing developmental priorities can avoid the choice of whether to gear development to the "needs" of the already privileged and the emerging middle class, or to work on behalf of, and in cooperation with, the masses of its impoverished citizenry to abolish human misery. Global hunger and poverty testify to the fact that most nations, including our own, have sought to develop for the benefit of the already privileged. But increased resistance among peasants and farmworkers, renewed demands for agrarian reform, the involvement of pastors, priests, and nuns in liberation struggles in Latin America, Asia, and Africa, a growing movement within the United States to demand better housing and health care as well as a reduction in military spending—all these developments testify to a growing consciousness of, and commitment to, new developmental goals.

Self-reliance is not a glamorous road to development. But it may in fact be the only road if one defines development in terms of meeting basic human needs, including adequate food, clothing, shelter, health care, and employment, and if one includes also a diversity of culture and the right to participate in decisions that affect one's life. Self-reliance involves forsaking certain technologies, luxury consumer items, and other goods and services commonly associated with affluence or the "good life" in favor of other values and goals. It begins with a commitment to people and to an economy of necessities. Such an economy is designed to maximize employment by utilizing locally available resources and skills and to distribute the benefits of production equitably—not according to market demand, which invariably skews both production and consumption in favor of the rich.

Earlier we described three characteristics common to many poor countries seriously affected by the world food crisis: their economies are integrated into the international free-enterprise system; production is determined on the basis of comparative advantage; and their economics are internally free-enterprise. Self-reliance would alter each of these characteristics. A country pursuing a self-reliant development path will necessarily withdraw, at least partially, from the international free-enterprise system. It will determine agricultural and industrial production according to locally available resources, skills, and needs. And it will distribute goods and services through a mechanism other than market demand.

As Denis Goulet forcefully argues in his book *The Uncertain Promise: Value Conflicts in Technology Transfer,* "austerity understood as 'sufficiency for all as first priority' is the only path which can directly attack the poverty of the poorest majorities."[1] This necessarily involves less and not more integration, less and not more imports of technology, less and not more exports based on comparative advantage. Goulet writes:

> The existing global economic order is uncongenial to the pursuit of equity and equality because its wheels are lubricated by forms of competition founded on comparative efficiency. . . . Therefore, whenever a national development plan in some poor country requires a high degree of integration with the global or regional export market, a whole gamut of supportive infrastructure investments is ipso facto rendered necessary so as to assure competitive efficiency. *Choosing integration implies selecting technology which is capital intensive and of standardized international quality. It also signifies plant scales opposed to the requirements of small and medium industry as well as an agricultural policy which favors small minorities within the agricultural sector to the detriment of the poorest and least productive.*[2]

Over the past thirty years we have witnessed a persistent movement toward large-scale multinational enterprises scanning the globe in search of cheap labor, resources, and markets. This movement has been accompanied by the tendency toward *monoculture.* By monoculture we mean the undermining of economic, cultural, and ecological diversity; the nearly universal acceptance of technology as the bearer of a salvation that has stripped citizens in the United States and throughout the world of traditional values and sources of meaning; the narrow association of efficiency with productivity without concern for compassion, justice, the abolition of mass misery, or the survival of the ecosystem; the association of development with mass consumption and quantitative rather than qualitative growth; and the undermining of decentralized local developmental approaches in favor of highly centralized, large-scale enterprises.

Self-reliance provides an important alternative to monoculture and the further internationalization of economic production. It fosters a developmental path in which people matter by affirming that people are precious and not "surplus." By gearing development to meeting basic human needs and by adopting technologies that harness locally available resources and skills, self-reliance gives common people a sense of their own power, creativity, and possibility. As Goulet writes:

> . . . a deliberate option in favor of austerity, with its attendant emphasis upon self-reliance, might lead nations to do without certain technologies if these can be acquired only at intolerable costs in money, in dependency, or in conflict with equity goals. Abstention from imports can encourage local and regional innovation, using less costly materials, less highly trained personnel, and more readily mastered techniques. To the objection that this approach condemns a nation to a subordinate role on the world scene, it must be answered that the 'high technology' strategy does not abolish misery among masses, create employment, or facilitate genuine development.[3]

Perhaps the most convincing argument in favor of self-reliance is that few countries can afford the vulnerability of food dependency. Unless nations reorder their developmental priorities so as to enable them to meet the basic nutritional needs of their overall population from indigenous resources, they will be less than independent. Food dependency is a frightening prospect, given the United States' waning political and economic power, its dependency upon food exports to lessen the impact of balance-of-trade deficits, and its apparent willingness to utilize food as a weapon. Equally important, the United States is currently overtaxing its agricultural resources. If we take into account possible future energy and environmental constraints, the United States may not be a reliable supplier for long.

Self-reliance has several important implications for the agriculture of poor countries. First, in a self-reliant developmental strategy agricultural production will be geared to internal market needs first, and will seek to maximize employment opportunities. It is virtually impossible to conceive such a development without land reform of a radical nature. The redistribution of land, and perhaps a reorganization of agricultural production into cooperatives, would make it possible to mobilize surplus population—those in the labor force who are currently unemployed or underemployed—to improve the land, build small-scale irrigation projects, construct roads and storage facilities, and cultivate the land more intensively. This will not only lead to increased food production, better distribution of income, and therefore to less hunger, but it will also stem the flow of rural migrants to urban areas and reduce population growth.

Second, agriculture in a self-reliant economy will provide a major impetus for the development of small- and medium-scale industries to provide necessary farm implements and other goods such as shoes, clothing, and housing materials for the rural population. Given the abundance of labor and the relative scarcity of capital in many poor countries these inputs would be expected to enhance the productivity of labor rather than displace it. By locating industries in rural areas and encouraging the development of technologies appropriate to locally available resources, skills, and needs, a further reduction in rural migration could be expected.

Finally, self-reliance implies a reduction in luxury imports or other capital-intensive imports and thus lessens the need to subordinate food production for local consumption to export production for the purpose of earning foreign exchange. This does not mean that poor countries will no longer export agricultural products; it does mean that they will do so from a position of strength, and that export earnings will not be used to finance the luxury consumption of elites at the expense of an impoverished minority.

We should note in passing that the United Nations' call for a New International Economic Order (NIEO), which the United States has strongly opposed as too radical, doesn't significantly address the question of self-reliance. While a new international economic order is necessary, present proposals for the most part affirm strategies of development based on integration, specialization, and production on the basis of comparative advantage. In calling for reductions in trade barriers, more stable commodity prices for raw materials, easier access to foreign technologies, better terms of aid, and rapid expansion of industrialization, poor countries are demanding a bigger piece of the global economic pie. They are not thereby addressing the values, cultural assumptions, and economic priorities that dominate the international system. Although a discussion of the NIEO is beyond the scope of this book, some of its proposals may have a positive impact on the world's poor. However, I think it is essential that we hear the voices of the oppressed within the Third World rather than the voices of government and business leaders who at the present time often profit at the expense of their people.

To summarize, self-reliance is an alternative to further internationalization of production. A natural outgrowth of choosing an elitist developmental path is that a nation will attach primary importance to integration into the international market system rather than to self-reliance. The choice for integration—a choice we should remember has been influenced by such tools of neocolonialism as aid, military assistance, and intervention—necessarily leads to a spiral of decisions that foster inequality for the reasons given below.

1. In order to compete in world markets, a poor country will often tie its developmental hopes to an outside power. This generally involves a commitment to industrial and agricultural production for export and to the production of consumer goods for members of the privileged classes rather than production geared to meeting basic human needs.

2. Efficiency, which is calculated on the basis of narrow definitions of productivity and comparative advantage, generally fails to factor in undesirable social costs as well as the waste of human and other natural resources.

3. The technology on which integration, productivity, and exports depend is generally capital-intensive and serves such values and objectives as centralization of power, mass production, and complex organization. Lower-scale technologies that depend upon utilization of local resources and skills, and that foster decentralization, simplicity, job creation, and wealth distribution as well as the local production and consumption of goods are either undermined or ignored.

If nations adopt self-reliance as a priority developmental path, this does not mean an end to international trade. It will, however, lead to a reduction in world trade, and radically alter the nature of the international system. In my view self-reliance is the key to ending world hunger, and is the only reasonable foundation on which an interdependent world can be built. So long as world trade is based primarily on the principle of comparative advantage, the poor will be victimized. The principles of internationalization of production and comparative advantage must be subordinated to other principles, which stress the desirability of using locally and regionally available resources to meet basic human needs, and which affirm the importance of economic, cultural, and ecological diversity. Self-reliance affirms the desirability and possibility of local and regional innovation and creativity, the development of indigenous technologies, and the calculation of efficiency based on human, ecological, and cultural well-being.

Self-reliance at Home

The value assumptions and technological choices central to self-reliant developmental strategies are not appropriate only for poor countries seeking to abolish mass misery. Present and future energy and environmental constraints, problems associated with the centralization of power, dependence on complex technologies, and the need for economic, cultural, and ecological diversity—all testify to the need for self-reliance in our own country as well. Foreign expansion, commitment to unlimited growth, and the deceptiveness of power associated with military might, mass consumption, and large-scale technologies and enterprises have lulled our nation into a false sense of omnipotence. The irony is that our nation and its leaders are at one and the same time powerful and powerless.

The United States is the world's leading military power; its bases dot the globe, and its weapons can ravage any city. Foreign troops armed with American weapons can put down rebellions that threaten American corporate interests. But there are a billion impoverished people throughout the militarized globe, and resistance movements continue to struggle against foreign domination and internal elites. The United States produces a nuclear weapon every eight hours, but global security or that of the American people are not enhanced as a result. The number-one military nation is not number one in providing health care to its own citizens; it is not number one in life expectancy; nor is it number one in reducing infant-mortality rates.

The nation that has described food as a weapon is curiously incapable of providing its citizens with a nutritionally adequate diet. The militarization of food, regarded by many of our nation's leaders as a symbol of power, arises out of weaknesses in the American trade position and the moral fabric of the nation. Agribusiness and agripower are accompanied by the demise of agriculture. Millions of small farms disappear, and the values of their former owners slowly erode and die in our big cities. As farming and food marketing become highly technologized and centralized, our farmers and consumers are made more vulnerable. Chemical overdoses, soil erosion, regional food dependency, reliance upon expensive and increasingly scarce resources—all these factors reveal profound weaknesses that are temporarily masked by narrow definitions of efficiency and references to food power.

The United States is the world's largest user of energy, a fact once applauded by President Nixon as an indication of strength. Today it looms as a profound weakness. Most visible is the fact that the United States imports nearly 50 percent of its oil, and this is a leading factor in the nation's trade deficit. Equally important is our failure to view the energy crisis as an opportunity to reassess the meaning of development. The values and assumptions of unlimited growth, specialization, centralization of power, mass consumption, high technology, and the corresponding insensitivity to things on the human scale as well as to the need for ecological, cultural, and economic diversity have all been fed by cheap energy.

The crisis of American power, including the energy crisis, is an opportunity for us to question long-accepted values and assumptions, and to seek solutions that affirm decentralization and human-scale technology as priority values. If one listens carefully for voices of change throughout the country, there is a tremendous clamor seldom heard by an insensitive ear. Groups such as Clergy and Laity Concerned (CALC), the American Friends Service Committee, ACORN, Earthwork, the Coalition for a New Foreign Policy, Rural America, National Land for People, the National Family Farm Coalition, small-farm energy projects, local food coops, community gardens and canneries, local food self-reliance institutes, solar-energy projects, farm and farmworker organizations, farmers' markets, organic growers' associations, and others are all working on positive alternatives to today's alienating society.

No doubt these groups do not as yet have a well-articulated vision, and communications among them are still limited. Nevertheless, they exist today as visible symbols of new hopes and possibilities. The parable of the mustard seed seems an appropriate statement of the present situation and future possibility:

> The kingdom of heaven is like a grain of mustard seed which a person took and sowed in a field; it is the smallest of all seeds, but when it has grown it is the greatest of shrubs and becomes a tree, so that the birds of the air come and make nests in its branches (Matt. 13:31–32).*

The mustard seed is small and unassuming, yet it grows into a great shrub capable of sheltering the birds of the air. I think it is significant that the kingdom is not compared to the cedars of Lebanon, symbols of majesty and power. The mustard seed grows into a sturdy shrub, neither majestic nor mighty, yet of great value. The seeds of change, carefully nurtured, will sprout as a mustard seed into a movement for social change predicated on the desirability of self-reliance.

The evolving grass roots movement for social change within the United States should not be dismissed or diminished because of the policies pursued by our nation's leaders. They have opted for big-power solutions that reinforce highly centralized, corporate-dominated developmental strategies. "Food for crude" is a slogan commonly heard in Washington, D.C. Food power, itself an expression of weakness, is used to cover over a weakness equally profound. In the coming decades America's land and water resources will be subjected to an onslaught from corporate America, particularly from the energy companies, unprecedented in our history: the strip mining of coal, coal gasification, development of shale oil, uranium mining (this will particularly affect Native Americans and their land, where approximately 50 percent of "domestic" uranium ore is located), the storage of nuclear wastes from both nuclear weapons and power facilities, and the spread of nuclear power plants throughout the countryside—all have profound implications for our land and water resources and for the culture of our nation.

These so-called solutions to America's "energy crisis" graphically illustrate that the centralization of the decision-making power itself undermines self-reliance and militates against authentic development. The top fifteen oil companies account for approximately 84 percent of the nation's oil-refining capacity, 72 percent of the natural-gas production and reserve ownership, 30 percent of domestic coal reserves, and 20 percent of coal-production capacity, plus 50 percent of the uranium reserves.[4] To the oil companies the nation's energy crisis is not a crisis of values or distorted economic priorities; it is rather an opportunity for a further centralization of their power, technological development, and profits.

Instead of developing alternative energy sources that are more in harmony with the natural environment, the solutions proposed by the oil companies further stretch the outer limits of the environment, and lead to even greater centralization of power. Increased reliance on coal, as we previously discussed, involves the destruction of agricultural land and water resources. Appalachia is already paying a severe price in terms of human health (the black lung disease) and environmental destruction (strip mining, soil erosion, water and air pollution, and flooding). Converting coal into liquid or gaseous fuel is a highly capital-intensive proposition, involves sophisticated centralized technology, and thus recommits the nation to an energy future dominated by the corporate giants. The same can be said about nuclear power, which is technologically complex, expensive, and unsafe. The nuclear accident at Three Mile Island near Harrisburg, Pennsylvania, in April 1979 confirmed the safety hazards of nuclear power. As Dr. Helen Caldicott has written in her book *Nuclear Madness*, if corporate and government leaders continue their pronuclear course "the nuclear facilities stand to inherit the earth."

As a physician, I contend that nuclear technology threatens life on our planet with extinction. If present trends continue, the air we breathe, the food we eat, and the water we drink will soon be contaminated with enough radioactive pollutants to pose a potential health hazard far greater than any plague humanity has ever experienced. Unknowingly exposed to these radioactive poisons, some of us may be developing cancer right now. Others may be passing damaged genes, the basic chemical units which transmit hereditary characteristics, to future generations. And more of us will inevitably be affected unless we bring about a drastic reversal of our government's pronuclear policies.[5]

There is overwhelming evidence that the nation's crisis of values as well as its social, economic, environmental, and energy crises are linked to an economy that demands growth, encourages specialization and concentration of power, promotes consumption as the way to happiness, and fosters inequality. Despite much evidence of the negative effects of such policies, our corporate, military, and governmental leaders continue to lead the nation down a path toward destruction. I can think of no greater arrogance than for the United States to pursue security through the expansion of its nuclear arsenal, or for this nation which in the course of several decades produced a dustbowl to proceed on a nuclear-energy course when there is now no satisfactory solution to the problem of disposing of nuclear wastes that need to be stored for 250,000 years before they lose their toxicity.

The big-power solutions proposed by our nation's leaders provide further evidence of the poverty of their power. Over the long term this will give rise to more and more individuals and groups demanding fundamental change. For example, the decision to develop nuclear power is meeting increased resistance from a variety of groups including CALC, the Mobilization for Survival, the Clamshell Alliance, and the Union of Concerned Scientists. More and more people are recognizing the need to set limits and reorder developmental priorities. The writer of Proverbs 30:8–9 recognizes the importance of setting limits:

> . . . give me neither poverty nor riches;
> feed me with the food that is needful for me,
> lest I be full, and deny thee,
> and say, "Who is the Lord?"
> or lest I be poor, and steal,
> and profane the name of my God.

There are both upper and lower limits to our needs. To violate these limits on either end is to flirt with idolatry and court disaster. Both excessive consumption and deprivation negatively affect our bodies and spirits. In a similar vein, it is as inappropriate to farm with a stick as it is to ravage the plains with 200-horsepower tractors, and as it is equally absurd to try to generate electricity with a candle as it is to do so with nuclear power. Self-reliance is not a commitment to a primitive aestheticism but a return to values of simplicity, caring, durability, and permanence. It is important to recognize that many of the changes in the American economy since World War II have increased corporate profits without improving the quality of life. They have resulted in pollution, energy waste, centralization of economic power, erosion of democracy, and a movement away from self-reliance. Millions of rural people have been forced into urban areas, and food is more highly processed and packaged and travels longer distances to our table but is less nutritious. While soil has been eroded and underground water supplies poisoned with run-off from chemical fertilizers and pesticides, the quality of the average American diet has declined. In both agriculture and industry, technologies have been adopted because they are more profitable and not because they serve human needs, use energy efficiently, conserve resources, or protect the environment.

Self-reliant development subordinates corporate profitability to the production of basic goods to meet human needs. Efforts would be made to utilize locally available resources and skills, develop technologies fostering local employment, encourage local decision-making, and preserve the quality of the environment. A self-reliant economy would necessarily be decentralized and based on renewable energy resources. For this reason solar energy is an appropriate foundation for self-reliance. The advantages of solar energy and its appropriateness for a self-reliant developmental path are described by James W. Benson of the Council of Economic Priorities of New York:

> I think it is very clear by now that most decentralized solar energy technologies are less expensive than any other technology that exists, except conservation. And the only reason they seem less economic is because of the hidden subsidies that exist for almost all other technologies . . . with oil getting the lion's share over the last several decades. Nuclear power got something like $17 billion. . . . That doesn't even count the existing subsidies in the form of tax breaks and limited liability on nuclear accidents. . . . So, solar energy is really *economic* today. . . .
>
> As far as *employment* and solar energy goes, solar will create 2 to 5 times as much employment per dollar invested, and the employment itself will be where unemployment currently exists—in those skill levels—and the employment will last longer and be more locally autonomous for the construction, operation, and maintenance of solar energy equipment. As to the *environmental* considerations, I just don't think there's any

question that solar energy and conservation are the most environmentally benign ways of supplying energy. No other can
match solar energy in this regard.

The *social* implications are . . . most interesting and most
important. Solar energy is certainly *more democratic* because it
falls on everyone everywhere and it's in *decentralized,
human-scale* forms. It's understandable; it can be installed and
maintained by users if they wish, or by home-improvement
people for those who aren't handy.

The *regional impacts* are equally as important. Solar energy
provides a *greater diversity* of energy supply systems. The
Nation's energy system becomes more decentralized and less
vulnerable. There's *more regional autonomy. The regions
don't have to rely on Federal grants and large, multinational
corporations for them.* There's *greater adaptability and flexibility* if regions are not locked into a particular technology for
20, 30, or 40 years of the life of the power plant itself. Then, too,
you have the problem of the unknowns that are associated with
the leftovers and wastes after the useful lives of the plants have
expired.

*We're being given more and more energy that we're really
not asking for.* The country is being electrified. The idea is to
turn our energy supply into 100 percent electricity. . . . When
energy demand forecasts are made, they're based on the wants
of institutions and organizations, rather than upon real needs.

. . . I think solar energy—and moving into a solar energy
future—will give us *greater national security* through reduced
imports and through decentralization of our energy supply system, making it much less vulnerable to sabotage and destruction. Our unfavorable balance of payments will be reduced and
eventually eliminated. There will be more employment; two to
five times more employment per dollar invested. . . . There
will be *less inflation,* because solar energy does not use a
"fuel." There will be less demand on depleting resources and,
again, the country can move in a direction that is more democratic because people will be making decisions for themselves.[6]

Solar energy is economical and environmentally sound; it creates
employment and reduces inflation; its available in decentralized,
human-scale forms and is compatible with democracy; it allows for
greater diversity, adaptability, and flexibility; it encourages regional
autonomy and promises to give us greater national security. The
greatest obstacle to solar energy and to self-reliance is corporate
power. The major reason that the development of alternative energy

sources such as solar energy are subordinated to oil, coal gasification, and nuclear power is that solar energy is ideally suited for a decentralized, self-reliant developmental path. It represents a genuine threat to the corporations that depend on unlimited growth, thrive on the centralization of power, and have a vested interest in further internationalization of economic production. This helps explain why in the federal energy budget for fiscal year 1979 "nuclear power by itself receives more money than has ever been spent on all of the solar resources—wind, biomass, and direct solar electric—in the history of the Republic."[7]

It also explains why we can expect much of the federal money that goes into solar energy research to be directed toward technologies such as solar satellites, which are capital intensive and highly centralized.

Self-reliance is a commitment to live within the boundaries of creation. It is therefore a commitment to reduce our claim on the world's resources. Without such a commitment the quality of our own lives will continue to deteriorate as well as the lives of poor people abroad. We can no longer afford—spiritually, morally, economically, or ecologically—to view the world as a corporation and the United States as its majority stockholder. To do so is to perpetuate hunger, poverty, and violence against the poor. Without a reduction in the claim of the United States on the world's resources, we can expect American policies, including aid, military assistance and sales, trade and investment, to lead to a further exploitation of the world's poor. For example, without self-reliance there is little likelihood that the United States human rights policies will be effective.

A recent State Department report informed Congress that human rights were being violated in varying degrees by most of the eighty-two countries that receive security assistance from the United States.[8] While the Carter Administration has restricted some military and economic assistance to "gross" violators, it has exempted "strategic" countries, and has shown almost no understanding of the relationship between American economic policies and human-rights violations. During a news conference while visiting Brazil, President Carter indicated that there is "no conflict between human rights on the one hand and the free enterprise system on the other." It was virtually "inconceivable" that American bank loans to Brazil would be restricted "under any circumstances." "This," he said, "would violate the principles of our own free-enterprise system."[9]

When Congress imposed some restrictions on economic assistance to repressive governments, more aid was delivered to countries like South Korea, Chile, the Philippines, Indonesia, and South Africa through bilateral programs and multilateral agencies over which Congress had no control. Some 69 percent of American and multilateral foreign aid now reaching the Third World does so without a Congressional review of the allocations planned on a country-by-country basis. "In fiscal year 1976," according to a report from the Center for International Policy, "the Third World got $24.9 billion in direct credits, government-guaranteed loans, government-insured investments and official debt deferments from 15 separate U.S. bilateral programs and U.S.-supported multilateral agencies, of which Congress debated, authorized and appropriated country allocations for $7.7 billion, only 31 percent of the total."[10]

It is not my intention to recount all the mechanisms by which the United States maintains its economic empire. The point I wish to underscore is that so long as our nation remains committed to foreign expansion and unlimited growth, and so long as it is assumed that what is good for American corporations is also good for the American people, the net impact of overall American foreign and economic policies will be to protect American investments, to secure access to raw materials, markets, and cheap labor, and to undermine self-reliance at home and abroad. Ironically, American foreign expansion and the exploitation of Third World peoples, which puts a disproportionate share of the world's resources at the disposal of United States-based corporations, prevents liberation at home and abroad.

Conversely, a commitment on the part of the United States to a self-reliant developmental path will enable the American people to truly assist poor countries in their efforts to overcome mass misery. Aid to villages in the form of capital resources or small-scale technology to assist in the production of solar equipment that uses local resources and skills is certainly far superior as a policy to our present system of transferring nuclear plants to poor countries. Those of us committed to social change must not underestimate the latent idealism of the American people and the legitimate desire of many Christians to assist the world's poor. In fact, millions of Americans feel a sense of betrayal when they learn that our food is being used as a weapon, and that American aid programs often serve the interests of American corporations rather than the poor. This feeling of shock is often the driving force that pushes otherwise conservative Americans into the arena of social change.

The task of organizing for a future in which all people participate in development and thereby meet their basic needs is sobering. To remain hopeful enough to keep struggling is itself an act of courage and faith. It requires a sense of mission as well as a sense of humor. American Christians committed to solving the world food crisis, including the crisis of American culture and agriculture, must participate in organizing efforts to confront and transform both the military and agroindustrial complex. Equally important we must counter a powerful ideology that associates development with mass consumption, freedom with free enterprise, and efficiency with the specialization and centralization of power. What's more, all of us have to one degree or another internalized the values of growth, mass consumption, waste, and privatism. We are going to have to be patient with ourselves and one another as we work to overcome such values.

Both our values and our economic system are in need of *fundamental* change. This poses a difficult dilemma: while the need for systemic change is the urgent task of our time, organizing is by its very nature a slow process. This makes all organizing efforts, which in the beginning are piecemeal, seem futile in comparison to the actual needs. As a consequence people often feel powerless. Some drop out of the struggle; others never even enter it; still others engage in symbolic actions that communicate their views to a small group of people, but do little or nothing to broaden the base of people committed to social change.

An additional problem is that many people are frightened at the mention of fundamental change. This is understandable. Change, whether personal or social, is nearly always a painful process. Yet it is important to realize that we and our society are changing all the time. We have witnessed in our lifetime changes of a fundamental nature. Food has been transformed into a weapon; agriculture has been reduced to a mass-production business; healthy soil has been eroded and replaced by chemicals; economic production has been internationalized; freedom and development have been redefined; and national security has been measured solely in terms of military might. So it is the direction and quality of fundamental change that concerns us, not whether or not such change will occur.

As we work for systemic change, the values implicit in the solutions we seek must be embodied in the struggle itself. A movement for social change committed to building a society that respects human beings, utilizes technologies appropriate to the human scale, places human needs before profits, affirms decentralization, and fosters economic, cultural, and ecological diversity must embody these same values in order to be successful. We must recognize our own victimization within the present economic order, and respect and understand others who are victimized. Despite the urgent need for structural change, we must recognize that there are no shortcuts to transformation. We must allow ourselves time and space to be nurtured and to nurture others.

An ever present danger is that we will set our organizing sights too high. We must faithfully begin with a mustard seed and patiently await the development of a shrub, rather than set our sights on the cedars of Lebanon. We cannot realistically expect change to come from the top down. Between one quarter and one third of our United States senators are millionaires. Numerous others are approaching this magic income figure. Free enterprise has been good to them, and we can expect that they will resist changes toward self-reliance that might challenge their political and economic interests. We have been naive, I think, to believe that we can in any meaningful sense preserve democracy while concentrating wealth and decision-making power in the hands of a small minority. In a similar vein, movements for "corporate responsibility" that encourage stock-holders to monitor and influence the ethical conduct of their corporations are of limited efficacy. It is the logic and mandate of the free-enterprise capitalist economy that growth is essential and profitability the bottom line. One of the frightening things about the problems we face, such as hunger and poverty, the centralization of decision-making power, the concentration of wealth, the practice of regarding land as a commodity, overconsumption, the destruction of the environment, foreign expansion, and the movement from diversity to specialization, is that these problems are consequences, not of some conspiracy, but of the natural workings of a "free-enterprise" economy. Therefore, corporate responsibility within the framework of our present economic system may well be a contradiction in terms.

Pointing out the limitations of an approach to social change based on legislative and corporate responsibility is not meant to breed cynicism or despair. It is an honest assessment of the difficulties that must be faced as we probe solutions to systemic problems. People engaged in campaigns promoting legislative or corporate responsibility should not necessarily abandon them. Organizing, as we mentioned previously, is a slow process that is often piecemeal. The important thing to recognize is that the force for fundamental change lies with the people. A movement for social change is therefore by its nature a grass-roots movement.

Given the fact that systemic change is a process rather than a one-time event, it seems to me that organizing should consist of two interrelated components: education and action. The action should involve a specific goal that is achievable within a given period of time. The education component uses the particular action as an occasion to raise consciousness about the need for broader social change. For example, a group may set as the goal of one of its actions the establishment of a food co-op at the end of a six-month period. In forming a food co-op, there is a potential for building alliances among a variety of groups—local farmers seeking an outlet for their produce, low-income consumers looking for better-quality food at lower prices, senior citizens and others. The formation of such a co-op is likely to be educational in itself. Consumers may learn how to understand better the problems faced by farmers, and vice versa.

Decisions may have to be made about whether or not to offer certain food items, such as vegetables from Mexico or bananas from Ecuador. The co-op can thus become an occasion for wrestling with a wide variety of food issues, thus broadening the constituency committed to fundamental change.

The principle of an educational action can operate in a variety of ways, but a key ingredient is always grass-roots support. For example, the United States desperately needs to convert many industries now producing military hardware to the production of civilian goods. Senator George McGovern has introduced bills in favor of "peace conversion" into the Senate ever since 1963, but without much success. Simply stated, peace conversion is a shift from military-related production to production of goods designed to meet basic human needs. During the period of transition to socially desirable production, workers are guaranteed an adequate income as well as retraining. Peace conversion bills provide a form of legislative action around which to mobilize public support. In addition, the existence of such bills provides a handle by which to engage people in an educational process whereby they learn first hand about the beneficiaries of the military-industrial complex, the obstacles to peace conversion, the hidden costs of militarism to the nation, and the relationship between militarism and hunger. But these bills will continue to die in Congress without massive public support. Grass-roots organizing efforts to pressure local defense industries to undertake plans for conversion are critical to building support for national initiatives. Local activities of this kind will build a base for a larger movement. Broad-based coalitions of concerned groups, including organized labor (which increasingly recognizes that military spending is not a good vehicle for creating jobs), church groups interested in hunger-related issues, and local community groups demanding that limited federal money be used to meet community needs, will unite around the common demand for peace conversion.

Another example that underscores the need for organizing at the grass-roots level is related to the struggle to shift from agribusiness to agriculture. The United States urgently needs a "peace-conversion" equivalent for agriculture. A government-sponsored farm or agricultural conversion program would guarantee farmers an adequate income during the period of transition to more ecologically and socially responsible production. The conversion program would be based on the basic assumption that small farms should be the foundation of American agriculture, and that such a development would be both socially and economically desirable. Components of an agricultural-conversion program might include government support for the following goals.

1. *Land reform.* Large landholdings could be divided and acreage

limitations and residency requirements established. Procedures could be developed to facilitate the development of farm cooperatives among farmworkers and among surplus urban dwellers who wish to return to rural areas.

2. *Organic farming.* The aim should be to reduce the risk factor for farmers so as to encourage a shift away from chemical fertilizers and pesticides toward organic methods of production and pest control.

3. *Revitalization of regional agriculture.* Efforts should be made to encourage diversified production on a regional basis, including the maintenance of a genetically diverse seed base. Reductions in United States food imports (which hurt American producers) and reductions in interregional trade, accompanied by efforts to expand local production and marketing of agricultural products, could be part of a systemic effort to reduce regional food dependency.

4. *Human-scale technology.* Various technologies appropriate for use on small farms should be designed to supplement human labor and not displace it. This would involve a radical change in the values, assumptions, and priorities of land-grant colleges.

5. *Renewable sources of energy.* Resources such as energy from the sun and wind as well as gasohol and methane conversion for *use on farms* merit support. They would reduce farm costs and dependency on nonrenewable resources, and would be important components of a self-reliant developmental strategy on a larger scale.

6. *Reduction in the acreage of feed crops.* Attention should be given to the reduction of acreage planted with feed crops while at the same time providing assistance to farmers during the period of transition to the production of other commodities.

7. *Debt relief.* Indebtedness has forced many farmers to seek to survive by expanding the size of their operations. It also often serves as a disincentive to experiment with organic approaches to pest control and increased production. Reduction or cancellation of debt could be an incentive for farmers to participate in an agricultural conversion program.

8. *Adequate pricing policies.* The exploitation of farm workers, the victimization of small farmers, and the precarious position of many larger farmers is in large measure due to their inability to exact a fair price for their labor and the goods they produce in a monopoly-controlled market. Farm commodity prices must reflect actual costs of production. They should be set on a local or regional basis (reflecting soil and climate conditions), rather than on a national or international basis, and should be set high enough to insure a good standard of living for farmworkers and small farmers.

In theory, an agricultural-conversion program takes the short-term needs of farmers seriously while implementing changes needed to insure the long-term food security of the American people. The problem with this proposal is not that these changes aren't necessary, but that they will not be achieved from the top down. American governmental leaders regard food as a political tool. Corporate giants that sell energy-intensive farm inputs are not about to abandon their profits. Land-grant colleges receive much of their funding from agribusiness corporations, and the largest American landowners have as great a stake in resisting land reform as their counterparts do in poor countries.

The point we wish to make is that while the changes outlined above are necessary and even vital to the long-term security of the American people, they can be achieved only through grass-roots organizing. Local residents will no longer tolerate the poisoning of their water supplies. Small farmers will take over a local land-grant college and refuse to leave until their demands for gearing research to small-scale technology are met. Local co-ops will continue laying the groundwork for an alternative food system linking local producers with local consumers. Church members and other morally concerned Americans will organize a massive March on Washington to demand disarmament, the dismissal of Department of Agriculture officials who tolerate soil erosion, and the removal of Department of State officials who plan the nation's strategy of using food as a weapon. Local farmers and rural residents will design small-scale windmills and solar devices to make use of locally available resources. Churches will withdraw their investments from multinational corporations and invest in small-scale enterprises that foster self-reliance. And local workers and community groups will organize to establish worker and community ownership and control of public utilities and other local industries.

Perhaps the most important thing to keep in mind in the early stages of developing a social change movement (and we are in the early stages of such a movement in the United States today) is that *the purpose of organizing is to engage people in a process*. In other words, the process people go through as they seek to achieve particular goals is as important as the goals themselves. We mentioned previously that in the next several decades America's land and water resources will be subjected to an onslaught from corporate America unprecedented in our nation's history. One possible response to this situation would be for concerned individuals or groups to pull together a conference of land-use experts, draw up a land-use policy statement for the United States, and introduce appropriate legislation into Congress. The likely result of this process is that the bill will be defeated, proponents of the legislation will become disillusioned, and the corporate onslaught will proceed unabated.

However, it is possible to envision an entirely different response to the same set of social forces. Instead of relying upon experts and immediately plunging into the legislative arena, concerned individuals and groups could mobilize a "People's Commission" or "People's Initiative," on Food, Land, and Justice. A People's Commission would be organized and coordinated by grassroots groups and would enable people directly affected by present land-use and other development priorities to speak for themselves about problems and solutions. People's hearings could be held in local communities throughout each state. At these hearings consumers, welfare rights organizers, community gardeners, co-op organizers, cannery workers, farmers, and others could share problems and discuss common solutions. Participants in these local events could mobilize support for larger, state-level hearings, which could be held at strip mines, on land owned by black farmers, on Indian reservations, in migrant-worker camps, or at other sites that graphically illustrate the social costs of corporate power and priorities in America. At the state-level hearings, representatives from various groups could again share problems and discuss solutions. Individual testimonies could be videotaped for later use. Out of each state-level hearing people could be selected to attend a "National People's Convention" on Food, Land, and Justice. The goal of such a convention might be to develop a "Food and Land Policy for the United States."

At the same time people's hearings were being organized throughout the United States, various church-related agencies and/or other groups could facilitate a similar process among people's movements within Asia, Africa, and Latin America. The goals as well as the mechanisms by which to undertake such a process would of course have to be determined by the people's movements themselves. We could expect, however, that whatever the process, these groups would probably address the injustices perpetuated by American corporate investment and United States foreign policy. Built into domestic events could be a reminder of the commonality of struggle between oppressed people within the United States and Third World peoples. And at the National People's Convention representatives from Third World People's movements could be asked to participate (this would need to be carefully done so as not to endanger the lives of the participants) and help draft the Food and Land Policy for the United States.

Churches could play a significant role in a People's Commission on Food, Land, and Justice. A process of constituency education could begin with efforts to generate interest and involvement in local and state-level hearings and in the National People's Convention. Once the Food and Land Policy Statement was completed it could be widely discussed in American churches. Videotapes of personal testimonies and of the hearing sites (strip mines, migrant camps, Indian reservations, family farms) would provide a powerful educational tool. Also, a People's Commission on Food, Land, and Justice would present people of faith with the opportunity to reflect upon the spiritual, social, and economic significance of land and land-use. It could serve as an impetus for a people's theology based on our own experiences. Equally important, such an effort would challenge America's industrial culture and thus open up the possibility of evaluating basic values and needs while challenging corporate values such as centralization of power, giantism, and unlimited growth. It might also place the churches' commitment to lifestyle reassessment in a broader and more meaningful context.

There are numerous advantages to this grassroots approach to social change as compared to legislative or corporate responsibility campaigns. A primarily legislative thrust shifts the locus for social change away from the poor and the oppressed and away from the radicalizing process and into the legislative arena of liberal or conservative politics. Legislative and corporate responsibility campaigns, however well intentioned or designed, often reinforce an erroneous view that significant changes will occur by appealing to representatives in Washington, D.C., or to the board members of corporate America.[11]

A grassroots approach such as a People's Commission recognizes that change is a dynamic process that reflects the consciousness of the agents of change and their interaction with political groups and forces. While such a people's effort may eventually have legislative fallout, it avoids the pitfalls of "putting the cart before the horse." Change, it is understood, will be generated by people. Therefore, such a people's effort would nurture a radicalizing process of politicization and conscientization. By building on the initiatives, skills, and experiences of local and regional groups, and by engaging such groups in a common task, a People's Commission would be a vehicle for building relationships of trust, which are essential to any broader movement for social change.

A People's Commission on Food, Land, and Justice is not a blueprint for social change. It is meant as an *illustration* of a grassroots approach. It is important to underscore that only the people and groups involved in organizing around food, land, and justice issues could launch such an effort and determine specific goals and strategies.[12]

There is no blueprint for social change. What is clear is that we must broaden the base of public support for change. None of us has the strength or creativity to work effectively without the support and nurturing of others. Chances are there is a group like Clergy and Laity Concerned in your neighborhood (or people interested in starting one), or other concerned groups or individuals with whom it is possible to share anger, frustration, tears, joy, hope, creativity, and vision. Listen carefully for the voices of social change in your community and add your voice to it.

Many Americans have rightly perceived that within our present political and economic system they have little control over their lives. But they have wrongly perceived that they themselves are powerless. For power lies with the people. Within each of us is a source of intelligence and creativity waiting to be tapped. If the sources of strength of the American people are joined together, they could bring about the human and social transformation of our country.

Chapter 10

HUNGER AND THE
CRISIS OF FAITH

Many American Christians are deeply concerned about world hunger. When the world food crisis intensified in 1974, churches led the way in mobilizing relief efforts. Nearly all the major American denominations have ongoing programs to explore the root causes of hunger. Citizens groups such as Bread for the World and the Interreligious Taskforce on U.S. food policy have sought to mobilize public support for legislation to affect United States policy on hunger-related issues.

However, while American Christians by and large have demonstrated a concern about world hunger, they have been generally silent about its underlying causes. We have been concerned about the victims without examining deeply enough the mechanisms that created them. It seems that many American Christians are knowingly or unknowingly locked into a bitter contradiction: they break bread together (celebrate the Lord's supper) to symbolize the faith, hope, and unity of a believing community while at the same time they are indifferent to, or offer support for, corporate and governmental policies that are breaking the bodies and spirits of hungry people around the world. The apostle Paul in his first letter to the Corinthians expressed dissatisfaction because the Lord's supper was celebrated in isolation from the needs of the poor. Apparently during the common meal to which the Lord's supper was connected, members of the upper social classes feasted while members of the poorer classes went hungry. Paul's word to the Corinthians seems equally relevant today: "When you meet together, it is not the Lord's supper that you eat" (1 Cor. 11:20). This is a harsh judgement, but it seems unavoidable in light of a world food crisis that is a consequence of social injustice.

181

In a manner similar to Paul, John the Baptist shattered the complacency of the Jews of his day. As the multitudes approached him to be baptized, he called them a "brood of vipers," and admonished them: do not "presume to say to yourselves, 'We have Abraham as our father' . . ." (Luke 3:7–8). According to John, the people were wrong to assume that salvation was a hereditary privilege. By so presuming they blocked the transformation that needed to take place in their own lives. John insisted that the choice for or against salvation was now, and that it involved their active participation. This was made clear several verses later when the perplexed multitudes asked him: " 'What then shall we do?' And he answered them, 'If you have two coats, share with those who have none; and if you have food, do likewise' " (vs. 10–11).*

I am suggesting that the existence of a world food crisis, including the crisis of American agriculture, shatters the assumptions of our faith. We must not presume to say to ourselves that we have Jesus Christ as our brother, or that Jesus Christ is our savior. Living in a nation that in many ways has caused, aggravated, and exploited hunger, we would be presumptuous if we assumed that we have understood or been faithful to the Gospel message. This is particularly true because biblical study and social analysis reveal that hunger is a consequence of social injustice; yet most American Christians do not regard justice as central to their faith. In fact, when I raise questions of social justice with American Christians concerned about world hunger, particularly questions challenging the role of American corporate and governmental policies, I am often accused of being unpatriotic and unfaithful. Criticism of the nation is perceived as a criticism of God, and justice is regarded as something alien or peripheral to the biblical message and its summons to faith.

The world food crisis is evidence of a profound crisis of faith. The biblical writers are clear that faith generally reflects the social fabric of the nation. The ramifications of social injustice quickly spread to the temple, where faith tends to reinforce rather than transform the structures of oppression. For this reason Amos announces that God's judgement will strike both temple (the center of religious life) and mansion (the embodiment of an economy of luxury built on the backs of the poor):

> "Hear, and testify against the house of Jacob,"
> says the Lord God, the God of hosts,
> "that on the day I punish Israel for its transgressions,
> I will punish the altars of Bethel,
> and the horns of the altar shall be cut off

and fall to the ground.
I will smite the winter house with the summer house;
and the houses of ivory shall perish,
and the great houses shall come to an end" (Amos 3:13–15).*

We would be naive, I think, to believe that the injustice so evident in this nation's aid, trade, and military policies has not influenced our understanding of Christian faith. How can we justify the following developments: the destruction of agriculture and victimization of small farmers; the glorification of values of bigness, growth, and the centralization of power; the association of freedom with free enterprise, and of development with luxury consumption; and the militarization of food and our overall economy? The absence of issues of justice among many American Christians is an indication that our faith may unconsciously reflect the dominant values of our society. In my view the world food crisis, including the crisis in American agriculture, will not be solved without a fundamental rethinking of the meaning of Christian faith, including a rediscovery of the centrality of justice and human transformation in the biblical message. In this chapter we shall take up the themes of biblical justice, explain their absence from many American churches, and describe their importance in the struggle for social change.

The Perspective of the Poor

The God of the Poor

The most visible victims of the world food crisis are by and large the poor. It is the poor who lack an income adequate to purchase food, who are denied access to land and other productive resources, and who have little decision-making power. Their fate is generally determined by the rich and powerful. The same was true in biblical times. Christians living in an age of injustice, hunger, and poverty must keep in mind the fact that the God of the Bible is an advocate of the poor. For the Israelites the God of the Bible was the God of the Exodus. The Egyptians "made the people of Israel serve with rigor, and made their lives bitter with hard service" (Exod. 1:13–14). The Israelites were the victims of Egypt's ill-fated policy of forced population control (Exod. 1:15–22). As an oppressed people they cried out to God, who heeded their cry by liberating them. "And the people of Israel groaned under their bondage, and cried out for help. . . . And God heard their groaning. . . . And God saw the people of Israel, and God knew their condition" (Exod. 2:23–25).

Then the Lord said, "I have seen the affliction of my people who are in Egypt, and have heard their cry because of their taskmasters; I know their sufferings, and I have come down to deliver them out of the hand of the Egyptians, and to bring them up out of that land to a good and broad land, a land flowing with milk and honey. . . . And now, behold, the cry of the people of Israel has come to me, and I have seen the oppression with which the Egyptians oppress them (Exod. 3:7-9).

It is the assurance of the Exodus that allows the poor to claim with confidence that "the Lord is on my side to help me" (Ps. 118:7). For the poor who are exploited and relegated to the "underside of history," the biblical message is good news because the Lord loves justice (Isa. 61:8); is a stronghold to the poor and needy (Isa. 25:4; Ps. 9:9); hears the desire of the meek, strengthens their hearts, and does justice to the orphan and the oppressed (Ps. 10:17-18); hears the groans of the prisoners and sets free those who are doomed to die (Ps. 102:20); hears the cry of the hungry (Ps. 107:4-6); raises the poor from the dust and lifts the needy from the ash heap (Ps. 113:7); and the Lord maintains the cause of the afflicted and executes justice for the needy (Ps. 140:12).

Those who oppress the poor insult their Maker (Prov. 14:31), and the Lord pleads the cause of the poor and despoils those who despoil them (Prov. 22:23). In the spirit of the Exodus the Psalmist writes with confidence:

> "Because the poor are despoiled,
> because the needy groan,
> I will now arise," says the Lord;
> "I will place them in the safety
> for which they long" (Ps. 12:5).

The New Testament affirmed God's special relationship to the poor. Jesus and his disciples were poor and lived among the poor. God's favor toward the poor was explicit in the Beatitudes (Luke 6:17, 20-23; Matt. 5:3f.). In the Magnificat Mary rejoiced because the Lord had "filled the hungry with good things, and sent the rich empty away " (Luke 1:53),* and Jesus announced that his mission was to "preach good news to the poor," "proclaim release to the captives," "set at liberty those who are oppressed" and "proclaim the acceptable year of the Lord" (Luke 4:18-19).

The Psalmist summarized God's special relationship to the poor:

Happy is the person whose help is the God of Jacob,
whose hope is in the Lord his God,
who made heaven and earth,
the sea, and all that is in them;
who keeps faith for ever;
who executes justice for the oppressed;
who gives food to the hungry.
The Lord sets the prisoners free;
the Lord opens the eyes of the blind.
The Lord lifts up those who are bowed down;
the Lord loves the righteous.
The Lord watches over the sojourners,
the Lord upholds the widow and the fatherless;
but the way of the wicked is brought to ruin (Ps. 146:5–9).*

Wealth and Plunder

God's special relationship to the poor is undoubtedly related to an intolerance for injustice. The prophets regarded wealth and exploitation of the poor as two sides of the same coin.

The Lord enters into judgment
with the elders and princes of the people:
"It is you who have devoured the vineyard,
the spoil of the poor is in your houses.
What do you mean by crushing my people,
by grinding the face of the poor?"
says the Lord God of hosts (Isa. 3:14–15).*

According to Jeremiah, the judgment against Israel was that "on your skirts is found the lifeblood of guiltless poor" (Jer. 2:34). The rich were like a "partridge that gathers a brood which she did not hatch" (Jer. 17:11); they store up violence and robbery in their strongholds (Amos 3:10; Micah 6:11–12), and they become wealthy through wickedness:

Like a basket full of birds,
their houses are full of treachery;
therefore they have become great and rich,
they have grown fat and sleek.
They know no bounds in deeds of wickedness;
they judge not with justice
the cause of the fatherless, to make it prosper,
and they do not defend the rights of the needy (Jer. 5:27–28).*

The wealthy plant iniquity, reap injustice, and eat the fruit of their lies (Hos. 10:13); they sell the righteous for silver and the needy for a pair of shoes (Amos 2:6–7), profit by cheating the poor in the marketplace (Amos 8:4–8), and trample upon the poor:

> Therefore because you trample upon the poor
> and take from them exactions of wheat,
> you have built houses of hewn stone,
> but you shall not dwell in them;
> you have planted pleasant vineyards,
> but you shall not drink their wine (Amos 5:11).*

Social Suffering and the Social Fabric

According to the biblical writers, the suffering of the poor reveals the religious and social fabric of nations. "The crucial manifestation of evil in Israel," writes James Luther Mays, "is the oppression of the weak. . . . Their suffering is the arresting circumstance that discloses the situation of the entire nation before Yahweh."[1] The story of the great judgment in Matthew 25:32ff. makes a similar point when it says that nations will be judged on the basis of whether they feed the hungry, clothe the naked, and so forth.

The suffering of the poor is an indication that there is something deeply wrong in the religious and social fabric of the nation. Just as a red light flashes a warning when a car is running without enough oil, the suffering of the poor flashes a warning that our political, economic, and religious systems are functioning without justice. When the poor were being trampled, the prophets conveyed the judgment of God: there is no knowledge of God in the land (Jer. 9:6); the poor are being exploited in the marketplace and dispossessed of their land (Amos 8:4–7); and the religious and political authorities are co-conspirators against God and the poor (Micah 3:9–11; Isa. 3:14–15).

The Bible was written from the "underside of history," that is, from the perspective of the poor and powerless. The rich are condemned for their exploitation of the poor, and the God of the Bible takes the side of the oppressed in the struggle for liberation (Amos 5:11–12; Luke 1:51–53). This is clearly a radical message that has been consciously or unconsciously suppressed in American churches. The Bible, which is *written* from the "underside of history," seems to be *interpreted* by dominant social groups whose faith becomes one component of a self-protecting ideology. To understand this, we must probe more deeply into the biblical message.

Co-opting Christian Faith

Idolatry

It is common today to pose the religious problem in terms of theism (belief in God) versus atheism (denial of the existence of God): there are believers and nonbelievers, and the mission of the Church is to evangelize. The Bible poses the religious problem in different terms: knowledge of the true God (I will define this shortly) versus belief in false gods (idolatry). Many people believe in one god or another, the question posed by the biblical writers is whether people believe in and know the God of the Bible. As Micah says:

> For all the peoples walk
> each in the name of its god,
> but we will walk in the name of the Lord our God
> for ever and ever (Mic. 4:5).

It is idolatry, defined here as belief in a god without knowledge of the true God, and not atheism that concerned Jesus and the prophets. And it is idolatry that accounted for their deaths. The religious problem, which has ominous political, economic, and theological implications, is that people worship and give allegiance to false gods, believing that they are being faithful to the true God. Jesus warns the disciples that the time is coming when they will be persecuted:

> They will put you out of the synagogues; indeed, the hour is coming when whoever kills you will think they are offering service to God. And they will do this because *they have not known God nor me* (John 16:2–3; emphasis added).*

Allegiance to false gods precludes knowledge of the true God. Jesus was crucified because he lived out his faith in God in history in a particular manner. He struggled throughout his life to discern the will of God, that is, to discern what it means to know God in history. And he was crucified because people rejected his life, which reflected a particular understanding of what it meant to know God. In the words of the fourth Gospel:

> Those who believe in Christ are not condemned; those who do not believe are condemned already, because they have not

believed in God's only Son. And this is the judgement, that the light has come into the world, *and people loved darkness rather than light, because their deeds were evil.* For every one who does evil hates the light, and does not come to the light, lest their deeds should be exposed. But those who do what is true come to the light, that it may be clearly seen that their deeds have been wrought in God (John 3:18–21; emphasis added).*

We tend to forget that *Jesus' crucifixion was a consequence of his life.* He proclaimed liberty to the oppressed (Luke 4:18–21), condemned the rich (Luke 6:24–26), and characterized the religious leaders of his day as the blind leading the blind (Matt. 15:14). He was executed both as a religious blasphemer (Matt. 26:65–68) and political agitator (Matt. 27:37). He was crucified because the God who was the subject of his faith declared inoperative the political and faith presuppositions of the people, particularly those of the dominant social groups.

It is possible at this point to make five observations about the relationship between idolatry and the death or exile of Jesus and the prophets:

1. Jesus and the prophets were killed by people who thought they were serving God. The executioners were people who *believed* in gods but *lacked knowledge* of the true God.

2. Evidence that those people did not know God is the fact that they killed or exiled God's messengers.

3. The executioners did not know God because they did not understand or accept what it meant to know God.

4. Jesus and the prophets understood what it meant to know God, and they tried to communicate this understanding to others.

5. Jesus and the prophets were killed or exiled because their understanding of what it meant to know God was rejected by the people.

These observations lead to a critical question: according to Jesus and the prophets, what does it mean to know God? Jeremiah answers this question: *to know God is to do justice!*

> Woe to one who builds a house by unrighteousness,
> and upper rooms by injustice;
> who makes a neighbor serve for nothing,
> and does not give just wages;
> who says, "I will build myself a great house
> with spacious upper rooms,"
> and cut out windows for it,
> paneling it with cedar,

and painting it with vermilion.
Do you think you are a king
because you compete in cedar?
Did not your father eat and drink
and do justice and righteousness?
Then it was well with him.
He judged the cause of the poor and needy;
then it was well.
Is not this to know me?
says the Lord.
But you have eyes and heart
only for your dishonest gain,
for shedding innocent blood,
and for practicing oppression and violence
(Jer. 22:13–17; emphasis added).*

Conversely Jeremiah says that in the absence of justice there is no knowledge of God:

They bend their tongue like a bow;
falsehood and not truth has grown strong in the land;
for they proceed from evil to evil,
and *they do not know me,*
says the Lord (Jer. 9:3; emphasis added).

Heaping oppression upon oppression, and deceit upon deceit,
they refuse to know me, says the Lord
(Jer. 9:6; emphasis added).

The prophet Hosea makes a similar claim:

Hear the word of the Lord,
O people of Israel;
for the Lord has a controversy with the inhabitants of the land.
There is no faithfulness or kindness,
and *no knowledge of God in the land* . . .
(Hos. 4:1; emphasis added).

The prophets also announce that without knowledge of God, worship and sacrifice are empty rituals because without justice the basis of their worship is themselves:

I hate, I despise your feasts,
and I take no delight in your solemn assemblies.

> Even though you offer me your burnt offerings and cereal
>   offerings,
> I will not accept them,
> and the peace offerings of your fatted beasts
> I will not look upon.
> Take away from me the noise of your songs;
> to the melody of your harps I will not listen.
> But let *justice* roll down like waters,
> and *righteousness* like an ever-flowing stream
>   (Amos 5:21–24; emphasis added).

Hosea made a similar point but substituted knowledge of God for justice:

> For I desire steadfast love and not sacrifice,
> *the knowledge of God*, rather than burnt offerings
>   (Hos. 6:6; emphasis added).

Jesus's life and teaching were consistent with the message of the prophets. We have already noted that he proclaimed liberty to the oppressed, condemned the exploitation of the poor by the rich, and ridiculed the Pharisees for leading the people astray. But in the story of the great judgment in Matthew Jesus states most clearly that to know God is to do justice to one's neighbor:

> Before the lord will be gathered all the nations, and the Lord will separate them one from another as a shepherd separates the sheep from the goats; the sheep will be placed at the right, but the goats at the left. Then the Lord will say to those at the right, 'Come, O blessed of God, inherit the kingdom prepared for you from the foundation of the world; for I was hungry and you gave me food, I was thirsty and you gave me drink, I was a stranger and you welcomed me, I was naked and you clothed me, I was sick and you visited me, I was in prison and you came to me.' Then the righteous will answer, 'Lord, when did we see thee hungry and feed thee, or thirsty and give thee drink? And when did we see thee a stranger and welcome thee, or naked and clothe thee? And when did we see thee sick or in prison and visit thee?' And the Lord will answer them, 'Truly, I say to you, as you did it to one of the least of these my brothers and sisters, you did it to me' (Matt. 25:32–40).*

According to Jesus and the prophets, to love and to know God is to love and to do justice to one's neighbor. The radical message for which the Son of God was crucified, and the prophets killed or exiled, is that the God of the Bible cannot be known or loved directly. Love and knowledge of God are mediated through one's neighbor. This does not mean that prayer and worship are not important. On the contrary, prayer is essential if we are to discern the will of God, and worship testifies to the transcendence of God. However, without a concrete commitment to a justice that alters the condition of one's neighbor, both prayer and worship are empty rituals that glorify false gods.

We can now go back and reformulate our fifth observation about the relationship between idolatry and the death of God's messengers: Jesus and the prophets were rejected by the people because Jesus and the prophets insisted that there is no knowledge of God without justice. If knowledge of God demands justice, we can understand John's assertion that Jesus brought light into the world, but that the people preferred darkness because of their evil deeds. They believed in a god that both tolerated injustice and could be known and loved directly through worship and sacrifice. It was in service to this god that those who knew God were executed.

The absence of the themes of biblical justice and issues of justice in many American churches takes on a somber meaning in light of our discussion of idolatry. The world food crisis, including the crisis of American agri*culture*, does not call into question the existence of God. It poses the problem of whether American Christians know, worship, and give allegiance to the God of the Bible or to some other god. If we are to know God, we cannot short-circuit our commitment to alter the condition of our neighbor, nor can we be indifferent to the structures that oppress them. The struggle for human liberation, our own and that of Third World peoples, involves a commitment to social justice and a return to authentic biblical faith.

The Dangers of Wealth

Americans have long taken pride in the wealth of our nation and in that of individual Americans. But according to the biblical writers, wealth is dangerous because it fosters idolatry. Wealth encourages belief in a god, but militates against knowledge of the true God:

> "Do not lay up for yourselves treasures on earth. . . . For where your treasure is there will your heart be also. . . . No one can serve two masters; for either they will hate the one and love the other, or they will be devoted to the one and despise the other. You cannot serve God and mammon" (Matt. 6:19,21,24).

When a young man asked Jesus what he should do to inherit eternal life, Jesus told him to sell his possessions, to give them to the poor, and to follow him.

> At that saying his countenance fell, and he went away sorrowful; for he had great possessions.
>
> And Jesus looked around and said to his disciples, "How hard it will be for those who have riches to enter the kingdom of God! It is easier for a camel to go through the eye of a needle than for a rich person to enter the kingdom of God."
>
> And they were exceedingly astonished, and said to him, "Then who can be saved?" Jesus looked at them and said, "With human beings it is impossible, but not with God; for all things are possible with God" (Mark 10:22–23, 25–27).

Unfortunately we often focus on the apparent qualifier at the end of this passage rather than on the dangers and possibilities Jesus outlined. Our image is of God smuggling rich people into the kingdom. I doubt that Jesus had in mind some otherworldly qualifier when he affirmed that all things are possible with God. It is far more likely that he was making a statement: it is very difficult, though possible in the context of God's love, for rich people to hear and accept the word of God. Jesus made a similar statement in the story about the rich man and poor Lazarus (Luke 16:19–31). It is common to interpret this passage as consoling the poor with the promise of heaven, but it is really directed to the rich. Once again Jesus was less than optimistic that the rich would accept the word of God, which demanded that they should radically change their lives: "If they do not hear Moses and the prophets, neither will they be convinced if some one should rise from the dead" (v. 31).

In the parable of the sower (Luke 8:4–15), the rich received the word of God like thorns that choked the word (v. 14):

> And as for what fell among the thorns, they are those who hear, but as they go on their way they are choked by the cares and riches and pleasures of life, and their fruit does not mature.

Why is it so difficult for rich people to accept the word of God? The biblical writers suggested three reasons. First, wealth has a sort of mesmerizing effect on the rich. They are able to celebrate their prosperity isolated from the poverty and needs of others. Life goes well for them; they are comfortable and complacent. Jesus tried to break down this complacency in his many teachings on wealth, including his "woe sayings" (Luke 6:24–26) and the following parable found in Luke 12:16–21:

And he told them a parable, saying, "The land of a rich person brought forth plentifully; and the rich person thought, 'What shall I do, for I have nowhere to store my crops? Ah, I will do this: I will pull down my barns, and build larger ones; and there I will store all my grain and my goods. And I will say to my soul, *Soul, you have ample goods laid up for many years; take your ease, eat, drink, be merry.' But God said, 'Fool! This night your soul is required of you;* and the things you have prepared, whose will they be?' So are they who lay up treasure for themselves, and are not rich toward God" (emphasis added).*

A second reason why rich people find it difficult to accept the word of God is that prosperity makes it nearly impossible for them to hear God's word as judgment. When the word of God challenges the assumptions on which their systems of politics and faith rest, they regard their wealth as a vindication of those assumptions. The prophets Hosea and Amos explicitly described this danger. Hosea notes:

A trader, in whose hands are false balances, loves to oppress.
[Yet] Ephraim has said, "Ah, but I am rich,
I have gained wealth for myself";
but all these riches can never offset the guilt
which has been incurred (Hos. 12:7–8).*

Amos condemns Israel's affluent society, which was built on the backs of the poor (Amos 6:1–6). In the first verse he proclaims God's judgment:

Woe to the carefree in Zion
and the confident in Mount Samaria,
the preeminent people of the first of nations
to whom the house of Israel comes.*

In the second verse Amos records the response of the upper classes, which because of their affluence are unable to hear God's word. They tell Amos that if he would compare the prosperity of Israel to that of surrounding nations he would surely see the absurdity of proclaiming God's judgment:

[Amos], cross to Calneh and look;
go from there to great Hamath;
then go down to Gath of the Philistines;
Are they better than these kingdoms,
or their territory greater than yours?*

After noting their response, Amos records verses 3–6:

> Woe to those who lie on ivory beds,
> and sprawl upon their couches;
> who eat lambs from the flock,
> and calves from the stall,
> who improvise to the sound of the harp,
> like David they compose for themselves melodies,
> who drink from great wine bowls,
> and with the best oil anoint themselves—
> *but they feel no pain*
> *at the ruin of Joseph* [*Israel*] (emphasis added).*

For members of the upper classes of Israel, their prosperity is evidence that Amos is a false prophet. Their wealth is an arrogant symbol of the viability of their political economy and religious cult. Wealth results in a tunnel vision narrowly focused on prosperity; this makes it nearly impossible for them to accept the word of God as a judgment.

Finally, it is difficult for the rich to accept the word of God because God's word demands justice. Justice poses problems because the biblical writers insist that wealth is usually gained by exploiting the poor (e.g., Hos. 12:7–8; Amos 5:11–15, 8:4–8). Thus God insists that unjust merchants and other rich Israelites are people "full of violence" (Mic. 6:11–12), and that the rich are "those who store up violence and robbery in their strongholds" (Amos 3:10). The point here is similar to that of the previous section on idolatry. People rejected Jesus and the prophets because Jesus and the prophets were insisting that knowledge of God depended on justice. For many the price of acceptance of God's message was too high. They preferred darkness to light because of their evil deeds. When Jesus says that we cannot serve God and mammon (Matt. 6:24), he forces us to choose between wealth and justice; we cannot have it both ways.

> And there was a man named Zacchaeus; he was a chief tax collector, and rich. And he sought to see who Jesus was, but could not, on account of the crowd, because he was small of stature. So he ran on ahead and climbed up into a sycamore tree to see him, for he was to pass that way. And when Jesus came to the place, he looked up and said to him, "Zacchaeus, make haste and come down; for I must stay at your house today." So he made haste and came down, and received him joyfully. And when they saw it they all murmured, "He has gone in to be the guest of a man who is a sinner." And Zacchaeus stood and said to the Lord, "Behold, Lord, the half of my goods I give to the

poor; and if I have defrauded anyone of anything, I restore it fourfold." And Jesus said to him, "Today salvation has come to this house, since he also is a son of Abraham. For the Son of man came to seek and to save the lost" (Luke 19: 2–10).

Before we close this discussion of the dangers of wealth, there is one other point to be made. It is common for rich people to react defensively when the dangers of wealth are discussed. This response is understandable. But it is regrettable that rich people often feel attacked and presume that the motives of their "attackers" are spiteful. It is interesting that Mark prefaced Jesus' suggestion that the rich man should sell his possessions, give them to the poor, and follow him (Mark 10:21), with these words: "*And Jesus looking upon him loved him, and said to him . . .*" It is because Jesus loved him that he issued the command.

To understand this, it is important to recognize that in all his teachings on wealth Jesus was interested in two interrelated liberations. First, he wanted to liberate the rich from the idolatry of their wealth. Second, Jesus was concerned with the liberation of the poor. We have noted previously that the biblical writers insisted that wealth is not accrued in a vacuum; it is gained by exploiting the poor. Jesus not only told the rich young man to sell his possessions but he instructed him to redistribute wealth to the poor on whose backs it had been accrued in the first place. When the rich young man refused to accept the word of God, he was, in John's words, "condemned already," because he had effectively blocked both his own liberation and the liberation of the poor.

The absence of themes of biblical justice and of issues of justice in American churches is probably related to the relative affluence of many congregations. My experience as an organizer is that wealthy congregations find it difficult to talk about, or to confront, the *causes* of the world food crisis. The international free-enterprise system has not only brought them prosperity but it has effectively removed them from the victims of that system. For the rich it seems inappropriate to raise questions about free enterprise, particularly in the context of Christian faith, which for them is a personal statement of their belief in God. Yet if we are to allow the word of God and the world food crisis to challenge the assumptions that undergird our faith and politics, we must recognize the dangers inherent in our affluence.

Depoliticizing the Biblical Message

To politicize means to "make political." Conversely, to depoliticize is to take something that is political and make it less political or nonpolitical. By and large most American Christians believe strongly that the biblical message and the role of the church transcend politics. "Politics," I have been told numerous times, "does not belong in the church." For example, several years ago some friends and I asked members of our church board for permission to do a worship service, including a sermon addressing the involvement of the United States in the Vietnam War. We were told that we could do a service addressing the general problem of war, but that we could not address questions related to American involvement in a specific war because this was a political issue that might alienate members of the congregation. The issue of Vietnam was not to intrude on the mission of the church which, according to the board, was to announce the gift of salvation through the death and resurrection of Jesus Christ.

The seemingly apolitical posture adopted by the board is representative of the vast majority of American Christians, including theologians, ministers, and lay people. The biblical message, according to the dominant view, transcends politics, economics, and history. The problem with an apolitical theology or interpretation of Scripture is that it ignores the fact that we do not read or interpret the Bible in a vacuum. Apolitical theology more often than not ends up being profoundly political. We know from history that faith and theology often serve the political and economic interests of the believing community. Slaveholders, for example, justified slavery on the basis of faith in a god who ordained slavery. In a similar way, American foreign expansion was often undertaken as if it had been divinely sanctioned. Senator Albert J. Beveridge of Indiana in an 1898 speech said:

> American factories are making more than the American people can use. American soil is producing more than they can consume. Fate has written our policy for us; the trade of the world must and shall be ours. . . . We will cover the ocean with our merchant marine. We will build a navy to the measure of our greatness. Great colonies, governing themselves, flying our flag and trading with us, will grow about our posts of trade. Our institutions will follow our trade on the wings of our commerce. And American law, American order, American civilization, and the American flag will plant themselves on shores hitherto bloody and benighted, by those agencies of God henceforth made beautiful and bright.

On another occasion Senator Beveridge spoke of the United States as God's "chosen nation":

God has . . . made us the *master organizers* of the world to
establish system where chaos reigns. He has given us the *spirit
of progress* to overwhelm the forces of reaction throughout the
earth. He has made us adept in government that we may administer government among savage and senile peoples. Were it
not for such a force as this the world would relapse into bar-
barism and night. And of all our race He has marked the American people as His *chosen nation* to finally lead in the *regenera-
tion of the world.* This is the *divine mission* of America, and it
holds for us all the profit, all the glory, all the happiness possible to man. . . . What shall history say of us? Shall it say that we
renounced that holy trust, left the savage to his base condition,
the wilderness to the reign of waste, deserted duty, abandoned
glory? No! They founded no paralytic government, incapable of
the simplest acts of administration. . . . They unfurled no re-
treating flag. That flag has never paused in its onward march.
Who dares halt it now—now, when history's largest events are
carrying it forward.[2]

Foreign expansion, which brought prosperity to the United States
while victimizing the poor, was undertaken with a sense of divine
mission. Not surprisingly, as the wealth of the nation grew, so too did
the American churches. Our situation parallels the idolatry described by Hosea during the prosperous years of Jeroboam:

> Israel is a luxuriant vine
> that yields its fruit.
> The more your fruit increased
> the more altars you built;
> as your country improved
> you improved your pillars (Hos. 10:1).*

While many churches claim to be apolitical today, they tend to
reinforce the dominant values of American society and reflect the
bias of their politically conservative members. The absence of
themes of biblical justice and issues of justice reflects the political
and economic interests of many congregations, which tend to con-
fuse patriotism with biblical faith. Issues of justice are political and
therefore excluded from the church. One can hardly expect justice
issues to have a central place in the life of the church when the
themes of biblical justice are absent or peripheral. It seems important therefore to unmask the churches' claim to political neutrality.
In the following scenarios I hope to demonstrate that it is impossible
for the church or its theology to be apolitical.

Scenario 1. It is "Social Concern Sunday" at your local church, and the topic is world hunger. Your minister or priest chooses the parable of the Good Samaritan (Luke 10:29–37) as the basic text of the sermon. After providing a few statistics on the magnitude of the world hunger problem, he or she describes the serious situation in the Philippines where poor weather has resulted in an unusually poor harvest. The good consciences of church members immediately stir as they hear the story of the Good Samaritan who helped the stranger who had been left beaten and stranded by the roadside. There is a near consensus when it is suggested that the congregation has a social responsibility to act as a Good Samaritan to hungry people in the Philippines. After the sermon a special offering is collected for hunger relief. Later the members thank the minister or priest for a fine sermon that reminds them of their Christian responsibility.

Scenario 2. The setting is much the same as that of Scenario 1. It is "Social Concern Sunday," the topic is world hunger, and the congregation, sermon text, and sermon are identical. The special concern is hunger in the Philippines, and a special offering is taken up for the relief of hunger. However, this is only the beginning of an unfolding drama. After the service members of the congregation come together during the coffee hour to discuss the sermon.

Mr. McGuire: Pastor Johnson, that was one of the finest sermons I have heard in some time. I am grateful that you brought this problem before the congregation, and I am pleased to contribute to the relief fund.

Miss Morgan: I agree. I think the situation there sounds terrible, and we must do what we can.

Ms. Roberts: Pastor Johnson, I hesitate to speak out, but feel as though I must. On Wednesday I returned from a three-month stay in the Philippines. With me this morning is Carlos Pérez, a citizen of the Philippines who recently fled his country. On my recent trip I spent a great deal of time in rural areas. While it is true that poor weather has contributed to hunger in the Philippines, there are other factors that seem to be more important. More and more land is being used to produce cash crops for export while the food needs of local people go unmet. Peasants and small farmers are forced off their land to make way for large producers that contract production with United States-based corporations such as Del Monte, Castle and Cooke, and United Brands. These corporations with a worldwide marketing network are not concerned about the poverty of the local people.

Mr. Jones: Here we go again—people bad-mouthing American corporations. Why don't you take your radical ideas somewhere else?

Ms. Roberts: I know that these are sensitive issues, and that some of our members are executives of companies that conduct operations in the Philippines. But what I saw with my own eyes is terrifying. Carlos here speaks almost no English, so I will try to tell his story. Members of Carlos's family have farmed the same land for generations. However, recently the authorities said that the family did not have a proper title to the land. Its members were forced to leave. Their land is now owned by a large farmer who produces bananas for Del Monte. When Carlos tried to organize other displaced farmers and peasants, he was arrested and tortured. Priests and nuns who have tried to be Good Samaritans by confronting the groups that victimize the poor have also been arrested. What disturbs me most is that the United States is giving substantial economic and military assistance to the government of the Philippines that makes this exploitation possible. The stable investment climate so prized by American businesses is being paid for with the blood of the Filipino people.

Mr. Langbar: I'm an executive of a corporation that does business in the Philippines. The agribusiness companies you ridicule as well as other United States-based corporations help the Philippines earn foreign exchange needed for development. American military assistance helps maintain stability, as you suggest, because it is necessary to counter a communist threat.

Mr. Garber: I have been in this congregation for more than thirty years. During this time I have learned that the best attitude in controversies of this type is a conciliatory one. These are political issues, and they should not be discussed in the church. The important thing for us as Christians is that, *for whatever reason,* people are hungry in the Philippines. Therefore, it is the responsibility of this congregation to avoid getting embroiled in politics. We must send relief aid to these people.

Many Members of the Congregation: Yes, that's right!

Scenario 1 is not uncommon. I have attended services like it many times, and I have preached sermons with a similar text and theme. Scenario 1 seems to be a perfect example of an apolitical church. The pastor and congregation are well intentioned, a sermon is preached, people become aware of the problem of hunger, they want to help, and a collection is taken for hunger relief. But Scenario 2 demonstrates that no church or theology can legitimately claim to be apolitical. Scenarios 1 and 2 are both political. In fact, the political and faith presuppositions of the congregation are the same in both scenarios. The only difference is that in Scenario 1 these presuppositions lie beneath the surface and remain nearly invisible whereas in Scenario 2 a citizen and visitor of the Philippines challenge these presuppositions and force them to the surface.

In the above scenarios it is possible to identify, with a certain amount of reading between the lines, the following political and faith presuppositions of the congregation:

1. The church is not the place to deal with political conflicts and issues.

2. It is okay to talk about the *problem* of hunger but it is not okay to discuss the *causes* of hunger, particularly if those causes challenge the interests of members of the congregation.

3. Multinational corporations are engines of development.

4. Hunger is a fateful accident, or it is the result of social forces unrelated to the economic well-being of citizens of the United States.

5. Christians are obligated to respond charitably to hungry people.

6. Theology is politically neutral; it does not interpret the biblical message in light of concrete events but transcends politics, economics, and history.

7. The mission of the church transcends politics; it is to preach salvation through Jesus Christ.

8. The church is interested in reconciliation made possible by the death and resurrection of Jesus; this reconciliation isn't related to questions of justice or injustice.

For the congregation these so-called apolitical presuppositions probably have the following *political* and ideological consequences:

1. The congregation, in fact, adopts a conservative political posture that perpetuates the structural causes of hunger and poverty.

2. The economic interests and political ideology of individual members are protected because they are insulated from criticism.

3. Theology becomes one component of a self-protecting ideology.

4. Hungry people are viewed as objects of charity rather than as victims of social injustice.

For hungry people in the Philippines the "apolitical" presuppositions of American Christians are likely to have the following *political* consequences:

1. American military and economic assistance will continue to reinforce unjust political and economic systems that oppress them.

2. More peasants and small farmers will be forced off the land.

3. Large producers will continue contracting production to United States-based multinational agribusiness corporations.

4. Acreage devoted to cash crops for export will increase while the food needs of local people are ignored.

5. Hunger will become a permanent feature in the Philippines. American Christians will have to continue to send relief aid, al-

though they may eventually feel powerless and blame overpopulation for the food crisis.

It is clear that it is impossible to divorce the church or theology from politics. "Apolitical" theologies end up by being conservative political theologies. But before we move on, it is possible to take Scenario 2 one step further. You will recall that Mr. Garber, a highly respected and conciliatory member of the congregation, received overwhelming support when he stated that the political issues raised by Ms. Roberts should not be discussed in church. For him the important thing was that, regardless of the reason why people are hungry in the Philippines, it was imperative for Christians to respond charitably to that need. The problem with this view is that *it assumes that charity is an apolitical act.*

Humanitarian assistance is always a political act that has political implications. To demonstrate this, we have only to consider that Ms. Roberts could have replied as follows to Mr. Garber's suggestion that the congregation simply send relief and therefore avoid political controversy:

Ms. Roberts: Mr. Garber, I do not think that sending aid is a way of avoiding controversy. On the basis of my observations, it is likely that the government of the Philippines will misuse church aid. For example, the friends and relatives of peasants and farmers involved in organizing protests are not allowed to receive aid. In addition, food aid in the past has served to reinforce the trend toward the production of cash crops for export, which fosters food dependency. Finally, in my view giving food aid to the Marcos regime relieves an unjust government of the necessity of providing relief services, thereby freeing up funds and resources that are used to repress and torture people who resist its policies.

So even charity is a political act. The only way for the church to cease to be political is to cease to be. If issues of justice are absent from many American churches, it is because by and large biblical and economic justice conflict with the perceived interests of many Christians. Economic injustice is tolerated because it is expedient. In such a setting it should not be surprising that, consciously or unconsciously, faith becomes a self-protecting ideology that insulates Christians from the world in which they are called to give witness.

Christian Faith and Social Change

The world food crisis, including the crisis of American agriculture, shatters the assumptions that undergird our faith and politics. We have somehow lost sight of the dangers of wealth and idolatry. In trying to depoliticize our faith we have placed it in the service of an economic system that victimizes the poor. This seemingly dismal assessment of Christian faith in the United States in fact opens up the possibility for spiritual renewal and social transformation. Many Americans take their faith *very* seriously. No doubt some will be outraged at the suggestion that faith has been unconsciously fused with patriotism, or that the god to which we give allegiance is not the God of the Bible. We would be naive, I think, to underestimate the conservative backlash to such a suggestion. After all, Jesus was crucified and the prophets were killed or exiled. Yet we would be naive and unfaithful if we denied the possibility of human transformation. With a growing consciousness that the international free-enterprise system is victimizing people at home and abroad, we can expect more and more Christians to commit themselves to the cause of global justice. Such a commitment will undoubtedly lead many to re-evaluate and reinterpret the meaning of authentic Christian faith.

Dynamic Love

The foundation of Christian faith is love. Foremost is God's love for us. The Incarnation (God's entering human history as a human person) testifies to God's commitment to human liberation. The crucifixion is evidence of the difficulty of the task. The resurrection is a symbol of hope. Because God loves us, we are capable of loving one another. As the author of John's First Epistle writes:

> Beloved, let us love one another; for love is of God, and those who love are born of God and know God. Those who do not love do not know God; for God is love. In this the love of God was made manifest among us, that God sent his only Son into the world, so that we might live through him. In this is love, not that we loved God but that God loved us and sent a Son to be the expiation for our sins. Beloved, if God so loved us, we also ought to love one another. No one has ever seen God; if we love one another, God abides in us and his love is perfected in us (1 John 4:7–12).*

Because of God's love for us, we are able to accept and love ourselves. This does not imply a destructive sort of narcissism, but rather a recognition that each of us is infinitely more precious than our alienating society would have us believe. None of us is surplus. We are sons and daughters of God, transformed by love and capable of social transformation. Thus Jesus indicated that we were to love our neighbor as ourself (Matt. 19:19). On two commandments depend all the law and the prophets: "You shall love the Lord your God with all your heart, and with all your soul, and with all your mind," and "You shall love your neighbor as yourself" (Matt. 22:37, 39).

If God's love is the starting point of faith, the condition of our neighbor is the yardstick by which we judge the effectiveness of our love and the authenticity of our faith. Biblical love is not a measure of our depth of feeling; it is the embodiment of our commitment to change the condition of our neighbor, which depends on our willingness to undergo a personal transformation.

> By this we know love, that Jesus laid down his life for us; and we ought to lay down our lives for our sisters and brothers. But if we have the world's goods and see our brothers or sisters in need, yet close our heart against them, how does God's love abide in us? Little children, let us not love in word or speech but in deed and in truth (1 John 3:16–18).*

Biblical love seeks to be effective. It is a love that flows from the awareness that the God who loves us is not indifferent to injustice, but takes the side of the poor and oppressed in the struggle for human liberation. A world in which a billion people are impoverished because of unjust social structures is a world in which the crucifixion is an ongoing historical reality (Matt. 25:42ff.). It is a world where Christian love must seek to overcome oppression. In this context it is important to remember that the liberation of the rich and poor is deeply connected. The Gospel is "good news" to both, but it is more difficult for the rich to hear its summons to faith.

The desire to make love effective necessarily leads Christians into the political and social arena. For too long American Christians have insisted that the biblical message and theology are apolitical. As a consequence they have avoided the analysis of social problems. While caring about hungry people, for example, they have been largely indifferent to United States corporate and governmental policies that victimize the poor. Today many American Christians who started, as I did, with a simple concern about world hunger, are following their concern to its logical conclusion. Our nation's involvement in social injustice has led many to ask the radical question posed by the multitudes: "What then shall we do?" The emerging answers are to rethink the meaning of faith, return to the biblical God of justice, and commit oneself to both a personal transformation and the growing movement for fundamental social change.

Throughout the world, priests, pastors, nuns, and other Christians are standing in the forefront of movements for social justice. In South Korea, the Philippines, Brazil, Chile, Guatemala, Peru, and elsewhere where people are denied basic economic, political, social, and cultural rights, Christians are being arrested, tortured, and murdered because they dare to align the Gospel with the struggle for liberation. Their courage and strength are giving hope to millions of people worldwide. Their message is clear: the God of the Bible to whom they give their allegiance and for whom they risk their lives is committed to the liberation of the whole person. Therefore the struggle for liberation, including economic self-reliance, political independence, cultural diversity, and spiritual renewal, is linked to authentic Christian faith.

The bitter exploitation of people in Latin America has given rise to a theology of liberation which insists that the starting point for theological reflection is the suffering of the poor. Theology is always a second act seeking to explain the meaning of Christian faith in the light of social structures that victimize the poor and in light of the struggle for liberation. The church, if it is to effectively witness to the love of God, must participate in the process of social transformation. As Gustavo Gutiérrez writes:

> In Latin America the world in which the Christian community must live and celebrate its eschatological hope is the world of social revolution; the Church's task must be defined in relation to this. Its fidelity to the Gospel leaves it no alternative: the Church must be the visible sign of the presence of the Lord within the aspiration for liberation and the struggle for a more human and just society. Only in this way will the message of love which the Church bears be made more credible and efficacious.[3]

Liberation theology has been harshly criticized by conservative critics who view it as a politicization of the faith. But no doubt a major reason why Americans find liberation theology discomforting is that the social oppression out of which it grew is in large measure caused by alliances between American corporations and the elites of poor countries. As Robert McAfee Brown writes:

> If we take liberation theology seriously, we will have to re-examine our jobs, since many of them, the minute we begin to explore their implications, will be found to be contributing to the ongoing oppression of other peoples. We will have to become uneasy with our affluent standard of living as we recall that it is enjoyed in a world where fifteen thousand people starve to death every day. We will have to question the whole fabric of our culture when we realize that those who weave it

stand on the broken backs of men and women who are paid exploitative wages to produce the luxury goods we don't really need. Here is a faith we want to doubt for fear it may be true. . . . Who, in such a situation, wants to confront the full impact of liberation theology? No one. And so, quite understandably, we prepare a variety of resistances to it.[4]

But the world food crisis, including the crisis of American agriculture, is leading more and more American Christians to question corporate power and priorities and the social, cultural, and religious fabric of the nation. A new and revitalized church is sprouting like a mustard seed out of the ashes of oppression inflicted by the old church and its bedfellow, corporate power. Spiritual renewal and political transformation are emerging as integrated movements that affirm the necessity, desirability, and possibility of social change.

Dynamic Faith

Christians have by and large regarded faith as an unquestioning belief or trust in Jesus as the Son of God. They have professed Jesus as the Christ and have centered their faith on the crucifixion and resurrection through which Jesus became the Christ, bore the sins of the world, and guaranteed our salvation. One has a sense that according to this view, Jesus entered the world fully conscious that he was and is the Son of God. His mission, of which he was aware, was to save humanity from sin by being crucified and later resurrected from the dead. His reward was that he would be worshiped throughout the ages by grateful followers. This view of Jesus reminds me of a script from *Mission Impossible*. It treats the believing community as a TV audience whose only responsibility is to turn to the correct channel, sit back, and enjoy the show. Jesus, the predestined Son of God, is our salvation! He is an actor, and we are his grateful observers!

The limitations of this view are that those who profess it generally place little importance on the historical life of Jesus and often turn him into an idol. It is important to realize that Jesus preached the kingdom of God and not himself. "And he went about Galilee, teaching in their synagogues and preaching *the gospel of the kingdom* and healing every disease and every infirmity among the people" (Matt. 4:23). The kingdom of God, according to Jesus, was breaking into history in a new and decisive way. His actions reflected the kingdom as he called people to faith by creating a new situation: he healed the sick, forgave sins, and announced his mission in terms of jubilee (Luke 4:18–19).

Jesus explicitly rejected a messianic role that enabled people to avoid participating in personal and social transformation, a role envisioned by most American Christians. In the temptation narrative (Matt. 4:1–11; Luke 4:1–13) he refused to turn stones into bread, to rule the kingdoms of the world, or to participate in a miracle at the pinnacle of the temple. Yet in his historical life he demonstrated great compassion for the hungry (Matt. 14:14f.; Luke 6:20ff.; 12:15ff.; 14:12); he ridiculed the Pharisees for neglecting justice (Luke 11:42); he drove the moneychangers out of the temple (Matt. 21:12f.); and he was regarded by the political authorities as such an important threat that they executed him as a political agitator (Matt. 27:37).

Jesus recognized the importance of creating an order within which people would be fed, he understood the need to revitalize the idolatrous temple, and he was fully aware that unjust political and economic structures and authorities were in desperate need of transformation. But he refused to become a magician who would miraculously solve all human problems. All of us, in a certain sense, long for such a savior who would effectively operate outside ourselves. But Jesus was not such a miracle worker. Instead, he dedicated his life to service in God's kingdom, thereby opening up new possibilities for us all. No longer must the poor be resigned to their fate, nor the rich bound by their wealth, nor religion chained to injustice and idolatry. It is possible, through God's grace and love, to be "born anew" (John 3:3). This is not some simplistic spiritual renewal. It is a total reshaping of one's thinking, life, and commitments in line with the new possibilities of the kingdom.

It is also important to underscore the following important point that was made by Jon Sobrino in his excellent book *Christology at the Crossroads*. While Christians often talk about faith *in* Jesus, it is equally important to talk about the faith *of* Jesus.[5] Throughout his life Jesus demonstrated his faith in God. His trust was absolute, and in this sense his faith was unyielding. Yet the actual fleshing out of the meaning of his faithfulness took place in history as he struggled to determine the will of God in particular situations of conflict. Jesus did not enter human history with a map outlining the course of his life to which he periodically referred to insure he was on the right path. He fasted and prayed in an effort to discern God's will. He proceeded in faith with all the uncertainties we face today as we struggle to discern the will of God for our lives in the midst of a world food crisis brought on by social injustice.

Only by respecting the faith of Jesus can we understand the meaning of authentic Christian faith. Jesus discerned the will of God in history and consequently proceeded on a path that led to the cross.

He was crucified because he took sides with the oppressed, thus opening up the possibility of liberation for both rich and poor. He revealed the hypocrisy of the Pharisees and the idolatry within the temple; he insisted that God was the Lord of history and unmasked the power of political authorities. And he insisted that there could be no knowledge of God without justice, that there was no easy liberation.

Above all, Jesus was and is the Son of God because of his unerring commitment to the will of God and his unyielding faith and trust. Even as it became clear that the kingdom was not arriving as speedily as anticipated, and that his death was imminent, Jesus was able to say: My God, "if it be possible, let this cup pass from me; nevertheless, not as I will, but as thou wilt" (Matt. 26:39). Jesus, who discerned the will of God throughout his life, now discerned that his life was culminating with a cross and not with the fulfillment of the kingdom. He went to the cross without the assurance of the resurrection; he proceeded on faith alone. On the cross Jesus saw his death as the death of his goals: "And about the ninth hour Jesus cried out with a loud voice . . . ,'My God, my God, why hast thou forsaken me' " (Matt. 27:46).

But the way of the cross was vindicated by the resurrection. God accepted the course of action that thrust Jesus into conflict with all the forces of this world that resist personal and social transformation. Jesus was the first to live out faith in its fullness. He was and is the Son of God. By entering history, by discerning the will of God, and by struggling to overcome all the forces of oppression, he showed us the way to God.

The faith, life, death, and resurrection of Jesus have profound implications for Christians living in a country that has in many ways caused, aggravated, and exploited the world food crisis. In today's world, where human hunger proves that the crucifixion is an ongoing historical reality, we who are committed to human liberation must proceed in faith. We know that Jesus is the Son of God. Such a proclamation is not a substitute for a dynamic faith that seeks to discern the will of God. It is a statement of our profound hope that, through the resurrection, God indicated that the locus of Christian faith and action is human history. The gap between the realization of the kingdom and the cross, which is so much in evidence in our present world of injustice and hunger, is not a legitimate reason for hopelessness or despair.

Human hunger is a consequence of social injustice. This hunger will be overcome to the degree that justice is built into the religious and social fabric of nations. In our own nation we cannot expect social justice without a rediscovery of the centrality of justice to biblical faith. Christians would be naive to expect the United States to become a "Christian nation," or to think that we will achieve through our own efforts alone the establishment of the kingdom of God on earth. But neither can we tolerate injustice while we claim to worship and give allegiance to the God of the Bible. As we seek human liberation we do so with the assurance that God, who is the source of our strength, shares our commitment. It is here that prayer and liberation are intimately linked. Prayer helps us to determine our way of acting in the world, and it calls on the power of God to intervene in a history that seems out of control.

As we seek to overcome the personal, corporate, and governmental obstacles to economic self-reliance, political independence, cultural diversity, and spiritual renewal, we proceed with the assurance of faith. We move forward in a spirit of humility with the knowledge that the kingdom is ultimately a gift. God's grace frees us to live today according to the possibility of the kingdom that at present is only partially fulfilled. We are invited by God to overcome the injustice at the root of the world food crisis, including the crisis of American agriculture. If we accept this invitation then we will hunger and thirst for justice, and we will live out authentic Christian faith through our commitment to liberation and to the risen Lord.

NOTES

Chapter 1   The Roots of Hunger

1. *The Holy Bible,* Revised Standard Version (New York and London: Thomas Nelson & Sons, New Testament, 1946, Old Testament, 1952). Unless otherwise indicated, all biblical quotations are from the Revised Standard Version. I have indicated added emphases. Biblical quotations marked with an asterisk (*) reflect my own adaptation of the biblical text in order to make the language inclusive of both men and women.

2. James Luther Mays, *Amos* (Philadelphia: The Westminster Press, 1969), p. 143.

3. Ibid., p. 45.

4. Ibid., p. 143.

5. *The Interpreters Bible,* 2 vols. (New York: Abingdon Press, 1956), 6:839.

6. Mays, *Amos,* p. 94.

7. Walter Wink, "Unmasking the Powers," *Sojourners Magazine,* October 1978, p. 10.

8. Ibid.

Chapter 2   The Economics of Hunger

1. Frances Moore Lappé and Joseph Collins, *Food First* (Boston: Houghton Mifflin Company, 1977), p. 78.

2. Walter Rodney, *How Europe Underdeveloped Africa* (London: Bogle-L'Ouverture Publications, 1972), pp. 171–72.

3. Richard J. Barnet and Ronald E. Müller, *Global Reach* (New York: Simon & Schuster, 1974), p. 190.

4. Richard K. Taylor, *Blockade* (Maryknoll, N.Y.: Orbis Books, 1977).

5. *New York Times,* 2 December 1974.

6. U.S. Senate, *Technical Assistance: Final Report of the Committee on Foreign Relations,* Report No. 139 (87th Congress, 1st Session, 12 March 1957), pp. 18–19; emphasis added.

7. William Appleman Williams, *The Tragedy of American Diplomacy* (New York: Dell Publishing Co., 1959), p. 235.

8. Richard J. Barnet, *The Roots of War* (Baltimore: Penguin Books, 1971), p. 152.

9. Quoted in Susanne Gowan et al., *Moving Toward a New Society* (Philadelphia: New Society Press, 1976), pp. 86–87; emphasis added.

10. Peter A. Toma, *The Politics of Food for Peace* (Tucson, Ariz.: University of Arizona Press, 1967), p. 144.

11. Ibid., pp. 106, 92.

12. Emma Rothschild, "Is It Time to End Food for Peace?" *New York Times Magazine*, 13 March 1977, p. 44.

13. *The New York Times*, 5 January 1971.

14. U.S. Senate, Committee on Agriculture and Forestry, *Hearings, Public Law 480* cited by Susan Demarco and Susan Sechler in *The Fields Have Turned Brown* (Washington, D.C.: The Agribusiness Accountability Project, 1975), p. 42.

15. *Agribusiness Manual*, (New York: The Interfaith Center on Corporate Responsibility, 1978), Section II, p. 13

16. Ibid., Section II, p. 14.

17. Hubert Humphrey (84th Congress, First Session, Senate Committee on Agriculture and Forestry: *Hearings: Policies and Operations of Public Law 480*, 1957), p. 129.

18. "U.S. Business vs. Malthus," *Forbes Magazine*, 1 March 1966, p. 25.

19. Directorate of Intelligence Office of Political Research, *Potential Implications of Trends in World Population, Food Production, and Climate* (Washington, D.C.: The Library of Congress, 1974), pp. 15, 39.

20. James W. Howe, *The U.S. and World Development: Agenda for Action 1975* (New York: Praeger Publishers, 1975), pp. 246–47. Also see *U.S. Foreign Agricultural Trade Statistical Report, Calendar Year 1977* (Washington, D.C.: Economics, Statistics, and Cooperative Service, U.S. Department of Agriculture, June 1978).

21. *The World Food Conference: Selected Materials for the Use of the U.S. Delegation to the World Food Conference* (Washington, D.C.: U.S. Government Printing Office, 1974), pp. 298–303.

Chapter 3   Hunger Today

1. Sterling Wrotman, "Food and Agriculture," *Scientific American*, September 1976, p. 38.

2. Laurence Simon, "Plantation Politics in the Dominican Republic," *New World Outlook*, New series, vol. 34, no. 3, Whole series, vol. 43, no. 10, November 1973, pp. 1–3.

3. Robert J. Ledogar, *Hungry for Profits* (New York: IDOC/North America, 1975), p. 75.

4. Patrick Hughes, ed., *Study Packet For the Slideshow* Guess Who's Coming to Breakfast. For a copy of the packet and information on the slide show, write the Packard Manse Media Project, Box 450, Stoughton, Mass. 02072.

5. *U.S. Foreign Agricultural Trade Statistical Report, Calendar Year 1977* (Washington, D.C.: Economics, Statistics and Cooperative Service, U.S. Department of Agriculture, June 1978), p. 222.

6. Alan Berg, *The Nutrition Factor* (Washington, D.C.: The Brookings Institution, 1973), pp. 65–66.

7. Lappé and Collins, *Food First*, pp. 254, 255, 257, and 170.

8. Ibid., pp. 289–90.

9. *Agribusiness Manual*, Section I, p. 7.

10. *Del Monte Annual Report*, 1977, p. 12.

11. *Del Monte Shield*, August 1977, p. 9.

12. *Agribusiness Manual*, Section I, p. 5.

13. Ibid., Section I, p. 6.

14. Ibid., Section I, p. 4. Also see, *People Toiling Under Pharaoh*, published by Urban Rural Mission, Christian Conference of Asia, 1976, p. 60.

15. Lappé and Collins, *Food First*, p. 253.

16. Susan George, *How the Other Half Dies* (Montclair, N.J.: Allanheld, Osmun & Co., Publishers, 1977), p. 10.

17. I strongly recommend the book *Food First* as a more complete study of export agriculture.

18. This quotation is taken from an interview with Orville Freeman in a recent documentary film about multinational corporations entitled "Controlling Interest." For information about the film write to Resolution, 630 Natoma Street, San Francisco, Calif. 94103.

19. Richard J. Barnet and Ronald E. Müller, *Global Reach* (New York: Simon & Schuster, 1974), pp. 31, 123, 175.

20. Susanne Gowan et al., *Moving Toward a New Society* (Philadelphia: New Society Press, 1976), pp. 76–77.

21. *Human Rights and the U.S. Foreign Assistance Program Fiscal Year 1978, Part I, Latin America* (Washington, D.C.: Center for International Policy, 1978), p. 33.

22. Ibid., p. 32.

23. José Míguez Bonino, *Doing Theology in a Revolutionary Situation* (Philadelphia: Fortress Books, 1975), p. 30.

24. *New York Times*, 12 September 1976.

25. Míguez Bonino, *Doing Theology*, p. 28.

26. *New York Times*, 14 December 1976; emphasis added.

27. David Vidal, "In Brazil Oil Imports Spur Drive to Export," *New York Times International Economic Survey*, 5 February 1978.

28. *New York Times*, 14 December 1976.

29. Ibid.

30. Study Document, Pastoral Committee of Bishops of Northeast Brazil for Third Conference of Latin American Bishops. Spanish translation published at Paris in *Liaisons Internationales*, no. 16, December 1977-February 1978.

31. Barnet and Müller, *Global Reach*, p. 149.

32. United Nations World Food Conference, *Assessment of the World Food Situation* (New York: United Nations, 1974), p. 68.

33. World Bank, *The Assault on World Poverty, Problems of Rural Development, Education, and Health* (Baltimore: Johns Hopkins University Press, 1975), p. 215–16, cited in *Food First*, p. 157.

34. David Pimentel et al., "Food Production and the Energy Crisis," *Food: Politics, Economics, Nutrition, and Research* (Washington, D.C.: American Association for the Advancement of Science, 1975), p. 122.

35. Berg, *Nutrition Factor*, p. 72.

36. *Assessment of the World Food Situation*, p. 68.

37. Barnet and Müller, *Global Reach*, p. 166.

38. Bette Shertzer, "Rural Women: Exploited and on the Edge," *Clergy and Laity Concerned Agrarian Reform Guide*, p. 15. The *Agrarian Reform Guide* is available for 50 cents plus postage from Clergy and Laity Concerned, 198 Broadway, New York, NY 10038.

39. Howard M. Wachtel, *The New Gnomes: Multinational Banks in the Third World* (Washington, D.C.: Transnational Institute, 1977), p. 11.

40. *New York Times*, 7 March 1978.

41. *New Internationalist*, August 1975, p. 1.

42. Howe, *U.S. and World Development*, p. 98.

43. *Assessment of the World Food Situation*, p. 54.

44. Barnet and Müller, *Global Reach*, p. 89.

Chapter 4   United States Military Power and the Third World

1. Ruth Leger Sivard, *World Military and Social Expenditures* (Leesburg, Va.: WMSE Publications, 1978), pp. 5, 18.

2. Richard J. Barnet, *The Roots of War* (Baltimore: Penguin Books, 1971), p. 152.

3. *Baltimore Sun*, 28 June 1967.

4. Speech before the National Foreign Trade Convention, 12 November 1946.

5. Austin Kiplinger, "The Round Table," *Chicago Journal of Commerce*, 2 March 1949; emphasis added.

6. Barnet, *Roots of War*, pp. 30, 34.

7. Thomas McCann, *An American Company: The Tragedy of United Fruit* (New York: Crown Publishers, 1976), pp. 39–40.

8. Richard J. Barnet, *Intervention and Revolution* (New York: World Publishing Company, 1969), pp. 229–30.

9. *Guatemala* (Berkeley: North American Congress on Latin America, 1974), p. 167.

10. Michael T. Klare, *Supplying Repression* (New York: Field Foundation, 1977), pp. 32, 36.

11. Susan Demarco and Susan Sechler, *The Fields Have Turned Brown* (Washington, D.C.: Agribusiness Accountability Project, 1975), p. 89.

12. Sivard, *World Military and Social Expenditures*, pp. 24–25.

13. Sydney Lens, *The Military-Industrial Complex* (Philadelphia: Pilgrim Press, 1970), p. 151.

14. *New York Times*, 7 October 1960.

15. *New York Times*, 27 August 1970. Also see Barnet, *Roots of War*, p. 66.

16. Barnet, *Intervention and Revolution*, p. 158.

17. Ibid., pp. 165–66.

18. Ibid., p. 177.

19. Klare, *Supplying Repression*, pp. 32, 20.

20. Barnet, *Intervention and Revolution*, pp. 168, 174.

21. Quoted in Susanne Gowan et al., *Moving Toward a New Society* (Philadelphia: New Society Press, 1976), pp. 86–87; emphasis added.

22. Robert McNamara, *The Essence of Security* (New York: Harper & Row, Publishers, 1968), p. 149.

23. Testimony before the House of Representatives, Committee on Foreign Affairs, *Hearings on the Foreign Assistance Act of 1967* (Washington, D.C., 1967).

24. Klare, *Supplying Repression*, p. 33.

25. U.S. Defense Security Assistance Agency, *Foreign Military Sales and Military Assistance Facts* (Washington, D.C., 1977), pp. 30–31. Quoted by Klare, ibid., pp. 36–37.

26. *Congressional Record*, 24 May 1965, pp. 112–30.

27. "Latin American Militaries, Two Models: Many Problems," *North American Congress on Latin America* (NACLA), January 1976, p. 9.

28. Ibid., p. 7.

29. Sivard, p. 9.

30. Alan Berg, *The Nutrition Factor* (Washington, D.C.: The Brookings Institution, 1973), p. 18.

31. U.S. Congress, Senate Committee on Armed Services, *Fiscal Year 1974 Authorization for Military Procurement . . . , Hearings*, 93rd Congress 1st Session 1973, Part I, p. 163, quoted by Klare, p. 34.

Chapter 5   The Impact of American Military Spending at Home and Abroad

1. Seymour Melman, *The Permanent War Economy* (New York: Simon & Schuster, 1974), p. 15.

2. Richard J. Barnet, *The Roots of War* (Baltimore: Penguin Books, 1971), p. 139.

3. William Appleman Williams, *The Tragedy of American Diplomacy* (New York: Dell Publishing Co., 1959), p. 237.

4. Barnet, *Roots of War*, p. 165.

5. *U.S. News & World Report*, 19 May 1950.

6. David Horowitz, *The Free World Colossus* (London: McGibbon & Kee, 1965), p. 23.

7. Sydney Lens, *The Military-Industrial Complex* (Philadelphia: Pilgrim Press, 1970) p. 44.

8. Ibid., p. 42.

9. Ibid., p. 12.

10. Michael Reich and David Finkelhor, "The Military-Industrial Complex: No Way Out," in *The Capitalist System* (Englewood Cliffs, N.J.: Prentice-Hall, 1972), p. 396.

11. Table is compiled from "The Fortune Directory of the 500 Largest

Industrial Corporations," *Fortune Magazine*, 8 May 1978; and from "The Defense Department's Top 100," *Newsletter: Council on Economic Priorities*, CEP Publication N7–5, 1 August 1977.

12. "The Defense Department's Top 100," *Council on Economic Priorities*, 26 January 1976.

13. Lens, *Military-Industrial Complex*, pp. 40, 45.

14. Ibid., p. 7.

15. Paul and Arthur Simon, *The Politics of World Hunger* (New York: Harper's Magazine Press, 1973), p. 188.

16. Ibid., p. 189.

17. *Congressional Record*, 23 May 1972, vol. 118, part 14, p. 18538.

18. Quoted in Seymour Melman, *Pentagon Capitalism* (New York: McGraw-Hill Book Company, 1970), p. 88; emphasis added.

19. Ibid., p. 80.

20. Melman, *Permanent War Economy*, p. 23.

21. "A Labor View of Foreign Investment and Trade Issues," *U.S. International Economic Policy in an Interdependent World*, Supplemental vol. 1 (Washington, D.C.: Government Printing Office, July 1971), pp. 914–17.

22. U.S. Commission on International Trade and Investment Policy, *United States International Economic Policy in an Interdependent World, Report to the President* (Washington, D.C.: Government Printing Office, July 1971), p. 170; hereafter cited as the Williams Commission.

23. Melman, *Permanent War Economy*, p. 102.

24. "A Labor View of Foreign Investment and Trade Issues," pp. 914–17.

25. Melman, *Permanent War Economy*, p. 69.

26. Williams Commission, p. 2.

27. Ibid., p. 3.

28. Ibid., p. 5.

29. Ibid., pp. 6–7.

30. Ibid., pp. 4–5.

31. Ibid., p. 7.

32. Ibid., p. 120.

33. Ibid., p. 118.

34. Ibid., p. 9.

35. Ibid., p. 4.

36. Ibid., p. 120.

37. Ibid., p. 834.

38. Ibid., p. 141.

39. Ibid., pp. 153–54; emphasis added.

40. Melman, *Permanent War Economy*, pp. 92–93.

41. Ibid., pp. 91–92.

42. "Foreign Military Sales Agreements FY–70 Through FY–76," Office of the Secretary of Defense, 20 August 1976.

43. Hal Sheets, "Big Money in Hunger," *Worldview*, March 1975, p. 10.

44. "Can Agriculture Save the Dollar," *Forbes Magazine*, 15 March 1973, p. 32.

45. *The World Food Situation and Prospects to 1985* (Washington, D.C.:

Economic Research Service, U.S. Department of Agriculture, Foreign Agriculture Economic Report No. 98, 1974), p. 3.

46. "Food Exports: Bailing Out the Empire," *North American Congress on Latin America*, October 1975, p. 7.

47. George McGovern as quoted in the Introduction to *Food and Population: The World in Crisis* (New York: Arno Press, 1975), p. viii.

48. Directorate of Intelligence Office of Political Research, *Potential Implications of Trends in World Population, Food Production, and Climate* (Washington, D.C.: The Library of Congress, 1974), p. 2; emphasis added.

49. Ibid., p. 15; emphasis added.

50. Ibid., pp. 33–34.

51. Ibid., pp. 39–40.

52. *New York Times*, 17 March 1975.

53. "U.S. Food Power: Ultimate Weapon in World Politics?," *Business Week*, 15 December 1975, p. 56.

54. Ibid., pp. 54, 56; emphasis added.

55. Directorate of Intelligence Office of Political Research, *Potential Implications*, pp. 3, 41.

Chapter 6   Is Overpopulation the Biggest Human Problem?

1. "The Fatal Math: The Doubling and Re-doubling of Populations," a fundraising pamphlet of the *Pathfinder Fund*, 1330 Boylston Street, Chestnut Hill, Mass. 02167.

2. Ibid.

3. In the order listed: *National Observer*, 30 March 1974; *New York Times*, 26 July 1974; *New York Times*, 15 September 1974; *Los Angeles Times*, 9 October 1974; and *New York Times*, 14 August 1974.

4. Paul Ehrlich, *The Population Bomb* (New York: Ballantine Books, 1968), p. 15.

5. Frances Moore Lappé and Joseph Collins, *Food First* (Boston: Houghton Mifflin Company, 1977), p. 4.

6. Ehrlich, *Population Bomb*, p. xi.

7. Mahmood Mamdani, *The Myth of Population Control* (New York: Monthly Review Press, 1972), p. 25.

8. Ibid.

9. Ibid., pp. 32–33.

10. *New York Times*, 30 May 1973.

11. *New York Times*, 22 October 1970.

12. Ibid.

13. Lester R. Brown, *By Bread Alone* (New York: Praeger Publishers, 1974), p. 38.

14. Lester R. Brown, *Human Needs and the Security of Nations* (New York: Foreign Policy Association, Headline Series 238, 1978), pp. 8, 10.

15. Brown, *By Bread Alone*, p. 145.

16. Brown, *Human Needs and the Security of Nations*, pp. 14–15.

17. Ibid., pp. 17–19.

18. Garrett Hardin, "The Immorality of Being Softhearted," *Stanford Alumni Almanac*, January 1969.

Chapter 7   Population Control in the Third World

1. Agency for International Development, *Population Program Assistance*, December 1971.

2. Richard Barnet, *The Roots of War* (Baltimore: Penguin Books, 1971), pp. 210–11.

3. Frances Moore Lappé and Joseph Collins, *Food First* (Boston: Houghton Mifflin Company, 1977), pp. 77–78.

4. *New York Times*, 26 July 1974.

5. Susan Cebeseto, "On the Causes and Solution to the Problem of World Hunger and Starvation: Comparative Evidence on the Development of China and India," a paper presented at the Annual Meeting of the American Sociological Association, New York, 31 August 1976, p. iv.

6. *New York Times*, 13 September 1974.

7. Susan Demarco and Susan Sechler, *The Fields Have Turned Brown* (Washington, D.C.: The Agribusiness Accountability Project, 1975), p. 61.

8. Samuel L. Parmar, "Self-Reliant Development in an 'Interdependent' World," *Beyond Dependency* (Washington, D.C.: The Overseas Development Council, 1975), p. 7.

9. Mahmood Mamdani, *The Myth of Population Control* (New York: Monthly Review Press, 1972), p. 25; emphasis added.

10. Ibid.

11. Alan Berg, *The Nutrition Factor* (Washington, D.C.: The Brookings Institution, 1973), p. 33.

12. Cebeseto, "Causes and Solution," p. 23.

13. Bonnie Mass, *Population Target: The Political Economy of Population Control in Latin America* (Brampton, Ontario, Canada: Charters Publishing Co., 1976), p. 37.

14. Quoted in Michael Hudson, *Super Imperialism* (New York: Holt, Rinehart and Winston, 1968), pp. 127–28.

15. "U.S. Program to Sterilize Millions," *St. Louis Post Dispatch*, 22 April 1977.

16. Capon Springs Public Policy Conference #2, Population and Food Policy, 22–24 February 1978.

Chapter 8   Hunger and the Crisis of Values

1. Quoted in "The Talk of the Town," *New Yorker*, 15 December 1975.

2. John Herbers, "Beneath the Streets, Old Cities Crumble and Decay," *New York Times*, 9 April 1978.

3. *Variations in Farm Incomes and Their Relation to Agricultural Policies* (Washington, D.C.: Agriculture Department, Chamber of Commerce of the United States, March 1945), pp. 9, 20, 21.

4. *An Adaptive Program for Agriculture*, a statement on national policy

by the Research and Policy Committee of the Committee for Economic Development (Washington, D.C.: Library of Congress Catalog Card No. 62–19145, July 1962), pp. 2, 3, 7, 19, 33–34, 59–60.

5. *Fact Book of U.S. Agriculture* (Washington, D.C.: U.S. Department of Agriculture Miscellaneous Publication No. 1063, Office of Communication, March 1976), p. 24.

6. "The New American Farmer," *Time* magazine, 6 November 1978.

7. *Fact Book*, p. 13.

8. *1977 Handbook of Agricultural Charts* (Washington, D.C.: U.S. Department of Agriculture, 1977), p. 8.

9. *Fact Book*, pp. 18, 13.

10. *1977 Handbook*, pp. 7, 14.

11. *Fact Book*, p. 16.

12. Ibid., pp. 2–3; emphasis added.

13. Jim Hightower, *Eat Your Heart Out* (New York: Vintage Books, 1975), pp. 11, 13, 17–19, 184; emphasis added.

14. *CDE Stock Ownership Directory: Agribusiness* (New York: Corporate Data Exchange, Inc., 1979). Library of Congress Number 78-61483.

15. Catherine Lerza and Michael Jacobson, eds., *Food for People Not for Profit* (New York: Ballantine Books, 1975), p. 165.

16. Michael Perelman, *Farming for Profit in a Hungry World* (Montclair, N.J.: Allanheld, Osmun & Co., 1979), p. 81.

17. Hightower, *Eat Your Heart Out*, p. 252.

18. "Some Problems Impeding Economic Improvement of Small-Farm Operations: What the Department of Agriculture Could Do," report to the Congress by the Comptroller General of the United States, 15 August 1975, p. 20.

19. Wendell Berry, *The Unsettling of America: Culture & Agriculture* (San Francisco: Sierra Club Books, 1977), pp. 33, 88.

20. *Time* magazine, 6 November 1978.

21. Walter Goldschmidt, "A Tale of Two Towns," in *Food for People Not for Profit*, pp. 70–72; emphasis added.

22. The Emergency Land Fund and the National Association of Landowners, "Problems Facing Minority Farmers and Landowners," *Clergy and Laity Concerned Agrarian Reform Guide*, p. 20. (Available from Clergy and Laity Concerned, 198 Broadway, New York, NY 10038; 50 cents plus postage.)

23. Barry Commoner, *The Poverty of Power* (New York: Bantam Books, 1977), pp. 151–155.

24. *Fact Book*, p. 30.

25. Ibid., p. 5.

26. *Time* magazine, 6 November 1978; emphasis added.

27. Daniel Zwerdling, "The Pesticides Plague," *Washington Post*, 5 March 1978.

28. Ibid.

29. Jack Anderson, "Foolish Farmers?," *Atlanta Journal and Constitution*, 20 August 1978.

30. Perelman, *Farming for Profit*, p. 53.

31. "National Farmers Union Washington Newsletter," 10 February 1978.

32. Ibid.

33. "Foreign Investors Flock to U.S. Farmlands," *Business Week*, 27 March 1978.

34. Anderson, "Foolish Farmers?"

35. Berry, *Unsettling of America* , pp. 9–10.

36. *Time* magazine, 6 November 1978.

37. *A Policy for Food and Agriculture in Massachusetts* (Boston: Executive Office of Environmental Affairs, Department of Food and Agriculture, 1976), p. 5.

38. Ibid., p. 4.

39. Michael Scully, "New Englanders Fight Food Dependency," *In These Times*, 19–25 January 1977.

40. Taken from minutes of the Northeast Task Force for Food and Farm Policy Conference of 29 July 1977, held at the Massachusetts State House, Boston. Conference Theme: "Averting Northeast Food Shortages in the 80's: Components of a Revived Agriculture."

41. Andy Kuhn, "Connecticut Food from Connecticut Farms?," *New Haven Advocate*, 20 April 1977.

42. Statistics are taken from personal correspondence with Randall J. Brown, Director, Agricultural Redevelopment, New York State. See also working paper no. 30, "Peri-Urban Agriculture: The New York Experience," NRE Economic Research Service, U.S. Department of Agriculture.

43. Press release from the office of New York Assembly Speaker Stanley Steingut, 2 October 1977.

44. "Farmland: Are We Running Out?," *Our Nation's Land and Water Resources*, U.S. Department of Agriculture Economic Research Service, August 1973.

45. "Report and Recommendations," Conference on the Future of Rural Pennsylvania and the Northeast/Appalachian Regions, 19–20 March 1978, p. 8. This conference was sponsored by the Institute for Community Services, Edinboro State College, Edinboro Pa.

46. Richard K. Taylor, *Economics and the Gospel* (Philadelphia: United Church Press, 1973), p. 74.

Chapter 9   Seeking Solutions for the World Food Crisis

1. Denis Goulet, *The Uncertain Promise* (New York: IDOC/North America, 1977), p. 164.

2. Ibid., p. 151; emphasis added.

3. Ibid., p. 163.

4. Bill Finger, Cary Fowler, and Chip Hughes, "Oil Tightens Its Grip," *Southern Exposure*, vol. 2, nos. 2–3 (Fall 1973), p. 158.

5. Dr. Helen Caldicott, *Nuclear Madness* (Brookline, Massachusetts: Autumn Press, Inc., 1978), p. 15.

6. "Domestic Policy Review of Solar Energy," *Consumer Briefing Summary* (Washington, D.C.: Office of Consumer Affairs, Department of Energy, 13 July 1978), pp. 7–8; emphasis added.

7. Ibid., p. 6.

8. *New York Times*, 13 March 1977.

9. *New York Times*, 31 March 1978.

10. "Foreign Aid: Evading the Control of Congress," *International Policy Report* (Washington, D.C.: Center for International Policy, January 1977).

11. Corporate responsibility campaigns are usually carried out outside the context of grassroots efforts. A notable exception is the campaign to change the unethical promotion practices of multinational corporations that market infant formula in areas of the world where a lack of clean water, literacy, and adequate income prevent its proper use. What began as a stockholder resolution against an American company has mushroomed into the largest non-union grassroots boycott in U.S. history. For more information about the infant formula campaign, write to: National Infant Formula Action Coalition (INFACT), 1701 University Ave., Minneapolis, Minn. 55414; or Interfaith Center on Corporate Responsibility, 475 Riverside Drive, New York, N.Y. 10021; or, Clergy and Laity Concerned, 198 Broadway, New York, N.Y. 10038.

12. As this book goes to press Clergy and Laity Concerned is taking the initiative in exploring with grassroots groups the possibility of a "People's Commission," or "People's Initiative," on Food, Land, and Justice. For information about recent developments write to: Clergy and Laity Concerned, Politics of Food Program, 198 Broadway, New York, N.Y. 10038.

Chapter 10   Hunger and the Crisis of Faith

1. James Luther Mays, *Amos* (Philadelphia: Westminster Press, 1969), p. 10.

2. John M. Blum et al., *The National Experience: A History of the United States* (New York: Harcourt Brace Jovanovich, 1963), p. 533; emphasis added.

3. Gustavo Gutiérrez, *A Theology of Liberation* (Maryknoll, N.Y.: Orbis Books, 1973), p. 262.

4. Robert McAfee Brown, *Is Faith Obsolete?* (Philadelphia: Westminster Press, 1974), p. 126.

5. Jon Sobrino, S.J., *Christology at the Crossroads* (Maryknoll, N.Y.: Orbis Books, 1978), pp. 79–139.

Index

CLERGY AND LAITY CONCERNED (CALC) is an action-oriented interfaith peace and justice organization—a nationwide network of women and men called to social action by religious faith and/or ethical principles. It is a not-for-profit, membership organization with a network of local chapters and action groups throughout the country.

Through its publication CALC REPORT (published eight times yearly) and through speakers and other resources, CALC assists individuals and groups who wish to work effectively with others for social change.

To receive information on membership, on how to form a CALC Chapter or Action Group, or on present organizing efforts, please write to:

Clergy and Laity Concerned
198 Broadway
New York, NY 10038

DEMONSTRATE YOUR CONCERN

Inform your political representative

This book raises important issues that need to be addressed by our public officials.

To send a copy to the local, state, and/or federal official of your choice, send only the price of the book and the intended recipient's name and address to:

Orbis Books
Maryknoll, NY 10545

(continued from back cover)

"I do not believe that there is a way
to satisfy your spiritual hunger for the meaning of life
without dealing with the material hunger
of the majority of the human family.

"Don't read Hermann Hesse,
don't travel to India
without knowing what the causes of hunger are
and who lives well from it.
Don't come later and tell me that nobody told you.

"Nikolai Berdyaev has said
that my own hunger is a material problem;
the hunger of my neighbor, however,
is a spiritual question to me.

"The author of this analysis, Jack Nelson, sees,
like the prophet Jeremiah,
'the blood of the guiltless poor' right on our shirts.
We cannot wash this blood away,
in blaming nature, the drought,
overpopulation, and underdevelopment.

"World hunger has its roots
in the economic and military policy
of the U.S. and other rich nations.
To wash the blood away
would mean to join the struggle of the poor.

"We cannot be hungry for them,
but it is possible to share their hunger for justice.
You need this hunger to grow, too."

Dorothee Sölle, *Union Theological Seminary, New York*

Jack A. Nelson is a graduate of St. Olaf College in Northfield, Minnesota, where he majored in political science. As an undergraduate student he traveled and studied in Ethiopia, India, Sri Lanka, Taiwan, and Japan. He did his theological training at Union Theological Seminary in New York City, where he received a Master of Divinity degree.

Jack has published articles in a variety of journals including *Christianity and Crisis, CALC Report, Sojourners, The Lutheran Standard, New World Outlook, Food Monitor,* and *Forty Acres and a Mule.* He has experience as a co-op organizer and publishes bi-monthly columns for food co-ops throughout the country.

He is presently the national coordinator of the Politics of Food Program with Clergy and Laity Concerned, a grassroots interfaith peace and justice organization with a nationwide network of local chapters and action groups. CALC members bring moral, ethical and religious values to bear on problems of political, economic, and social injustice.